D1212299

THE MYTH OF MEASURABILITY

THE MYTH OF MEASURABILITY

EDITED BY PAUL L. HOUTS

HART PUBLISHING COMPANY, INC. • NEW YORK

BF
431
.M87

NEW YORK, NEW YORK 10012

ISBN NO. 08055-1218-7 (PAPERBACK 08055-0312-9)
LIBRARY OF CONGRESS CATALOG CARD NO. 76-54045

MANUFACTURED IN THE UNITED STATES OF AMERICA

PREFACE

In 1975, The National Association of Elementary School Principals devoted two issues of its journal, *Principal,* to the subject of standardized testing. While periodic but isolated critiques of standardized testing had been appearing in the literature for years, the two issues taken together presented a unique and strong brief against standardized testing and caused considerable controversy and comment, both in the press and within the education community.

In enabling the articles from the two issues of *Principal,* and several other articles published subsequently, to be published in book form and to reach a wider audience, we would like to extend our appreciation to the Ford Foundation for its kind support and assistance, and to the authors whose articles appear in the following pages for their generous permission to reprint their material.

P.L.H.

CONTENTS

INTRODUCTION: STANDARDIZED TESTING IN AMERICA

> *In every child who is born, under no matter what circumstances, and of no matter what parents, the potentiality of the human race is born again; and in him, too, once more, and of each of us, our terrific responsibility towards human life; towards the utmost idea of goodness, of the horror of error, and of God.*
>
> James Agee

For the past several decades, standardized testing has been a growth industry in this country, and if we look to the future, the forecast for the industry is, as the Wall Street people like to say, bullish. Last year alone, over 40 million elementary and secondary school children underwent standardized testing at a cost of well over a quarter of a billion dollars. These figures by themselves should be good reason to make us pause and question what we are doing. But there are even more cogent reasons, for these figures cannot convey the effects the tests have on the lives of children. The tests wield great power, whether it be in helping to determine which children shall be put in special education classes, which children shall go to college, or even which shall enter a given profession.

Moreover, the figures do not represent the other costs that cannot be measured in dollars and cents; that is, the emotional costs to children and parents, the costs in school or learning time, the costs in staff time and energy to administer the tests, and now—in these days of accountability—the costs to teachers and principals whose competency may well be judged on the basis of the test results.

For all of these reasons, in the articles that follow, we shall be taking a close look at standardized testing, and in the process, we hope to raise a number of questions about both the tests and their use (or misuse, as the case may be). Of these many questions, two seem to us to be particularly important. First, do the tests measure what they are supposed to measure? And second, is the current use of standardized tests consistent with what must be a central task of any democracy—to reduce as much as possible the inequities in our social system?

By exploring the first question, we hope to learn something about the tests themselves, their use, and the test makers. The second question is more difficult, for it requires that we learn some things about ourselves and how we operate as a nation.

We begin with intelligence testing. Descended from the experiments of Alfred Binet and nurtured by an age that believed in fostering the "preservation of Favored Races in the Struggle for Life" (to use Charles Darwin's words), large-scale IQ testing first came into its own during World War I. It was a tidy arrangement, particularly for a nation committed to an egalitarianism of sorts. Here was a handy mechanical device that would help us sort people according to their ability. We would have an aristocracy of talent, not of birth, thus carefully preserving the sanctity of our national charter. Not strangely in the historical weather of the time, the notion that each man had a native intelligence—one that could be measured and that remained relatively constant from birth—passed from mere popular acceptance to a state of almost mystical belief, one that persists to our own day.

From its very inception, however, a geological fault has run through the dogma of IQ. Walter Lippmann detected it as early as the 1920s, when he wrote: "Because the results are expressed in numbers, it is easy to make the mistake of thinking that the intelligence test is a measure like a foot rule or a pair of scales. . . . But 'intelligence' is not an abstraction like length and weight; it is an exceedingly complicated notion which nobody has as yet succeeded in defining." Lippmann foresaw how easily the test could be turned into "an engine of cruelty" and went on to warn us that, "if the impression takes root that these tests really measure intelligence, that they constitute a sort of last judgment on the child's capacity, that they reveal 'scientifically' his predestined ability, then it would be a thousand times better if all the intelligence testers and all their questionnaires were sunk without warning in the Sargasso Sea."

In the spring of our belief, Lippmann's words had little effect. We might now smile a wintry smile at our naiveté, except that we continue to believe that we can measure intelligence when we have never defined it. Our progress has been that of transcendence, not advance. As Sheldon White points out, what we have here is an "affair in which magic, science, and myth are intermixed." To that we would add that our science has been at best weak and more than a little tainted by politics.

Where, then, do we go? Mr. Lippmann's Sargasso Sea is far, but we believe it is not too far to go to rid ourselves of the damage that the IQ tests continue to bring about. It may not be easy to end wide-spread use of IQ testing, for myths and customs linger and they are difficult to exorcise. Still, although the reader will find varying opinions within this book, we believe there should be an end to such obligatory testing. In view of the many defects of the so-called intelligence tests, it is difficult to imagine that, as a profession, we shall miss them. A careful look at the existing tests should assure most everyone that such instruments cannot possibly measure anything so wonderfully variegated as human ability. As for the idea that the tests can measure the hereditary intelligence of human beings, it is here we believe the greatest harm has been done. The scientists and social scientists who have perpetuated such theories deal us a cheap hand.

But even without the IQ tests, we are left with a bevy of standardized tests that purport to effectively measure student achievement in the major areas of study.

Dazzled by the apparent success of the Army Alpha Test designed for use during World War I, schools, colleges, and organizations during the early 1920s quickly seized on psychological testing as a useful and convenient device for sorting students, which was then (rightly or wrongly) perceived as an important and legitimate function of the schools. Intelligence testing was quickly followed by the development of achievement testing, and by 1929, more than five million tests were being administered annually.

Today that figure has mushroomed in keeping with an inflationary age. According to estimates by the National Education Association, at least 200 million achievement test forms are used each year in the United States, and this number represents only about 65 percent of all the educational and psychological testing that is carried out.

These are hardly small numbers, nor are the earnings that accompany them. The Bank of New York's Research Division reports that gross earnings for testing for the three major test publishers and one scoring company totaled $105 million in 1974. The $105 million, incidentally, does not include the giant but nonprofit Educational Testing Service, or the numerous other smaller but still significant commercial test publishers.

But as was pointed out, such figures—startling as they are—simply mask the enormous impact of the tests on the lives of children and parents and, in an age of accountability, on the careers of educators. Testing is far from an incidental matter in a young person's life. In the course of a child's public schooling, from kindergarten through high school, he or she will almost certainly take as many as six full batteries of achievement tests—and very possibly as many as a dozen—in addition to other standardized tests, such as reading readiness and IQ.

In view of this one must ask, why so much testing? How effective is it? Are the current tests really providing us with valuable aids in the instructional process? For that, after all, should be their true function. The articles in this book certainly indicate otherwise: they point to serious defects in the tests themselves. But the problem goes deeper. As Ralph Tyler recently pointed out, " . . . at a time when the need for universal education was developing, the testing movement furnished both an ideological and an instrumental basis for the practice of schools and colleges in sorting students rather than educating them. . . . Furthermore, the testing movement promoted the simplistic notion that important outcomes of schooling could be adequately appraised by achievement tests. The ease with which objective tests can be given, scored, and summarized tempts school administrators to collect these data as the sole comprehensive and comparable information available about student learning."

In fact, the temptation has become irresistible. The reading scores of the New York public schools are published in the *New York Times*, and the scores have even come to govern hiring policies. Moreover, other cities now follow a similar practice in releasing scores to the press. Recently, one northeastern city even saw fit to publish not only the mean achievement test scores for each of its schools, but the mean IQ scores as well! And so the public judges its schools, its educational system, on scores that are misleading at best; government and foundation projects are often considered a success or failure by virtue of the test scores that accompany their evaluation reports; and indeed, educational policy making is being influenced by testing at all levels, a situation not unlike an airline pilot being directed by a defective instrument panel.

However, because the need to identify children's abilities and talents and the accompanying need to assess their progress remain with us, we must face a series of nettlesome but critical questions about the standardized tests themselves. Can they be improved? Can we develop effective alternatives to standardized tests? Can we develop a wider variety of tests that will help to identify and promote (and thereby celebrate) the great diversity of abilities and talents within our student population? Finally, and perhaps we should put the question first, is any reform of standardized testing realistic, or is it in conflict with the realities of the market-place? Testing is, after all, big business in this country. A significant amount of money is involved, and interlocking economic forces are at work. We seldom approach the problems of testing from an economic standpoint, but it might yield some interesting (and surprising) results if we were to do so.

Yet it would be naive to believe our problems are the result of some sinister cabal of test makers foisting tests on a helpless public; they are merely businessmen responding to (and often creating) a market, as businessmen always have, though the marketplace is hardly free of irresponsible practice. Nor do our problems stem from the fact that the tests themselves are not particularly good, which they are certainly not.

Rather, our current predicament stems from another factor. As a society, we are beginning to work on a new series of assumptions: that the purpose of education is not to sort people but to educate them; that in a knowledge society, we need to expose as many people to education as possible, not to exclude them from it; that human beings are marvelously variegated in their talents and abilities, and it is the function of education to nurture them wisely and carefully; and not least, that education has an overriding responsibility to respect and draw upon cultural and racial diversity.

In the final analysis, the current reliance on standardized testing can only prevent schools from operating under these new social and educational conditions. By its very nature, standardized testing must continue to skew our entire educational enterprise. As Lewis Mumford has so wisely remarked, "In letting depersonalized organizations and automatic contraptions take charge of our lives, we have been forfeiting the only qualities that could justify our existence: sensitiveness, consciousness, responsiveness, expressive intelligence, human heartedness, and (alas, one cannot use this word now without wincing) creativity." These, we believe, are also the qualities that justify every teacher's and principal's professional life.

Do we need testing? Of course we do. But we need many more kinds of tests that meet our current educational and social needs. Can we develop them? Of course. The education profession has met equally difficult challenges, and many effective forms of evaluation are already well known to teachers and principals. Can the testing companies help in such future test development? Perhaps. Most any endeavor can benefit from broad participation and a wide range of viewpoints and knowledge. But we believe it is now imperative for the education profession to take the initiative in developing alternatives to the current standardized tests. Testing must be returned to the education profession itself.

PAUL L. HOUTS

THE MYTH OF MEASURABILITY

SOCIAL IMPLICATIONS OF IQ

SHELDON H. WHITE

Sheldon H. White is a member of the Faculty of Education and chairman of the Program in Personality and Developmental Studies, Department of Psychology and Social Relations, Harvard University, Cambridge, Massachusetts.

He has served as a consultant to the National Institute of Mental Health in Bethesda, Maryland; Educational Testing Service in Princeton, New Jersey; the Children's Television Workshop; and the Harvard Project Nutrition.

Mr. White was a member of the National Advisory Council for the Education of Disadvantaged Children and a member of the advisory board of the National Laboratory for Early Childhood Education.

In addition, his articles and writings have appeared in many professional journals.

Existing instruments (for measuring intellect) represent enormous improvements over what was available twenty years ago, but three fundamental defects remain. Just what they measure is not known; how far it is proper to add, subtract, multiply, divide, and compute ratios with the measures obtained is not known; just what the measures obtained signify concerning intellect is not known. We may refer to these defects in order as ambiguity in content, arbitrariness in units, and ambiguity in significance.

Edward L. Thorndike

The meaning and wisdom of intelligence testing is much debated today. This is as it should be, because our ideas about intelligence and our practices of testing for it have significant influence on the way we educate children. Unhappily, too much of the debate stays within a kind of magic circle. We argue about whether intelligence is given at birth or whether it can be changed. We discuss whether or not there are culture-fair procedures for measuring intelligence. We consider how much schools should or should not be guided by intelligence tests. But all of these discussions are curiously restricted. Staying within the magic circle, we hover about the notion that there is a single, generalized human capability that may be called "intelligence." I say hover because I believe that most of us have serious doubts about there being some single "it" in human ability.

The central question in intelligence testing is not whether one can give a child some games, puzzles, and questions and statistically predict how well he will do in future games, puzzles, and questions. Everyone knows we can do that, at least to some extent. And everyone knows that we can predict from the games, puzzles, and questions of the test to those embodied in school classrooms, at least to some extent. The central question is whether the child's performance on the games, puzzles, and questions—those of the test and those of the school—reflects some essence in the child so significant that it should be considered to be merit, general ability, or promise for society. It is here where we have doubts. Those in the schools have some doubts about the tests as definitive measures of intellectual ability, and those outside the schools have some more generalized doubts about "school smartness."

Why, with our doubts, do we confine our arguments within the magic circle? We do so, I believe, because the circle defines a zone within the mythic structure and rationalized practices of our society. If we stay within such a zone, we can debate means, not ends. If we step outside the magic circle, however, we suddenly open unsettling questions about the values inherent in our social arrangements and equally difficult uncertainties about what is right and fair in the practices of the public and institutional side of children's socialization.

Intelligence tests are not ordinarily discussed as components of a mythic system. They are ordinarily addressed as technology, as instruments, or as measuring devices. They are considered to be science, not magic. But a consideration of the history of intelligence testing suggests strongly that the tests have not won their way by their technological merits—indeed, that a technology of intelligence measuring has not been invented and probably could not be. Much of the historical sequence looks like a history of the dissemination of an imperfect technology that moves into currency because of its social utility.

•

The intelligence test was invented in the first decade of this century at a time when American social arrangements were changing, particularly arrangements for the upbringing of children. It was also a time when major activity patterns of American psychology were being established. We cannot fully understand the forms and the growth patterns of American psychology unless we understand the emerging discipline in the social milieu of that period.

Barbara Tuchman's book *The Proud Tower*[1] conveys dramatically just how different that time was from our own. The movement of Western societies was clearly toward industrialization, urbanization, automation, and bureaucratization. But the last rites in the transfer of power had not taken place; there were still remnants of an older social order. Most of the kings and queens of Europe were in place. There were aristocracies. The aristocrats were dilapidated, nervous, even fatalistic, but they still had a little power. Most of their ancient power was in the hands of the merchant princes, with whom they shared a love-hate relationship. Of course, the United States had no king and no titles, but it did have an establishment that could get along comfortably with the titled establishments of Europe.

One can read Nicholas Murray Butler's autobiography, *Across the Busy Years*, to get an impression of the life of a pillar of the American establishment at that time. Butler was active in the widespread conversions of American colleges into American universities near the turn of the century. In 1901, becoming president of Columbia University, he entered into the company of the leadership of American affairs. He enjoyed, as he delicately puts it, "worldwide contacts and associations of the greatest possible charm and importance." He visited frequently at the White House. He was offered opportunities to become a bank president, a railroad president, a governor, a senator. He traveled abroad regularly and was involved in the machinations of international affairs. His autobiography radiates a coziness and a comfort that we can hardly imagine today—a leader born in a time when leaders could imagine they were born to lead, an American aristocrat from Paterson, New Jersey.[2]

Contrast Butler with the harassed, short-lived college president of our time and you have one aspect of the difference between then and now. Now consider another difference. There was then explosive radicalism, anarchism, the Wobblies, and the fighting trade unions. For more than a hundred years the common man had been coming, since the American and French revolutions, since 1848, since Marx. There was still something a little adventurous and dangerous about active espousal of his cause, but the fight for the common man was in the open. The battle was engaged.

If we examine the entries in the three-volume documentary history *Children and Youth in America*, we then get a sense of what the common men were fighting about. Volume II of that history contains excerpts that describe the life of the American poor farm family, the immigrants, the blacks, the Indians, and the mining families at the turn of the century. We find chronicles of low wages, long hours, hunger, uncertain work, poor housing, child labor, and poor health. We find Eleanor Roosevelt relating how, as a little girl, she was taken by her father to help serve Thanksgiving dinner at the Children's Aid Society:

> *I was tremendously interested in all these ragged little boys and in the fact, which my father explained, that many of them had no homes and lived in little wooden shanties in empty lots, or slept in vestibules of houses or public buildings or any place where they could be moderately warm. Yet they were independent and earned their own livings.*[3]

Eleanor Roosevelt was being initiated into the then genteel practice of social work, in the tradition of Jane Addams. Social work was one of the few ways by which, voluntarily and on the impulse of charity, selected individuals crossed the large gulf between the haves and the have-nots.

In the first decade of this century, then, we find a social order more split than our own. The aristocrats were more clearly set off as aristocratic. The common man was a little more common. But bridges were being built between them. There were renegotiations of the social contracts of that society, and those renegotiations ultimately tended to blur together the aristocrats and the anarchists. Many of those renegotiations involved social work directed not at the individuals but the institutions of society, and those renegotiations changed the socialization of children in our society:

- Common schooling was coming. Compulsory schooling had been argued for unsuccessfully since before the Civil War. Now a series of compulsory attendance laws were passed between 1880 and 1917, and attendance at school became a requirement. But there was still a conflict between common schooling, conceived of as a homogenizing agent, versus vocational schooling, conceived of as training and disciplining a labor force, just as there was conflict between child education and child labor. In 1900, although twenty-eight states had compulsory school attendance laws, about 1.7 million children under sixteen were still in employment. In the decades to come, however, common schooling would grow and child labor and vocational education would subside.

• Child welfare was coming. There had been a long series of private, city, and state moves against abuse, neglect, and abandonment of children. In the early 1900s, the issue of children's rights became a national issue. The first of the decennial White House Conferences on Children was convened by President Theodore Roosevelt in 1909. The Children's Bureau was established in 1912. There ensued a series of state conventions in the decade of the 1910s to reconsider and strengthen state-level laws and practices concerning the treatment of children.

• The "whole child" professions were coming. There were efforts to create a science of education and, on that science, found a true profession of teaching. To this end, schools of education were incorporated within the universities. The young Nicholas Murray Butler, assistant in philosophy, ethics, and psychology, was trying to teach pedagogics and trying to bring together Columbia College and Teachers College, a liaison that was effected in 1900. Not only teaching, but other professions relevant to the care and socialization of children were being established—social work, pediatrics, and a variety of other school or health related career lines. A new division of responsibility and labor was being established, reallocating the child-rearing responsibilities of family and society. Some traditional parental rights and responsibilities were being reassigned to the professions.[4]

It was amidst the social arrangements and the social changes of that time that American psychology was born. I believe that most of us share a misunderstanding about the history of American psychology. We see it too much as something that was created in intellectual and scientific history, rather than as something that was given life and form by American social concerns in the 1900s. The new American psychology emerging at the opening of the nineteenth century took an abrupt turn away from the philosophical psychology originally imported from the German universities. A set of psychological enterprises erupted into prominence in the American universities that are not easily traced back to one lineage.

If we stick with the traditional analysis of American intellectual history, then the decade from 1900 to 1910 appears to be a decade of brilliance. We find within the confines of that decade the abrupt emergence of men, ideas, and enterprises that were quite distinct from the German philosophical psychology, that squelched its growth in short order, and that superseded it to become the basis of American psychology today. It was indeed a decade of brilliance, but there was something else. During this period, certain images, ideas, and inquiries were afloat in the intellectual world that were struck by the heat and light of social movement and were crystalized into institutionalized forces. Society started investing in public knowledge of human behavior because it was making a major new set of investments in public responsibility for human socialization and human development. In fact, if we examine the new psychologies that erupted in the 1900s, we find that they were stimulated by the social concerns of the time, particularly by contemporary interests in creating professional, scientific bases for children's education and socialization.

Consider learning theory. In 1898, Thorndike published his first monograph on animal associative learning. By 1904, Pavlov had announced his turn from the study of digestion toward the study of phychic reflexes, and by 1909 we find

Pavlov's work under discussion in American journals in a paper by Yerkes and Morgulis. By 1913-14, Thorndike had published the three volumes of his *Educational Psychology* and Watson had published his "Psychology as the Behaviorist Views It." The learning theory movement was now in place.

Note that in Thorndike's mind, learning theory was the cornerstone of a science of education; in Watson's mind, behaviorism was the cornerstone of a science of child rearing. These were the themes of clinical psychology and personality theory. In 1896, Lightner Witmer founded the Psychological Clinic at Pennsylvania. In 1909, William Healy founded what was to become the Institute for Juvenile Research at Chicago. These were the beginnings of the child guidance movement. It was in 1909 that G. Stanley Hall brought Freud, Jung, Ferenezi, and Jones to participate in the twentieth anniversary celebrations of Clark University. Theories about the importance of early human personality development, and clinical activity related to these theories, emerge at the beginning of American psychology.

The theme of child study began with G. Stanley Hall's educational psychology. Hall founded the Pedagogical Seminary in 1891. He studied the contents of children's minds from 1894 to 1903. (By the middle of the first decade of this century, there was a sizable bibliography on child study, which was the work of many hands.) This movement waned during the First World War, but took life again as the Child Development Movement in the late 1920s and early 1930s and finally became the foundation for the basic and applied efforts that are characteristic of psychological research with children today.

Finally, there was the theme of mental testing. The Binet and Simon instrument, first developed in 1905, was the culmination of a long series of efforts toward the development of mental tests. It shortly became accepted as an intelligence test. Learning theory, clinical psychology, personality theory, and child study were all put in place in the dawning psychology of that day because of the special feeling that new social sciences would help in designing new social contracts. But nothing so instantly leaped into use and relevance as mental testing. The relevance of mental testing to the social needs of that period was particularly striking, and it merits some extended discussion.

•

One of the most interesting things about Binet and Simon's invention is the contrast between the curious indefiniteness of the invention compared with the curious definiteness of its social acceptance. What did Binet's test measure? According to Binet and Simon:

> *It seems to us that in intelligence there is a fundamental faculty, the alteration or the lack of which is of the utmost importance for practical life. This faculty is judgment, otherwise called good sense, practical sense, initiative, the faculty of adapting one's self to circumstances. To judge well, to comprehend well, to reason well, these are the essential activities of intelligence. A person may be a moron or an imbecile if he is lacking in judgment; but with good judgment he can never be either. Indeed the rest of the intellectual faculties seem of little importance in contrast with judgment. . . .*[5]

Binet and Simon are here trying to discount the value of the sensory and memory mental testing that had preceded them. Their affirmation of judgment appears in a paper in which the basic items of the Binet-Simon scale are presented, and one can easily examine the items to see if they are valid according to the stated criterion of judgment. The items do not look like items that tap only judgment; one would guess they identify a complex of entities.

Binet and Simon were not completely sold on judgment as the sine qua non of intelligence. In writings before and after the above quote, indeed in the very same paper, Binet sponsored a curiously vacillating series of verbal definitions of intelligence, with little apparent relationship among them. Spearman, in his *The Nature of "Intelligence" and the Principles of Cognition* reviews some of Binet's definition variations and finally concludes: "It would seem as if, in thus inconstantly flitting hither and thither, Binet can nowhere find a theoretical perch satisfactory for a moment even to himself."[6]

Spearman also reviews some of Simon's writings about intelligence, independent of Binet's, which only compound the problem. In the very delivery of their instrument, Binet and Simon initiated a situation with which we are quite familiar today—intelligence testing, definite procedure, explicit test items, and countable and scorable behaviors. But this procedural definiteness is shrouded in a never ending series of feeble, wandering verbal statements of what the items and the behaviors are all about.

The development of the Binet-Simon instrument was certainly not a simple fruition of theoretical inquiry. The instrument was precipitated by a practical social problem in the selection of children. It was submitted to the minister of public instruction in France in 1905 after he requested a study of measures to assure the benefits of education of defective children. The test was submitted to assist in a question of social selection. This question was probably, then as now, one that was individually poignant and politically tricky for those individuals having to make the decision. Not all psychologists, teachers, and psychiatrists were happy about the theory or the practice of the tests. They are not happy today. But the tests moved slowly into use.

A bureaucratic society must, for many of its activities, categorize or classify people. Those responsible for such classifications are under relentless pressure to justify their sorting of people on universal grounds that are at least argumentatively objective and fair. It seems most likely that the intelligence tests came into use in the 1920s and 1930s for much the same reason that they were used for preschool evaluations in the 1960s—not because of strong belief in them, but because there were no alternatives and something had to be used. The public became aware of the mental testing movement at the time of World War I, when grading men for military service was initiated. Brought into prominence and given commercial development, the series of offspring of the rather rudimentary venture of Binet and Simon, became the basis of the large and diversified enterprise of psychological testing we find in our society today.

But, throughout this period of social growth, that seed of paradox first visible in the Binet-Simon work remains. In 1927, when Thorndike and his colleagues reviewed the theory of intelligence testing, they found that the tests had improved, but they still could not determine, any more than Binet, what was being measured by the tests or what was meant by "measurement."[7]

In 1958, David Wechsler commented on the attempts over decades to define intelligence:

> *Some psychologists have come to doubt whether these laborious analyses have contributed anything fundamental to our understanding of intelligence while others have come to the equally disturbing conclusion that the term intelligence, as now employed, is so ambiguous that it ought to be discarded altogether. Psychology now seems to find itself in the paradoxical position of devising and advocating tests for measuring intelligence and then disclaiming responsibility for them by asserting that "nobody knows what the word really means."*[8]

Either Thorndike's or Wechsler's judgment could apply today.

In short, if one reviews the situation persisting from

Binet through Thorndike to the present, we find that we have in some astonishing way managed to continuously upgrade a technology for directing an uncertain measurement paradigm toward an undefined entity. If we look at an intelligence test as a piece of technology, an invention, or an outcome of science, then I do not believe we can understand this. We advance on understanding the problem somewhat if we consider that the growth of intelligence testing has largely come through recurrent human needs to justify selection and classification of people. But even this does not seem sufficient. There are a good many practices of social classification for which we do not use tests. And despite the fact that there are by now thousands of tests, no test has been assigned its own magic circle quite so decisively as the intelligence test. No test is given more credence. No test has been implicated as deeply in usage and in serious discussion of education and society. What we deal with here, I believe, is an affair in which magic, science, and myth are intermixed.

•

In some classic essays in cultural anthropology, Bronislaw Malinowski has attempted to capture the place of magic, science, religion, and myth in primitive societies. He discusses the cultural practices of the Trobriand Islanders. Reacting against some descriptions of primitive peoples, which would picture them as wholly immersed in superstition and magic, he argues that the Trobriand Islanders have scientific knowledge, and that they recognize a distinction between practice based on knowledge versus practice that must be based on magic. The Trobrianders must contend with natural forces in a variety of their cultural activities—in gardening, building boats, fishing, warfare, and in care of the sick. Where they understand and can control what they are doing, they use science; where they do not understand, they are very apt to interject magic. "It is most significant," Malinowski says, "that in the lagoon fishing, where man can rely completely upon his knowledge and skill, magic does not exist, while in the open-sea fishing, full of danger and uncertainty, there is extensive ritual to secure safety and good results."[9]

Overriding the knowledge, magic, and beliefs of the Trobrianders are stories—fairy tales, legends, and sacred tales or myths. Malinowski argues that these bring order and unity to the Trobrianders' body of social experience, uniting and justifying:

> *The cultural fact is a monument in which the myth is embodied; while the myth is believed to be the real cause which has brought about the moral rule, the social grouping, the rite, or the custom. Thus these stories form an integral part of culture. Their existence and influence not merely transcend the act of telling the narrative, not only do they draw their substance from life and its interests—they govern and control many cultural features, they form the dogmatic backbone of primitive civilization.*[10]

Our culture went through some serious changes around the turn of this century. The time was much marked by appeals to science and reason. But is it possible that we could not have accomplished those changes entirely on those grounds? If we concede that the Trobriand Islanders had a little science, then we might entertain the possibility that today we supplement our science with a little magic. If we hold that the Trobriand Islanders unify and justify their social practices using myths, we might also suspect that our ancestors, putting behind them the social values associated with the myth of creation, might have rebuilt social explanations and justifications around the evolutionary narratives newly offered to them by scientific work. One reason for believing in this possibility is precisely the peculiar transcendental status of the notion of intelligence during the period we are considering.

Our notion of intelligence has transcended questions of definition and proof. In all the diverse writings about intelligence, there is a curious resemblance to the medieval proofs of God. Hundreds strive to define or measure its ineffable essence, sometimes with epic labors such as those of Piaget or Guilford. Who sanctified intelligence and made it prior to proof? The likelihood is that Herbert Spencer gave the term "intelligence" ideological sanctification. The likelihood is that subsequently changing American social practices at the turn of the century wove intelligence testing in as part of a new act of procedures for assigning social status.

More than a hundred years ago, Spencer stated that the be-all and end-all of human evolution was the growth of intelligence, sentience, and elaborated knowledge of the world. He argued that, if one arranges the phylogenetic tree in the way we usually do, with natural history moving toward man and culminating in man, then the basic dimension of phylogenesis is intelligence. To evolve is to become more intelligent; to become more intelligent is to evolve.

Spencer had an enormous vogue as the prophet of an evolutionary vision of the design of a society. Sir Francis Galton, a contemporary, was interested in eugenics (scientific human breeding to advance the race). It was in the interest of eugenics that he made his tries at "anthropometry" that were the beginning efforts at mental testing. But Herbert Spencer preached a social eugenics, society governed by fitness and rewarding and promoting fitness, and it was probably he who provided the climate for the ultimate acceptance of such testing. Hofstadter's *Social Darwinism in American Thought*[11] traces the Spencerian embodiment of evolutionism in social thinking. In the 1870s and 1880s Herbert Spencer's writings were so dominant in discussions of society and politics that they virtually sank into the unconscious of American political deliberation, ceased to be an argument, became obvious, and became common sense. They remain strong even today. They form the core of the "market mentality" satirized in the recent best-seller, *Nixon Agonistes;*[12] that is, the notion that the social arena must be seen as a competitive arena where the strong survive and the weak die. The Spencerian philosophy formed a scientistic core for outlooks that we today characterize as elitism, racism, and imperialism. Hofstadter's review emphasizes the alignment of Social Darwinism with conservative political forces in the nineteenth century, and this seems fair. Spencer seems to have courted the wealthy. But there was much of the evolutionary philosophy built into the liberal politics of the time. Progressivism had its Social Darwinism, too.

People approached the social changes of the turn of the century with their minds formed by Spencer and the advocates of Social Darwinism. Before Binet, or Thorndike, or Cattell, or even Galton, people had made up their minds about the centrality of intelligence as the epitome of human merit. When the tests came along, they were not required to prove their way. The tests could not then—and they cannot now—prove their way. They were exemplifications, definitions, and manifestations of an entity whose scientific and social sanctity was given.

•

I have very briefly rehearsed the ideology of the time. Now consider the import of that ideology on the social business of the turn of the century. American society was in the process of constructing more egalitarian arrangements. The actors on the American scene—aristocrats, workers, anarchists, immigrants—were in search of new rules and procedures for the allocation of social benefits and social status. Without relinquishing their belief in aristocracy—that there are better men and worse men—people sought to abolish favoritism based on inheritance, or land, or property. They felt that the only right and fair aristocracy should be one of merit. To a society concerned in finding ways in which the best might rule, Social Darwinism offered the extremely important definition of bestness. Bestness was intelligence. Bestness was developed by education. Spencer did not speak of intelligence as solely an innately fixed trait; he saw schools and, more generally, cognitive development as adding to and enlarging human intelligence. Thus Spencer's arguments were important factors in several of the trends that enhanced the place of education in the social scene at that time: 1) the coming of common schooling; 2) the elaboration of colleges into universities; and 3) the general feeling that social science and social scientists must take a more central role in social governance. John Dewey, in his writings, expresses the almost mystical progressive feeling prevalent at that time: that science, education, good government, public morality, all interpenetrate; so that to foster one is to foster all the others.

The argument then is that the intelligence test exploded into public acceptability and public use not because of its merits, but because it could be seized on as part of a more fair and more just system of social contracts. The test could be used as part of the system for allocating social opportunity. Needless to say, the tests could not have been so accepted if the people in power at that time saw the tests as potentially destroying their children's power. But the IQ tests of that time had the rather happy property of being a conservative social innovation. They could be perceived as justifying the richness of the rich and the poverty of the poor; they legitimized the existing social order. At the same time, they played a slowly subversive role, so that some of the actors—the Germans and the Irish and the Italian and the Jewish immigrants—could see their second- and third-generation offspring move toward social status.

All this being true, if it is, how do we get out of the

magic circle we have created? How do psychologists cease being priests of the mysteries of intelligence, rationalizing a semimystical system of social allocation whose present defects have begun to seriously outweigh any benefits gained from previous use? How do educators reduce the incessant pressures to negotiate and explain the gaps between the myths and the realities of education? There are probably no absolute answers and no safe way out. I believe, however, it is now time for us to construct some new testing to replace the traditional IQ and achievement testing; and I also believe that everything—new ideology, new social contracts, new data—is coming into place to permit us to do this.

We are in an active period in rebuilding social contracts. This, I believe, is the deeper meaning of the poverty programs of the 1960s and the ferment that continues now concerning education, health care, family assistance, day care, and so forth. In diverse ways, we are seeking to redefine the rights and responsibilities of children, parents, teachers, physicians, social workers, courts, and governmental agencies.

As one might expect, this social change is accompanied by a change in the mythic system—in Malinowski's terms, a new "dogmatic backbone." We are into the politics of pluralism. The old mythic system held that humans were arranged in a linear hierarchy of excellence, blending the ancient human format of an aristocratic order with newer social provision for a competition of merit. The pluralisms of early twentieth century America were to be resolved by the melting pot; that is, all species of Americans were resolved into one species. In this context, the fair fight for social place could take place on universal standards of IQ and the open competition of the schools.

There is much to be admired in this conception. It was a vision of a socially fair system, within which the practice of intelligence testing could take an honorable place. It was not important to understand the tests, because they were so reasonable in intent that one could only see them as a benign "white magic." Furthermore, various intercorrelations among IQ, school achievement, income, and socioeconomic status (SES) always turned out positive—a little loose, but positive—thus mixing a little science with the magic.

We are now moving to relinquish this mythic structure and to replace it with another. The fundamental move is to disentangle excellence from chosenness. It is simply not true that human beings manifest one kind of excellence, that society rests on one order of human excellence, or that schools should be in the business of promoting one kind of excellence. If we step outside the magic circle for a few moments and look beyond the sacred trinity of IQ, school achievement, and SES, we can recognize the everyday, scientific realities on which a new and pluralistic mythic structure might be based.

Our test data do not tell us that one order, one linear arrangement of human ability prevails. Our test data tell us that humans have diverse, correlationally distinct abilities. Our data from cognitive development, from psychoneurology, from human learning, and from memory studies tell us that humans have multiple knowledge systems, multiple systems of representation, multiple gnostic centers, multiple short-term and long-term memories, and multiple laws of learning.

Our experience with society tells us that there is more than one order of social status. Humans give and receive respect on diverse grounds. Status based on money is not exactly the same as status based on education, and neither begins to classify the diverse social hierarchies based on vocational and political competencies.

Our experience with schooling tells us that children show diverse patterns of giftedness and achievement. This is true within the simplest form of the elementary school as a place to foster reading, writing, and mathematics. The similarities and differences among children concerning these skills are only lightly portrayed by a linear arrangement of grade-point-equivalent scores on a standardized achievement test. If one's conception of an elementary school includes all those other diverse aspects of training that are or might be put into the curriculum, it seems obvious that sooner or later the outcomes sought will be beyond the capacity of a single ordinal number.

I believe that the pluralistic picture I have been sketching is quite obvious. Certainly, no one should be surprised by the idea that children have diverse abilities, that schools foster diverse achievements, or that society uses diverse competences. Furthermore, I doubt that many will have trouble with the idea that a single valued intelligence test is simplistic. So let me, finally, turn to the central question: can we reform intelligence testing? Yes, I believe we can. But only to some extent.

Considering all the problems with intelligence testing, it is tempting to argue that we ought to throw the tests out as illogical and mischievous. It seems possible to do that. The Soviet Union officially banned all intelligence testing in 1936, and, so far as I know, it has gotten along without it ever since. But we might have problems doing that. Intelligence tests moved into usage because of difficult and real problems that bureaucracies had in their basic business of categorizing people. Suppose we were to throw out the tests and put the decisions they serve entirely in the hands of human judgment and estimation? What problems would arise from human bias, carelessness, and incompetence? How intense and how hurtful would be the problems of conscience and politics that afflict the decision maker who holds the power to help or hurt a child by choosing whether the child will go to a special class, receive extra remedial help, or qualify for higher education or a job? These are the problems now eased by the science-plus-magic of intelligence testing. The problems attendant on categorizing people are endemic in bureaucracies. On the one hand, we have national commissions deploring and viewing with alarm the problems of labeling children; and on the other hand, we have commissions calling for more widespread diagnosis of early handicaps (as though we could find true positives without false positives, or as though we could diagnose without labeling).

I believe we must imagine that the reform of intelligence testing can best be accomplished by the widespread adoption of plural tests of human mental abilities. Those giving mental tests have for some time recognized that human test performance tends not to be uniform but, in part at least, seems to be broken up, so that clusters of items tend to go upward and downward together in groups, setting themselves apart as intercorrelating entities. This kind of observation has brought forth various proposals that a plurality of human mental abilities exist—such things as verbal ability, spatial ability, reasoning, numerical ability, idea fluency, mechanical knowledge and skill, and so forth. Some relief might come from this body of pluralized mental testing.

One problem facing this kind of option, however, is that diverse testers do not agree on the number and kinds of diverse abilities humans have. A second problem, probably the source of the first problem, is that the conception of the human's competence as a profile on an *n*-ability set of scales is much too simple. But, despite such problems, the invention and use of such a system of characterizing differences among children would have considerable social benefits. It would provide a larger magic circle, encompassing significantly more of the reality one encounters in schools. It would also provide a considerably richer mixture of science in the midst of the magic.

We would, through use of such a system, recognize in some official sense that human excellence and human social utility come in diverse forms. We would encourage the diversification of the aims and goals of education—a matter well worth pursuing. And if we still argued about the hereditariness versus environmentalness in our new multiple system—the modern counterpart of traditional disputation about predestination versus good works—we would at least see, within the argument, the vision of multiple roads to salvation.

Human beings have trouble finding intellectual formats within which to comprehend the variety of dimly perceived similarities and differences that float by in experience. The discovery or reception of promising formats is a good deal of what cognitive development, education, and science are all about. One of the simplest and easiest formats available to humans is the simple, linear ordinal arrangement. It can be used by seven-year-olds. It comes easily to the mind. There has been a recurrent human tendency to picture the universe as filled with creatures of all possible degrees of perfection. Lovejoy in his *The Great Chain of Being*[13] traces this three-thousand-year-old tradition and shows how, in the nineteenth century, Darwinism simply brought about the transposition of the format on an evolutionary and biological scale. Now we find it applied to humans and social affairs. The fact that the format is ancient may only mean that it is easy, not inexorable. Once upon a time the fifteenth century alchemists, not knowing much about matter, imagined all elements to exist on a linear order of nobility—gold and silver the most noble of all. They saw their problems in terms of this format. For example, they saw the problem of transmuting lead into gold as essentially the problem of freeing lead from impurity and baseness.

In a strikingly similar fashion, today we envisage the solution of many educational problems as simply a matter of removing from some children their impurity or baseness—elevating the IQ, removing deficits or disadvantages, closing the gap, or accelerating their cognitive development. It is my hope that we will come to accept the notion that people are quite as complicated as chemical elements, that it takes a multidimensional format to begin to comprehend their similarities and differences. Seeing people in this way, we may come to think in new and useful ways about what the possibilities of better education might be.

NOTES

1. B. Tuchman, *The Proud Tower* (New York: Macmillan Co., 1966).
2. N. M. Butler, *Across the Busy Years* (New York: Charles Scribner's Sons, 1939).
3. R. H. Bremner, ed., *Children and Youth in America: A Documentary History,* vol. II (Cambridge, Mass.: Harvard University Press, 1971), p. 34.
4. S. H. White et al., *Federal Programs for Young Children* (Washington: U.S. Government Printing Office, 1973), chap. 2; S. H. White, "Socialization and Education—For What and by What Means?" in *Raising Children in Modern America,* ed. N. B. Talbot (Boston: Little, Brown and Co., in press).
5. A. Binet and T. Simon, "The Development of the Binet-Simon Scale," in *Readings in the History of Psychology,* ed. W. Dennis (New York: Appleton-Century-Crofts, 1948), p. 417.
6. C. Spearman, *The Nature of "Intelligence" and the Principles of Cognition* (London: Macmillan Co., 1923), p. 10.
7. E. L. Thorndike et al., *The Measurement of Intelligence* (New York: Teachers College Bureau of Publications, 1927).
8. D. Wechsler, cited in R. D. Tuddenham, "The Nature and Measurement of Intelligence," in *Psychology in the Making: Histories of Selected Research Problems,* ed. L. Postman (New York: Knopf, 1962).
9. B. Malinowski, *Magic, Science and Religion and Other Essays* (Glencoe, Ill.: The Free Press, 1948), p. 12.
10. Ibid., p. 85.
11. R. Hofstadter, *Social Darwinism in American Thought* (Boston: Beacon Press, 1955).
12. G. Wills, *Nixon Agonistes: The Crisis of the Self-made Man* (New York: Houghton Mifflin, 1970).
13. A. O. Lovejoy, *The Great Chain of Being: A Study of the History of an Idea* (Cambridge, Mass.: Harvard University, 1936).

THE POLITICS OF IQ

LEON J. KAMIN

Leon J. Kamin is Dorman T. Warren Professor of Psychology at Princeton University, Princeton, New Jersey. Mr. Kamin is an experimental psychologist whose major research interests have been in the areas of animal conditioning and learning.

This article is adapted from Mr. Kamin's book The Science and Politics of I.Q. *Reprinted with the permission of the author and publisher from Kamin, L.J.* The Science and Politics of I.Q. *Hillsdale, N.J.: Lawrence Erlbaum Associates, Publishers, 1974.*

Leon Kamin's book The Science and Politics of I.Q. *presents a detailed analysis of the classical IQ studies that have led many contemporary scholars to conclude that IQ scores are largely determined by heredity. Following his review of studies of separated identical twins, of kinship correlation, and of adopted children, Kamin concludes that, "There exist no data which should lead a prudent man to accept the hypothesis that IQ test scores are in any degree heritable." Kamin argues that the current upsurge of hereditarian theories has political and social, rather than scientific, roots. The adaptation from the book reprinted here focuses on the social history of IQ testing in America. We believe that in this instance, history contains a very pointed contemporary moral.*

The Editor

The first usable intelligence test was developed in France by Alfred Binet in 1905. The basic facts are known to everybody who has taken a college course in psychology, and are available in any textbook. The French minister of public instruction had commissioned Binet to develop a testing procedure that could help to identify students whose academic aptitudes were so low as to necessitate their placement in "special schools."

The test developed by Binet was very largely atheoretical. He viewed it as a practical diagnostic instrument and was not concerned to "make a distinction between acquired and congenital feeblemindedness."[1] Binet in fact prescribed therapeutic courses in "mental orthopedics" for those with low test scores. His chapter on "The Training of Intelligence" began with the phrase "After the illness, the remedy," and his judgment on "some recent philosophers" who had given their "moral support" to the idea that "the intelligence of an individual is a fixed quantity, a quantity which one cannot augment" is clear: "We must protest and react against this brutal pessimism."[2]

With this orientation, it is perhaps as well that Binet died in 1911, before witnessing the uses to which his test was speedily put in the United States. The major translators and importers of the Binet test were Lewis Terman at Stanford, Henry Goddard at the Vineland Training School in New Jersey, and Robert Yerkes at Harvard. These pioneers of the American mental testing movement held in common some basic sociopolitical views. Their "brutal pessimism" took a very specific political form, manifested by their enthusiastic memberships in various eugenic societies and organizations. They arrived at the remarkable conclusion that the questions asked of children by the Binet test provided a fixed measure of "innate intelligence." The test could thus be used to detect the genetically inferior, whose reproduction was a menace to the future of the state. The communality of their views—and their divergence from Binet's—can best be illustrated by quotations from their early writings.

The Americanized "Stanford-Binet" test was published by Terman in 1916. The promise of the test was made explicit at the outset:

> *...in the near future intelligence tests will bring tens of thousands of these high-grade defectives under the surveillance and protection of society. This will ultimately result in curtailing the reproduction of feeblemindedness and in the elimination of an enormous amount of crime, pauperism, and industrial inefficiency. It is hardly necessary to emphasize that the high-grade cases, of the type now so frequently overlooked, are precisely the ones whose guardianship it is most important for the State to assume.*[3]

Terman asserted that "there is no investigator who denies the fearful role played by mental deficiency in the production of vice, crime, and delinquency." The cause of mental deficiency—and by implication of crime—was transparently clear. "Heredity studies of 'degenerate' families have confirmed, in a striking way, the testimony secured by intelligence tests."

The test, in Terman's view, was particularly useful in the diagnosis of "high-grade" or "border-line" deficiency; that is, IQs in the 70 to 80 range. That level of intelligence

> *is very, very common among Spanish-Indian and Mexican families of the Southwest and also among negroes. Their dullness seems to be racial, or at least inherent in the family stocks from which they come ...the whole question of racial differences in mental traits will have to be taken up anew and by experimental methods. The writer predicts that when this is done there will be discovered enormously significant racial differences in general intelligence, differences which cannot be wiped out by any scheme of mental culture.*

> *Children of this group should be segregated in special classes. . . . They cannot master abstractions, but they can often be made efficient workers. . . . There is no possibility at present of convincing society that they should not be allowed to reproduce, although from a eugenic point of view they constitute a grave problem because of their unusually prolific breeding.*[4]

The theme will reappear, so it is of interest to note that Terman did not draw a simple distinction between the white and the "colored" races. The "dull normals," with IQs between 80 and 90, were said to be "below the actual average of intelligence among races of western European descent. . . ." The "New Immigration" from southeastern Europe was already, by the time Terman wrote, a matter of considerable national concern. The distinction between the "races" of western and southeastern Europe was made forcefully by Madison Grant's influential *The Passing of the Great Race,*[5] and Terman's attribution of a high intelligence level to "races of western European descent" was clearly made in the light of concern over immigration policy.

Professor Terman's stern eugenical judgment fell, in any event, even-handedly on the very poor of all colors. Writing in 1917 under the heading "The Menace of Feeble-Mindedness," he observed that

> *. . . only recently have we begun to recognize how serious a menace it is to the social, economic and moral welfare of the state. . . . It is responsible . . . for the majority of cases of chronic and semi-chronic pauperism. . . .*

> *. . . the feeble-minded continue to multiply . . . organized charities . . . often contribute to the survival of individuals who would otherwise not be able to live and reproduce. . . .*

> *If we would preserve our state for a class of people worthy to possess it, we must prevent, as far as possible, the propagation of mental degenerates . . . curtailing the increasing spawn of degeneracy.*[6]

The violence of Terman's language stands in melancholy affirmation of Binet's earlier reproof to teachers of the "feeble-minded":

> *The familiar proverb which says: "When one is stupid, it's for a long time" seems to be taken literally, without criticism, by some schoolmasters; those who disinterest themselves in students who lack intelligence; they have for them neither sympathy nor even respect, as their intemperance of language makes them say before these children such things as: "This is a child who will never accomplish anything . . . he is poorly gifted. . . ." Never! What a large word!*[7]

The views of Henry Goddard, who began to use the Binet test in 1908, did not differ in any important particular from those of Terman. The test data, to his mind, could be used to provide statistical support for the already demonstrated proposition that normal intelligence and "weak-mindedness" were the products of Mendelian inheritance. Perhaps the foremost of the "heredity studies of 'degenerate' families" cited by Terman was Goddard's lurid tracing of the family lines descended from one Martin Kallikak. With respect to the social menace of hereditary feeble-mindedness, Goddard had in 1912 predated Terman: " . . . we have discovered that pauperism and crime are increasing at an enormous rate, and we are led to pause and ask, 'Why?' Even a superficial investigation shows us that a large percentage of these troubles come from the feeble-minded."[8] The "troubles" had evidently caught the attention of alert social scientists who labored long before Professors Banfield or Herrnstein.[9]

The sociopolitical views of the early mental testers are perhaps nowhere more clearly revealed than in Goddard's invited lectures at Princeton University in 1919. There Goddard discoursed on the new science of "mental levels." That new science made possible the accurate assessment of the mental levels both of children and of adults, and those levels had been fixed by heredity. The new science had generated data of profound social significance, and in particular, it invalidated the arguments of gentlemen socialists:

> *As for an equal distribution of the wealth of the world that is equally absurd. The man of intelligence has spent his money wisely, has saved until he has enough to provide for his needs in case of sickness, while the man of low intelligence, no matter how much money he would have earned, would have spent much of it foolishly and would never have anything ahead. It is said that during the past year, the coal miners in certain parts of the country have earned more money than the operators and yet today when the mines shut down for a time, those people are the first to suffer. They did not save anything, although their whole life has taught them that mining is an irregular thing and that when they were having plenty of work they should save against the days when they do not have work. . . .*
>
> *These facts are appreciated. But it is not so fully appreciated that the cause is to be found in the fixed character of mental levels. In our ignorance we have said let us give these people one more chance—always one more chance.*[10]

The progress from Binet's position is staggering. The feebleminded, the paupers, and the unemployed coal miners now seem scarcely distinguishable. This is something more than the "brutal pessimism" protested by Binet. Whatever else we call it, this was a perversion of psychological "science." There are few more vivid examples of the subordination of science to political and economic ideology.

The point of view of the third major importer of Binet's test, Robert Yerkes, is sufficiently indicated by his 1917 appointment as chairman of the Committee on Inheritance of Mental Traits of the Eugenics Research Association. The relation of IQ to heredity and to economic factors is made clear in Yerkes's prescription for how "to make a true diagnosis of feeble-mindedness. . . . Never should such a diagnosis be made on the IQ alone. . . . We must inquire further into the subject's economic history. What is his occupation; his pay . . . we must learn what we can about his immediate family. What is the economic status or occupation of the parents? . . . When all this information has been collected . . . the psychologist may be of great value in getting the subject into the most suitable place in society. . . ."[11]

To be diagnosed as feebleminded during this period, and to be assigned to a "suitable place," was not an enviable lot. There were few fine discriminations drawn, as we have seen, among the criminal, the poor, and the dull-witted.

This was the social climate into which Terman, Goddard, and Yerkes introduced the intelligence test. The judgments of psychologists were to have grave social consequences, for the measurement of the fixed mental level was to have a role in determining who was set free and who was jailed; and it was to aid in determining who was sufficiently fit to be allowed to reproduce. There is no record, however, to the effect that the pioneers of American mental testing experienced the awe reported by the physicists who first split the atom.

•

The early history of testing in America fixed on the

Binet test an apparently indelible genetic interpretation. The hereditarian interpretation shared by Terman, Goddard, and Yerkes did not arise as a consequence of the collection of IQ data. Their involvement in the eugenics movement predated the collection of such data. There was, at the time they wrote, no quantitative genetics; there was in fact no tenable theory of how mental traits might be inherited. The notion that dependency, defectiveness, weakmindedness, and other social ills were attributable to the genes was, in America, an idea whose time had come.

We can trace the force of that idea—and its utter divorce from any meaningful scientific data—in the successful efforts of the eugenicists to enact sterilization laws. The rise of the mental testing movement coincided precisely in time with the passage of such laws by a large number of states. These sterilization laws, many of which—but not all—were never enforced, had two features in common. First, they were to be applied exclusively to inmates of publicly supported corrective or "charitable" institutions. Second, they asserted as a matter of fact that various forms of "degeneracy" were hereditarily transmitted.

The first bill actually passed by a legislature was in Pennsylvania. The year, ironically, was 1905, the year in which Binet first published his test. The bill was described as an "Act for the Prevention of Idiocy," but it was vetoed by Governor Pennypacker. The first fully enacted law was passed by Indiana in 1907. The law's preamble, with slight modification, appeared repeatedly in sterilization laws subsequently passed by other states. The preamble stated very simply, "Whereas, heredity plays a most important part in the transmission of crime, idiocy, and imbecility."[12] This legislative fiat occurred before Terman and Goddard sketched out in detail the interrelations among crime, feeblemindedness, and dependency. They were in large measure following the lead provided by the would-be behavior geneticists of the state legislatures.

The advancement of human behavior genetics seemed

now to lie in the hands of politicians, and few could resist the temptation to contribute to science. To Indiana's list of traits in which "heredity plays a most important part," New Jersey added in 1911 "feeble-mindedness, epilepsy, criminal tendencies, and other defects."[13] The Iowa legislature in the same year provided for the "unsexing of criminals, idiots, etc." The "unsexing" provision, however, went beyond any valid eugenic need, and a scientifically sounder measure was adopted by Iowa in 1913. The new bill spelled out the "etc." of the 1911 law, providing for "the prevention of the procreation of criminals, rapists, idiots, feeble-minded, imbeciles, lunatics, drunkards, drug fiends, epileptics, syphilitics, moral and sexual perverts, and diseased and degenerate persons."[14]

Presumably, the Supreme Court of the State of Washington had in mind the work of the pioneer mental testers when it upheld the Washington sterilization law on 3 September 1912. The court pointed out that "modern scientific investigation shows that idiocy, insanity, imbecility, and criminality are congenital and hereditary. . . . There appears to be a wonderful unanimity of favoring the prevention of their future propagation."[15]

The scientific documentation offered by the mental testers that degeneracy and feeblemindedness were heritable did not occur in a vacuum. Their views were responsive to social problems of the gravest moment. Their "findings" were politically partisan, and they had consequences. We can see clearly with hindsight how ludicrously beyond the bounds of science those views and "findings" extended. They fixed on the succeeding generations of psychometricians, equipped with more sophisticated scientific tools, a clear predisposition toward a genetic interpretation of IQ data. That predisposition is still with us.

Though sterilization measures were fitfully enforced against the poor—most notably in California—they had no major impact on American society; in fact, the sterilization laws may have been largely dead letters. In another sphere, however, the mental testing movement was deeply involved in a major practical accomplishment. The findings of the new science were used to rationalize the passage of an overtly racist immigration law. The mental testers pressed on the Congress scientific IQ data to demonstrate that the "New Immigration" from southeastern Europe was genetically inferior. That contribution permanently transformed American society and is not without contemporary relevance.

•

The United States, until 1875, had no federal immigration law. The 1875 law, and all subsequent amendments until 1921, placed no numerical limitation on immigration. The first federal law simply listed a number of excluded classes of individuals. The 1875 list was modest—it barred coolies, convicts, and prostitutes.

The control over immigration developed slowly, and at first by the gradual addition of new excluded classes. There was also a "gentlemen's agreement" with Japan, and circuitous regulations having to do with the longitudes and latitudes from which immigration was debarred served to assure an appropriate racial balance. There was, however, no discrimination drawn among the various European countries that provided the bulk of immigration. Throughout the nineteenth century, the preponderance of immigration flowed from the countries of northern and western Europe.

With the turn of the century, however, the "New Immigration" from southeastern Europe began to assume massive proportions. The English, Scandinavian, and German stock that had earlier predominated was now outnumbered by a wave of Italian, Polish, Russian, and Jewish immigrants. The popular press and the literary magazines of the period were filled with articles questioning the assimilability of the new and exotic ethnic breeds. There arose a public clamor for some form of "quality control" over the inflow of immigrants. This at first took the form of a demand for a literacy test; but it could scarcely be doubted that the new science of mental testing, which proclaimed its ability to measure innate intelligence, would be called into the nation's service.

The first volunteer was Henry Goddard, who in 1912 was invited by the United States Public Health Service to Ellis Island, the immigrant receiving station in New York harbor. The intrepid Goddard administered the Binet test and supplementary performance tests to representatives of what he called the "great mass of average immigrants." The results were sure to produce grave concern in the minds of thoughtful citizens. The test results established that 83 percent of the Jews, 80 percent of the Hungarians, 79 percent of the Italians, and 87 percent of the Russians were "feeble-minded."[16] By 1917, Goddard was able to report in the *Journal of Delinquency* that "the number of aliens deported because of feeble-mindedness . . . increased approximately 350 percent in 1913 and 570 percent in 1914. . . . This was due to the untiring efforts of the physicians who were inspired by the belief that mental tests could be used for the detection of feeble-minded aliens. . . ."[17]

This accomplishment of the fledgling science won sympathetic attention from the Eugenics Research Association. That society's journal, *Eugenical News*, was edited by the biologist Harry Laughlin. Writing in his journal in 1917, Laughlin observed: "Recently the science of psychology has developed to a high state of precision that branch of its general subject devoted to the testing of individuals for natural excellence in mental and tempermental qualities. When the knowledge of the existence of this science becomes generally known in Congress, that body will then be expected to apply the direct and logical test for the qualities which we seek to measure. . . ."[18]

This appears to have been a relatively modest proposal,

presumably pointing toward the use of mental tests in detecting would-be immigrants who fell into the debarred classes. There were, however, historical forces at work that were to catapult the science of mental testing to new levels of public acceptance, and that were to provide the scientists of the Eugenics Research Association with opportunities scarcely imaginable in early 1917. The United States was soon to enter the First World War, and mental testing was to play a critical role in determining the ethnic and racial composition of the republic.

The president of the American Psychological Association when the country declared war was Robert Yerkes, who suggested that the major contribution of psychologists to the war effort might be the mass intelligence testing of draftees. The proposal was accepted by the military, and a group of psychologists quickly developed a written group intelligence test—"Alpha"—which could easily be administered to large bodies of men. The work on test development was planned by a committee whose membership included Terman, Goddard, and Yerkes.

The tests appear to have had little practical effect on the outcome of the war. They were not in fact much used for the placement of men. The testing program, however, generated enormous amounts of data, since some two million men were given standardized IQ tests. The mental tests were widely publicized. Public interest was doubtless excited by the finding that the "mental age" of the average white draftee was only thirteen.

Following the war, an intensive statistical analysis was performed on the scores of some 125,000 draftees. The results of this analysis, together with a detailed history of the testing program, were published in 1921 by the National Academy of Sciences, under Yerkes's editorship.[19] The publication of the data occurred in the same year in which Congress, as a temporary measure, first placed a numerical limitation on immigration.

The World War I data provided the first massive demonstration that blacks scored lower on IQ tests than did whites. That, however, was not a matter of pressing concern in 1921. The chapter in the Yerkes report with immediate impact was that on "Relation of Intelligence Ratings to Nativity," which summarized IQ results for a total of 12,407 draftees who had reported that they were born in foreign countries. A letter grade, ranging from A through E, was assigned to each tested draftee, and the distribution of grades was presented separately for each country of origin.

The chapter observed: "The range of difference between the countries is a very wide one. . . . In general, the Scandinavian and English speaking countries stand high in the list, while the Slavic and Latin countries stand low . . . the countries tend to fall into two groups: Canada, Great Britain, the Scandinavian and Teutonic countries [as opposed to] the Latin and Slavic countries. . . ."[20]

There occurred in 1920 a massive influx of experimental psychologists, who had worked during the war under Yerkes, into the Eugenics Research Association. The secretary of that association, Harry Laughlin, was appointed "Expert Eugenics Agent" of the House Committee on Immigration and Naturalization of the U.S. Congress. The Division of Anthropology and Psychology of the National Research Council established a Committee on Scientific Problems of Human Migration under Yerkes' leadership. The function of that committee was to remove serious national debate over immigration from politics, and to place it instead on a firm scientific basis.

The first research supported by the National Research Council's committee was that of Carl Brigham, then an assistant professor of psychology at Princeton University. The Princeton University Press had already published in 1923 Brigham's *Study of American Intelligence*. The book is a landmark of sorts. Though it has disappeared from contemporary reference lists, it can be argued that few works in the history of American psychology have had so significant an impact.

The empirical contribution made by Brigham consisted of a reanalysis of the army data on immigrant intelligence. The performance of Negro draftees was taken as a kind of bedrock baseline; fully 46 percent of the Poles, 42.3 percent of the Italians, and 39 percent of the Russians scored at or below the Negro average. The most original analysis, however, centered about the "very remarkable fact" that the measured intelligence of immigrants was related to the number of years that they had lived in America. This had been demonstrated by pooling the scores of immigrants from all countries, and then subdividing them into groups categorized according to the years of residence in America prior to being tested. This analysis indicated that foreigners who had lived in the country twenty years or more before being tested were every bit as intelligent as native Americans. Those who had lived in the country less than five years were essentially feebleminded. To some analysts, this finding might have suggested that IQ scores were heavily influenced by exposure to American customs and language, but that was not the tack taken by Brigham.

"We must," Brigham declared, "assume that we are measuring native or inborn intelligence. . . ."[21] The army psychologists had, after all, deliberately devised a "Beta" test, as well, to measure the genetically determined intelligence of the illiterate and the foreign-speaking. "The hypothesis of growth of intelligence with increasing length of residence may be identified with the hypothesis of an error in the method of measuring intelligence. . . ." That hypothesis was not likely to be congenial to a mental tester, and Brigham quickly disposed of it with a number of statistical and psychometric arguments. With this accomplished, "we are forced to . . . accept the hypothesis that the curve indicates a gradual deterioration in the class of immigrants examined in the army, who came to this country in each succeeding five year period since 1902."

Forced by the data to this conclusion, Professor Brigham was at no loss to provide a clarifying explanation—"the race hypothesis." He proceeded to estimate "the proportion of Nordic, Alpine and Mediterranean blood in each of the European countries," and to calculate the numbers of immigrants arriving from each country during each time period. These combined operations produced a sequential picture of the blood composition of the immigrant stream over time. There was thereby unearthed a remarkable parallelism; as the proportion of Nordic blood had decreased, and the proportions of Alpine and Mediterranean blood increased, the intelligence of the immigrants was deduced to have decreased. This is a nice example of the power of correlational analysis applied to intelligence data. Brigham made no attempt to discover whether, *within* each of the "races," measured intelligence had increased with years of residence in America. The conclusion he reached followed in the footsteps of the testing pioneers who had taught him his trade. He urged the abandonment of "feeble hypotheses that would make these differences an artifact of the method of examining" and concluded forthrightly that "our test results indicate a genuine intellectual superiority of the Nordic group. . . ."

The final paragraphs of the book raised the eugenic spectre of a long-term decline in the level of American intelligence as the consequence of continued immigration and racial mongrelization. "We must face a possibility of racial admixture here that is infinitely worse than that faced by any European country today, for we are incorporating the negro into our racial stock, while all of Europe is comparatively free from this taint. . . . The decline of American intelligence will be more rapid than the decline of the intelligence of European national groups, owing to the presence here of the negro."[22]

With national problems of this magnitude, nothing short of a radical solution seemed likely to be of much avail. From this stern logic, neither Professor Brigham nor his sponsor, Professor Yerkes, shrank. The mental testers brought the facts not only to the Congress, but also to the thoughtful reading public. Their relevance to immigration policy was made entirely explicit.

The Johnson-Lodge Immigration Act of 1924 was enacted after the conclusion of the congressional hearings. There had already been enacted, on a temporary basis, a 1921 law embodying the principle of "national origin quotas." The number of immigrants admitted from any given country in one year had been limited to 3 percent of the number of foreign-born from that country already resident in the United States, as determined by the census of 1910. The Johnson-Lodge Act established national origin quotas as a permanent aspect of immigration policy, and it reduced the quota to 2 percent; but most important, *the quotas were to be based on the census of 1890.*

The use of the 1890 census had only one purpose, acknowledged by the bill's supporters. The "New Immigration" had begun after 1890, and the law was designed to exclude the biologically inferior D— and E peoples of southeastern Europe. The new law made the country safe for Professor Brigham's Nordics, but it did little for the safety of Alpines and Mediterraneans. The law, for which the science of mental testing may claim substantial credit, resulted in the deaths of literally hundreds of thousands of victims of the Nazi biological theorists. The victims were denied admission to the United States because the "German quota" was filled, although the quotas of many other Nordic countries were vastly undersubscribed. The Nazi theoreticians ultimately concurred with biologist Laughlin's assessment that, in the case of D— and E people, "Cost of supervision greater than value of labor."

•

There is a moral to be drawn from this melancholy history. The immigration debate, together with its European victims, is long since dead—but only to be replaced by a curiously similar issue. The major domestic issue of our own time, as our politicians remind us, is "the welfare mess." The welfare issue, like immigration, contains within itself a tangle of the most profound racial and economic conflicts. Today's psychometricians tend to approach questions of race and economics rather more gingerly than did those of the 1920s. There are some, however, who are again prepared to serve as teachers to the Congress, and to supply arguments to meet the opposition. These teachers once again assert that their effort is only to remove racial and economic conflicts from politics, and to place them on a firm scientific basis.

We see today that the psychologists who provided "expert" and "scientific" teaching relevant to the immigration debate did so on the basis of pitifully inadequate data. There is probably no living psychologist who would view the World War I army data as relevant to the heritable IQ of European "races." There are few who now seem much impressed by the data on "Italians in America" summarized by Rudolf Pintner in his 1923 text, *Intelligence Testing.*[23] Professor Pintner had called attention to the "remarkable agreement in the median IQ for the Italian children" in six separate studies. That median IQ was 84, a full 16 points below the average American. There is probably no psychometrician today prepared to assert that that 16-point deficit was produced by inferior Italian IQ genes. That does not prevent the same mental testers from pointing gravely to the possible genetic significance of Professor Jensen's recent survey of the contemporary IQ literature. That survey led Jensen to report: "The basic data are well known: on the average, Negroes test about 1 standard deviation (15 IQ points) below the average of the white population, and this finding is fairly uniform across the 81 different tests of intellectual ability used in these studies. . . ."[24] This kind of finding, like Goddard's earlier report that 83 percent of Jewish immigrants were feebleminded, cannot be ignored by thoughtful citizens.

The notion that IQ is heritable has been with us for so long that it is difficult for us to step back and appreciate fully the assumptions involved in that conclusion. The World War I army Alpha test contained such multiple choice items as "The Brooklyn Nationals are called the Giants . . . Orioles . . . Superbas . . . Indians," and "Revolvers are made by Swift and Co. . . . Smith and Wesson . . . W. L. Douglas . . . B. T. Babbitt."[25] The Italian or Hebrew immigrant who could not answer such questions was thereby shown to have defective genes. The Stanford-Binet asked fourteen-year-olds to explain the following: "My neighbor has been having queer visitors. First a doctor came to his house, then a lawyer, then a minister. What do you think happened there?" Professor Terman explained that a satisfactory answer must normally involve a death: "The doctor came to attend a sick person, the lawyer to make his will, and the minister to preach the funeral."

There were, however, "other ingenious interpretations which pass as satisfactory." For example, "A man got hurt in an accident; the doctor came to make him well, the lawyer to see about damages, and then he died and the preacher came for the funeral." The following answer was failed by Professor Terman. "Somebody was sick; the lawyer wanted his money and the minister came to see how he was."[26] Professor Terman's high-quality genes evidently made him better disposed toward the good intentions of lawyers than did the genes of his failing respondent. To Professor Terman, it seemed more logical that a minister at the house next door is there to preach a funeral rather than to inquire after the welfare of an ill parishioner.

To the degree that items in IQ tests are not so monstrously arbitrary as those we have just cited, they largely consist of arithmetical and vocabulary materials together with skills of logical analysis, which are largely learned in school. Those who cannot answer have not learned what in theory the schoolteachers wished to teach them. They are usually the same people who have failed to learn that lawyers do not want the money of their clients and are primarily useful to help one bequeath one's fortune. From this—and the fact that this failure to learn what one should seems to run in families—we are asked to conclude that a low IQ score indicates a genetic defect. The tests in fact seem to measure only whether one has learned, and believed, what Professor Terman and his colleagues have learned and believed. To the degree that one has, one may reasonably look forward to enjoying the kind of success that Professor Terman enjoyed. The assumption that one who has not learned these things was prevented from doing so by his bad blood is both gratuitous and self-serving.

The worst contemporary blood, if one regards the IQ as a mirror held up to the genotype, is black blood. The average IQ score of blacks is lower than that of whites. That fact, together with a very great score overlap between the black and white populations, has been documented in an enormous research literature. To some scholars, at least, racial differences in IQ have constituted a further demonstration of the IQ's genetic basis. But the dreary and at times revolting literature on race differences will not be reviewed here; there is no need to force oneself through it. There is no adequate evidence for the heritability of IQ within the white population. To attribute racial differences to genetic factors, granted the overwhelming cultural-environmental differences between races, is to compound folly with malice. That compounding characterized the mental testers of World War I, and it has not vanished.

The interpretation of IQ data seems never to be free both of policy implications and of ideological overtones. The IQ test in America, and the way we think about it, has been fostered by men committed to a particular social view. That view includes the belief that those on the bottom are genetically inferior victims of their own immutable defects.

The consequence has been that the IQ test has served as an instrument of oppression against the poor—dressed in the trappings of science, rather than politics. The message of science is heard respectfully, particularly when the tidings it carries are soothing to the public conscience. There are few more soothing messages than those historically delivered by the IQ testers. The poor, the foreign-born, and racial minorities were shown to be stupid. They were shown to have been born that way. The underprivileged are today demonstrated to be ineducable, a message as soothing to the public purse as to the public conscience.

These are, of course, political considerations. To pretend that the politics of IQ testing and the science of IQ testing are separable is either naive or dissembling. With respect to IQ testing, psychology long ago surrendered its political virginity. The interpretation of IQ data has always taken place, as it must, in a social and political context, and the validity of the data cannot be fully assessed without reference to that context. Tragically, it is this context that has been ignored by some scientists who do not recognize that their science and their politics are not clearly separable.

NOTES

1. A. Binet and T. Simon, "Sur la necessite d'etablir un diagnostic scientifique des etats inferieurs de l'intelligence," *L'annee psychologique* 11 (1905): 191.

2. A. Binet, *Les Idees modernes sur les enfants* (Paris: Flammarion, 1913), pp. 140-41.

3. L. M. Terman, *The Measurement of Intelligence* (Boston: Houghton Mifflin, 1916), pp. 6-7.

4. Ibid., pp. 91-92.

5. M. Grant, *The Passing of the Great Race* (New York: Scribner's, 1916).

6. L. M. Terman, "Feeble-minded Children in the Public Schools of California," *School and Society* 5 (1917): 165.

7. Binet, *Idees,* pp. 140-41.

8. H. H. Goddard, "How Shall We Educate Mental Defectives?" *The Training School Bulletin* 9 (1912): 43.

9. E. C. Banfield, *The Unheavenly City: The Nature and Future of our Urban Crisis* (Boston: Little Brown, 1970); R. J. Herrnstein, *I.Q. In the Meritocracy* (Boston: Atlantic Monthly Press, 1973).

10. H. H. Goddard, *Human Efficiency and Levels of Intelligence* (Princeton: Princeton University Press, 1920), pp. 99-103.

11. R. M. Yerkes and J. C. Foster, *A Point Scale for Measuring Mental*

Ability (Baltimore: Warwick and York, 1923), pp. 22-25.

12. H. H. Laughlin, *Eugenical Sterilization in the United States* (Chicago: Psychopathic Laboratory of the Municipal Court of Chicago, 1922), p. 15.

13. Ibid., p. 24.

14. Ibid., pp. 21-22.

15. Ibid., pp. 160-61.

16. H. H. Goddard, "The Binet Tests in Relation to Immigration," *Journal of Psycho-Asthenics* 18 (1913): 105-07.

17. H. H. Goddard, "Mental Tests and the Immigrant," *Journal of Delinquency* 2 (1917): 271.

18. H. H. Laughlin, "The New Immigration Law," *Eugenical News* 2 (1917): 22.

19. *Psychological Examining in the United States Army,* ed. R. M. Yerkes (Washington: Memoirs of the National Academy of Sciences, 15, 1921).

20. Ibid., p. 699.

21. C. C. Brigham, *A Study of American Intelligence* (Princeton: Princeton University Press, 1923), p. 100.

22. Ibid., p. 210.

23. R. Pintner, *Intelligence Testing: Methods and Results* (New York: Holt, 1923), pp. 351-52.

24. A. R. Jensen, "How Much Can We Boost I.Q. and Scholastic Achievement?" *Harvard Educational Review* 39 (Winter 1969): 81.

25. Brigham, *American Intelligence,* p. 29.

26. Terman, *Measurement,* pp. 316-17.

THE TROUBLE WITH IQ TESTS

JERROLD R. ZACHARIAS

Jerrold R. Zacharias is professor of physics emeritus at Massachusetts Institute of Technology, Cambridge, Massachusetts, and director of Project ONE, a group at Education Development Center, Newton, Massachusetts, that is producing a television series about mathematics.

Among Mr. Zacharias' previous positions are membership from 1952 to 1964 on the President's Science Advisory Committee and chairmanship of that committee's Panel on Educational Research and Development, 1961-67.

When I first thought about writing this article, I considered entitling it (with all due respect to Aleksander Solzhenitsyn) "The IQ Archipelago," for it is my belief that our efforts to measure so-called intelligence have had an imprisoning and destructive effect on the lives of children. In fact, I believe that the entire enterprise of "standardized," machine scored aptitude and achievement tests has been grossly misused and warrants our most serious reconsideration.

Close examination of the problems of standardized tests is particularly needed now. There is clear evidence that the influence of the tests on the present and future lives of children is mushrooming, and yet, with few exceptions, the tests have gone unchallenged in any serious way. One of those exceptions, however, is a particularly notable one, and because it points up so well both the difficulty of the tests themselves and the problems that face those who would examine and challenge them, I believe it warrants some mention here as an appropriate introduction to an exploration of IQ testing.

In 1962 Banesh Hoffmann, a professor of mathematics at Queens College, published a penetrating book entitled *The Tyranny of Testing.* I read it when it first appeared. I have read it twice since then, most recently just before starting to write this article. Hoffmann's first chapter begins:

> *On the otherwise unmemorable day, Wednesday, March 18, 1959, the* Times *of London printed the following letter to the editor:*
>
> *Sir,—Among the "odd one out" type of questions which my son had to answer for a school entrance examination was: "Which is the odd one out among cricket, football, billiards, and hockey?"*
>
> *I said billiards because it is the only one played indoors. A colleague says football because it is the only one in which the ball is not struck by an implement. A neighbour says cricket because in all the other games the object is to put the ball into a net; and my son, with the confidence of nine summers, plumps for hockey "because it is the only one that is a girl's game." Could any of your readers put me out of my misery by stating what is the correct answer, and further enlighten me by explaining how questions of this sort prove anything, especially when the scholar has merely to underline the odd one out without giving any reason?*
>
> *Perhaps there is a remarkable subtlety behind it all. Is the question designed to test what a child of nine may or may not know about billiards—proficiency at which may still be regarded as the sign of a misspent youth?*
>
> *Yours faithfully,*
> *T. C. Batty*
>
> *This question of the four sports makes a fascinating party game. . . . There is only one drawback: after a while the fun suddenly stops and the party*

becomes indignantly serious. This happens as soon as someone asks what sense there is in giving children such questions on tests; for then, right away, the fat is in the fire. Parents begin recalling similar questions that their own children had on tests. College students complain that such questions are by no means confined to children. Graduate students and older people push the age limit higher as they recount their own experiences. And soon there is an awed realization that there may, in fact, be no age limit at all.[1]

Hoffmann's book should have spearheaded an immediate, major, indignant revolt against the misuse of "standardized," machine scored aptitude and achievement tests. It did not. The standardized achievement test business flourishes, and we have continued on with the insidious undertaking of trying to measure "intelligence."

In fact, during the past several years, a controversy has been raging in some academic circles concerning the inheritance of intelligence—the so-called nature-nurture controversy—and there is by now a copious literature on the topic: at least a dozen books, a full congressional committee report, numerous magazine and journal articles, and an even greater number of pieces distributed by the informal, office-copier route. I have read a great many of them, glanced through some, and thrown some into a corner in anger. I have not been able to pass over the more mathematical treatments by pleading mathophobia. Since the social implications of this debate include the possibility of providing a scientific basis for racism, none of these arguments should pass without close examination.

On one side of the debate, the authors try to show differences in intelligence between averages of the IQ scores of large numbers of minority people and similar averages for majority groups. They claim that these differences result from the genetic pool of the group and not entirely from financial, educational, and social disparities.

On the other side, most investigators try to show that it is not possible to separate nature (inheritance) from nurture (environment).

The main defect in both sides, or either side, of this argument is that the protagonists pay so little attention to the quality of the data base. They revert to saying that the data are not very good, but let's use them anyway because they're all we have. If the resulting discussions were inconsequential or just frivolous, I would not fuss. But the discussions cannot be laughed off without analyzing the sources of the data, and it is just this data base that concerns me most. And since the basic data come from the tests—whether they be mass administered and machine scored, or individually administered and individually scored; whether they be called aptitude tests, intelligence tests, achievement tests, or mental maturity tests—I believe that there are flaws in the entire process.

•

The worst error in the whole business lies in attempting to put people, of whatever age or station, into a single, ordered line of "intelligence" or "achievement" like numbers along a measuring tape: 86 comes after 85 and before 93. Everyone knows that people are complex—talented in some ways, clumsy in others; educated in some ways, ignorant in others; calm, careful, persistent, and patient in some ways; impulsive, careless, or lazy in others. Not only are these characteristics different in different people, they also vary in any one person from time to time. To further complicate the problem, there is variety in the *types* of descriptions. The traits *tall, handsome,* and *rich* are not along the same sets of scales as *affectionate, impetuous,* or *bossy.*

As an old professional measurer (by virtue of being an experimental physicist), I can say categorically that it makes no sense to try to represent a multidimensional space with an array of numbers ranged along one line. This does not mean it is impossible to cook up a scheme that tries to do it; it's just that the scheme won't make any sense. It's possible to strike an average of a column of figures in a telephone directory, but one would never try to dial it. Telephone numbers at least represent the same *kind* of idea: they are all addresslike codes for the central office to respond to.

It is also possible to make a pretense of precision by taking averages over large amounts of data. Legend has it that a Chinese merchant wanted to know the height of the emperor of China. He asked a few people first, then hundreds, then thousands, then millions. Most had never seen the emperor, but they guessed his height. As the merchant gathered more and more guesses, the average value seemed to become more and more precise. But after all it was only the average of uninformed guesses, and no better. People who work with computers call this kind of procedure GIGO, meaning "garbage in; garbage out." I call it "The Height of the Emperor of China Syndrome." Sadly, the legend would be more appropriate to our problem if the merchant had added up in the averaging process the emperor's weight, his blood pressure, his waist diameter, and his birthday—all in appropriate units. Put this way, no sensible person would do it. Yet adding up a "general" score on an IQ test is not very different.

Implicit in the process of averaging is the process of adding. To obtain an average, first add a number of quantitative measures, then divide by however many there are. This is all very simple, provided the quantities can be added, but for the most part, with disparate objects, they cannot be. The problem also points to one source of my impatience with the so-called new math—that is, the business of sets. Draw a ring around any number of objects, similar or dissimilar, and count them. Now, everyone knows better than to do that and expect it to yield a sensible total. Take, for instance, a set consisting of one elephant, two bacteria, three kisses, and a pair of roller skates. How would you even begin to add them?

In the case of ability tests, we might count one each for a verbal analogy item, a numerical analogy item, a picture analogy item, a short computation item, an item that depends on being able to guess which definition of an English word the tester was thinking of, an item that depends on a ready use of symmetry properties, or any of the examples in this issue.

•

In moving away from analogy and fables to the realities of the tests, it is only natural to ask what values, skills, capabilities, interests, or aptitudes the existing tests are trying to discover or disclose. What do the individual numbers that make up average scores represent?

Obviously, individual test items lack focus and purpose. Many are inherently faulty besides. The proper way to demonstrate this would be to take a dozen or so complete tests and work them over, item by item. Since it is not possible to do so in the limited space here, let us look instead at some of the popular *categories* of test items.

One well-known type of item asks the student to find the missing digit in a string of digits, such as: 3, 4, 4, 2, 7, 2, 9, □. For me, this item tests how well I remember the express stops on the IRT subway from Herald Square to Teachers College. But that is not the skill the testers seek, nor the arbitrary rule they want the children to apply. They usually want the children to make successive subtractions until they find a simple order. This procedure is by no means the only procedure for arriving at an answer to the question, but it is what the testers seek. It is an easy skill for almost any child to learn, perhaps not as complex as tying his shoe or blowing his nose, but it looks intellectual. What does it tell? I, for one, do not know.

A variant of the above is the numerical, verbal, or pictorial analogy: A is to B as C is to (X or Y or Z). A typical numerical example could be 2 : 4 :: 6 : □. The answer could be anything at all, including 8, 12, or 36—really anything at all, unless

$$2 : 4 :: 6 : \square \text{ means } \frac{2}{4} = \frac{6}{\square}.$$

This analogy problem gets worse when the words carry no mathematical import. Consider item 15 in Figure 1:

Figure 1. Using the checklist on page 29, see how many difficulties you can identify in these analogy items. Source: Irving Lorge and Robert L. Thorndike, *The Lorge-Thorndike Intelligence Tests* (Boston: Houghton Mifflin Co., 1954).

1. forest → tree : garden →
A rake **B** gladiolus **C** blossom **D** flower **E** fruit

2. book → chapter : play →
F stage **G** scenery **H** cast **J** act **K** drama

3. handkerchief → linen : dress →
L dressmaker **M** cotton **N** style **P** apparel **Q** print

4. automobile → manufacture : home →
R rent **S** buy **T** build **U** mortgage **V** own

5. human being → arm : tree →
A trunk **B** twig **C** limb **D** foliage **E** growth

6. biology → microscope : astronomy →
F telescope **G** binoculars **H** lens **J** stratosphere **K** heavens

7. speaker → introduction : author →
L contents **M** index **N** digest **P** title page **Q** preface

8. laborer → wage : teacher →
R profession **S** work **T** fee **U** honorarium **V** salary

9. plaintiff → defendant : prosecution →
A litigation **B** decision **C** defense **D** replication **E** appellant

10. king → abdicate : president →
F disdain **G** retract **H** resign **J** veto **K** coup d'état

11. federal → congress : state →
L house **M** senate **N** representatives **P** constitution **Q** legislature

12. jeopardy → security : hazard →
R quarantine **S** safeguard **T** custodian **U** peril **V** convoy

13. distill → extract : precipitate →
A deposit **B** colloid **C** solidify **D** congeal **E** isotope

14. diffuseness → expansion : conciseness →
F terseness **G** condensation **H** laconicism **J** epithet **K** ellipsis

15. vindicate → acquit : stigmatize →
L prosecute **M** libel **N** arraign **P** condemn **Q** indict

15. vindicate → acquit : stigmatize →
L prosecute **M** libel **N** arraign
P condemn **Q** indict

Besides demonstrating that the test writers did not understand the legal implications of their question, I cannot discern what aspect of intelligence they are trying to disclose.

When, as in this last case, no word in the English language is exactly right, the testers retreat to the ploy called "best answer." As Hoffmann says on this point:

> *Rarely do the multiple-choice testers ask the candidate to pick the "correct" answer. Rather, they ask him to pick the "best" answer, or the answer that "best fits," or "is most nearly correct," or the like. This is not unrelated to the ambiguity that haunts the multiple-choice format. In a sense it is a sign of emancipation, a banner proclaiming escape from the true-false trap. But it is sometimes regarded as an excuse for laxity and license. Defenders of multiple-choice tests are apt to use it to condone imprecision and ambiguity. Complain to them, for example, that the wanted answer to a particular question is certainly not a correct one and is not really even a good one, and they will point out that all is well since it is nevertheless "the best."*[2]

Many, but not all, of these troubles can be traced to the mechanical convenience of multiple choice. Take, for example, what I call "non-sense" questions, which cannot be machine scored. In a test for six-year-olds that allows free responses, there appears this question: "What is the difference between a dog and a wolf?"[3] It particularly disappoints me that the poetic expression, "A dog is tameful," is considered wrong.

Another "non-sense" question is, "What is the difference between a bird and a dog?" I am sure that if I had been asked that as a child, I would have been puzzled indeed. Sometimes puzzlement is a more intelligent reaction than a trumped-up answer. However, there is something more seriously wrong with this popular type of question. Asking for *the* difference implies that there is one, and only one, point of difference. I am not recommending it, but the question could ask for *a* difference, or *some differences*.

As George Orwell once observed, our language "becomes ugly and inaccurate because our thoughts are foolish, but the slovenliness of our language makes it easier for us to have foolish thoughts." Orwell was speaking, as I recall, of politics, but tests, like politics, go astray with slovenly language.

•

At this point, let us look at the way test items are made, selected, validated, and finally printed. To adequately describe a typical procedure for preparing a "norm referenced," "standardized" test would require more space than I have to devote here. The nub of the issue, however, is that the test makers try to produce a "total instrument," each part of which serves the purpose of building up a bell shaped distribution curve of children's scores. Each test item is regarded as contributing to that process, rather than as an idea of its own that can be misread or not, misunderstood or not, used in diagnosis of trouble, or used to indicate the child's real perception or lack of it.

If a test item is missed by children who otherwise have high scores, the test item is made easier; more difficult if the other way. Both *easy* and *difficult* are defined statistically in terms of what fraction of the high, low, or medium scorers do this or that. A proper scientific approach would be to try to find many ways to study each of many children's understanding of an idea, and then ask if the test item shows that the children's understanding is consonant with what you already know (on the basis of other procedures) that their understanding is.

I am not saying that a scientific procedure is easy, but there is no decent statistical substitute for it. Statistical analysis does *not* apply. The careful validation of test items, item by item, requires intensive study of each item in a variety of ways, child by child. Adequate scrutiny of an item demands knowing not only what a child's response is, but also *why* he or she made that particular response.

Furthermore, to reflect differences due to heredity versus those due to environment, we would need data that tell a great deal about the individual lives and styles of the people involved—and these data would have to come from statistically valid samples. Yet we do not even know what kinds of data these would be, or how many dimensions we would have to analyze. Moreover, all of these data would have to be free of cultural bias.

Now, in an effort to short-circuit these necessary procedures, the proponents in the nature-nurture argument resort to saying that the intelligence or aptitude tests correlate with achievement test results, and so are valid. Of course they correlate—or at least they should—for they are almost the same tests! The correlation between early aptitude tests and later performance tests is due to the test construction, not to the people being tested. If a person can do this or that now, there is a great likelihood that he will be able to do this or that later. And so on, through college and career.

We must now turn to the correlation problem, for the achievement/aptitude correlations referred to above are not as good as perhaps they should be. Correlation coefficients are usually discussed in mathematical terms, and this handicaps the general reader. Let us see to what extent an early test helps to predict the same individual's score on a later test; for example, an IQ score as the predictor of performance in college. Let's call this pretest versus post-test.

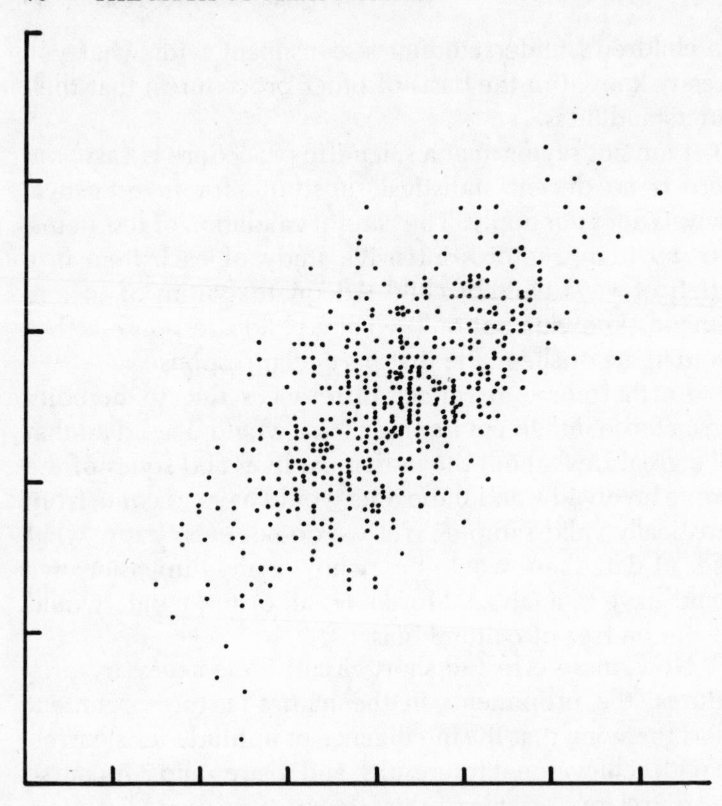

Figure 2. Scattergram representing two correlated normal distributions of data. The correlation coefficient represented by this diagram is 0.5, a quite usual correlation for tests appropriate to this discussion.

Figure 2 shows a scattergram for a possible post-test/pretest plot. There are 500 points, 1 for each of 500 people. Each dot on the diagram represents one person's pretest score along the horizontal axis, and his post-test score along the vertical axis. Tests are constructed on purpose so that a scattergram like this one bulges with dots in the middle, and thins out for high and low values.

Let us consider three students for whom we have only pretest scores—one high, one low, one medium—and suppose that this is all we know about any of them. Draw three vertical lines, one at each of three pretest scores, one high, one low, and one medium. Then you can reasonably well predict that the post-test scores for the high and low scorers are likely to be high and low, respectively. The high scorer obviously can handle tests of this sort; the low scorer clearly needs help. But for the student with a medium pretest score, all we can say about where his post-test point on the scattergram will fall is that it will be somewhere along a vertical line through his pretest score. No matter where on this line his post-test score falls, he will have plenty of company.

Thus post-test prediction could be almost anywhere, and this sort of prediction is of little if any use. For the child at either end of the performance spectrum, the test is saying only what every other indicator already says. For the child anywhere near the middle of the spectrum of performance, the test scores are little better than a lottery—but the child has to bear the subsequent burdens.

•

If all this is true, then, the reader may well ask, why have the public, and especially the school people, not reacted to the tests sooner and more violently? I believe there are three reasons.

First, educated adults are generally entertained by tests for children. It is fun to outpsych the tester, even if the mathematical items are tricky and the vocabulary items recondite or confusing. Just try working through (or playing through) a test on which no personal situation depends. It's as much fun as a crossword puzzle, and, for an adult, just as unthreatening.

The second reason for tests' survival is much more worrisome. It involves secrecy and secrecy's police force—the copyright laws. If not impossible, it is at least extremely inconvenient and time consuming for someone without proper credentials to obtain full sets of aptitude tests or achievement tests. And to appreciate the implications of a test fully, it is necessary to study the full test, not just an occasional test item here or there. In my view, this explains why Hoffmann's keen analysis of individual test items has not been taken seriously by many people.

The third reason is that tests fill a perceived need—namely, putting children in order—even though the need is wrong and the tests fill it very badly.

I have made a checklist to help analyze the pitfalls of tests from many points of view. To assist any reader who takes the trouble to try working over a full test, I have tried to make the list complete, but I would appreciate any additional suggestions.

Demands made on the student:

1. Disproportionate facility in reading and writing

2. The need for just the right level of sophistication or naivete

3. The need to understand the tester's language and jargon

4. The need to guess what the tester wants

5. The need for speed

6. The need to muster the compulsiveness to think, to finish, and to be fussy about putting the answer where it should be put

7. The need to tolerate boredom

8. The need to care about the results

Properties of the test from the student's point of view. Test items frequently are:

1. Ambiguous

2. Meaningless

3. Irrelevant to anything the student knows or cares about

4. Trivial, and therefore misleading

5. Misleading for other reasons

6. Time wasting, either in general or specifically, from the time allowed for completing the test

7. Overprecise or not precise enough

8. Unnecessarily complex in language

9. Seemingly tricky when there are not any tricks

10. Not 9

Properties of the test from the point of view of someone who knows the subject, the goals, and testing in general. Test items can be:

1. Illogical

2. Too tricky

3. Just plain wrong

4. Too complex, requiring too many different operations in series or in parallel

5. Unnecessary or irrelevant to objectives

6. Relevant to irrelevant objectives

7. Unrevealing

8. Poor pedagogic practice with respect to subject matter or method

9. Not useful for diagnosis

Effects on student may be:

1. Frightening

2. Rarely rewarding for any specialized genius, talent, or interest

3. Penalizing for specialized genius, talent, or interest

4. Misleading for tracking or grade level

5. Misleading in forming teacher's image of pupil

6. Unnecessarily damaging to student's self-image

Effects on class, school, or system may be:

1. Constraining with respect to content, method, and schedule

2. Misleading for tracking or grade level

3. Deleterious to morale of students, teachers, parents, administrators

4. Setting false standards for performance, for subject, or for goals of learning

5. Penalizing for a creative or imaginative teacher

Sources of the troubles. People who generate the test may be and often are:

1. Ignorant of the subject—such as mathematics, measurement, science, technology, art, literature, or even grammar

2. Unaware of, or unclear about, what they want the tests to disclose (naturally this could be due

to ignorance, stupidity, haste, or accident; hardly ever to ill will)

3. I don't know how to say this, but sometimes a test item reminds me that a camel has been described as a horse designed by a committee. You can place the blame squarely between the two humps of a Bactrian camel

•

For all of these reasons, I will conclude by proposing that we not retreat to catch phrases like, "I know these tests are not very good, but they are all we have." There are many other ways to assess a child's general competence. They may not look numerical or scientific, but they are known to every teacher and every school principal who reads this journal. I believe, therefore, that the administration of IQ tests as they now exist should cease and desist. There should be a major effort to find some reasonable collection of procedures so that the need felt by teachers, schools, systems, and parents can be satisfied without at the same time destroying any children, teachers, schools, systems, or parents.

NOTES

1. Banesh Hoffmann, *The Tyranny of Testing* (New York: Collier Books, 1964), pp. 17-18.
2. Ibid., p. 77.
3. Lewis M. Terman and Maud A. Merrill, *Stanford-Binet Intelligence Scale—Manual for the Third Revision—Form L-M* (Boston: Houghton Mifflin Co., 1962 impression).

THE BELL SHAPED PITFALL

PHILIP MORRISON

Philip Morrison is Institute Professor at the Massachusetts Institute of Technology, Cambridge, Massachusetts, where he has taught theoretical physics.

Mr. Morrison is also the regular book reviewer for Scientific American *and the author or coauthor of textbooks in physics at the high school, college and graduate school levels. He finally learned what good teaching means, he tells us, during eight years' work among gifted colleagues on the Elementary Science Study, 1964-72.*

In our days all of us bear a variety of numerical descriptions that are plain enough, if less conspicuous than the price tags in the store. We know well our age, street address, and present weight (maybe a mother recalls a weight at birth), and we sometimes even worry about numbers called blood pressure and income. In the school context, all children bear still another number, plain on the record, observed in everyday affairs. IQ.

What we make of all these numbers is a social phenomenon, not a truly arithmetical one. For they take on meaning insofar as we consider them in relation to similar numbers borne by our fellow citizens—men, women, children—wherever comparable. The street address is unique; no one meaningfully shares it, save family or neighbor; it is a marker, not a magnitude, even if an uptown address is better than a downtown one where you live. You are as old as you feel, but when you are the oldest person in sight, you feel different from when you find yourself in a congenial group of people who share many of your concerns and your memories. As for blood pressure—its numbers take on meaning only when the anxious question is answered, "Is that about normal, Doctor?"

The record of just how many out of any population being compared on a numerical basis share each value of the number is what the statisticians call the *distribution* of the statistic. There are all kinds of distributions. Perhaps the clearest impression of a distribution is gained by looking at a graph in which, for each value of the descriptive number plotted along the bottom edge of a graph field, the vertical height of the curve plotted tells how many persons shared that value. Look at Figure 1. There we plot the measured blood pressure of a sample of Londoners drawn from the general population. You see the sort of bell shaped curve familiar from classroom grades. The most "popular" value stands out a little, but it is flanked by plenty of cases nearly as common. Deviate from the "norm" by very much—either too high or too low—and you find little company. The curve falls smoothly off as the pressure goes above or below the mean value (which for this symmetric curve is the same as the most frequent value, as far as inspection can tell). The bell curves off rapidly; few have half the mean, or twice it. Many diverse phenomena follow this sort of pattern: the height of men (or women) at twenty years of age, say (see Figure 2); or the distance by which a marksman's bullet misses the bull's-eye; or the tearing strength of a sample of uniform cloth.

Since the great Karl Gauss, working in the time of Andy Jackson, mathematicians have known and admired this kind of distribution. They formulate it in all precision algebraically, and they can show that it must arise under certain idealized circumstances as the distribution of chance events. In that form, it is called either the Gaussian distribution, after its theorist; the normal curve, for its ubiquity; or sometimes the curve of error. For indeed the chance errors of careful measurement—the length of a stick measured with a ruler, for example—will approach such a distribution. (Psychometrics dotes on it, too, and most of the sophisticated operations that the test experts carry out depend on its well-known ideal properties.)

But of course by no means all interesting and important distributions are even approximately bell shaped, let alone "normal." (See Figures 3-5.) Count the days when the sky is cloudless, or is one-tenth, two-tenths, three-tenths, and so on, cloud covered. In London they found that the distribution of cloud cover in July was not at all bell shaped, but crudely the reverse—the curve is like a cup, a bell upside down. Few Greenwich summer skies are half cloudy, it seems; mostly the sky is either blue or entirely overcast. The number of children per family, to take another example, has a mean value a little bigger than two, but it stretches from zero to a dozen or more—not at all bell shaped. And the distribution of income is extended indeed, to accommodate the well-off, up to the vice president and his like, but it falls quickly off toward zero.

It should be remarked that each and every one of these results follows from a careful but rather simple measurement. We know what we are measuring in each case, and the means of measurement has been developed with little reference to the distribution that results. There is one grand exception: the tests that lead to the IQ. (See Figure 6.) With perhaps one exception that I can find—the pioneer—these tests have been composed of items *selected* after trial for observed conformity with the normal distribution. Items that showed little correlation with the overall expectations, or with the results of previous tests of the kind, have been systematically excluded. Even more, real care has been taken to enforce the stability of these results even after item selection was completed. For example, the spread of results for young children given the Stanford-Binet tests in the 1960 edition was too large compared with the results for other ages. Thereupon, the scoring scheme was adjusted to modify the measured distribution somewhat—the curve ex-

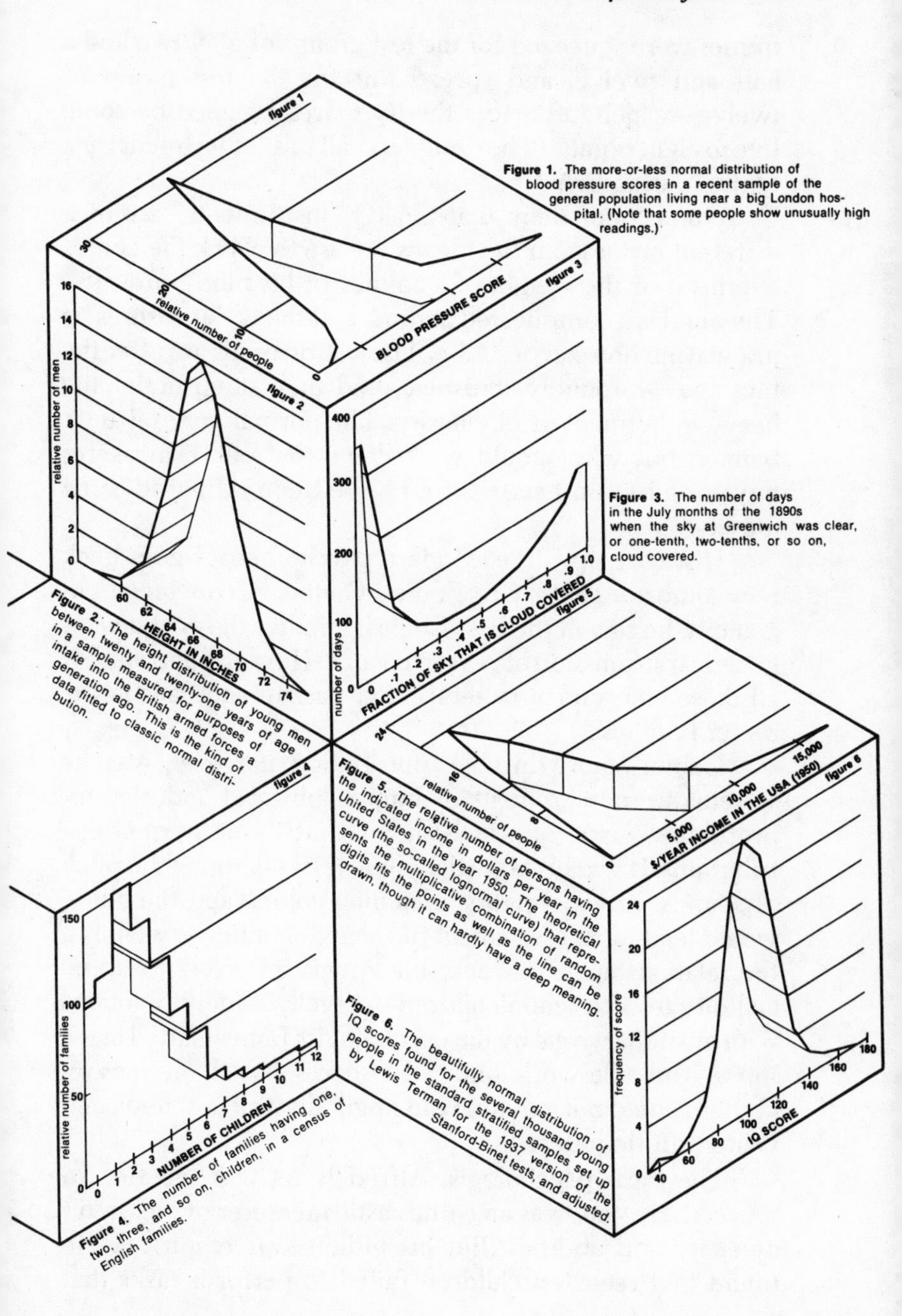

Figure 1. The more-or-less normal distribution of blood pressure scores in a recent sample of the general population living near a big London hospital. (Note that some people show unusually high readings.)

Figure 2. The height distribution of young men between twenty and twenty-one years of age in a sample measured for purposes of intake into the British armed forces a generation ago. This is the kind of data fitted to classic normal distribution.

Figure 3. The number of days in the July months of the 1890s when the sky at Greenwich was clear, or one-tenth, two-tenths, or so on, cloud covered.

Figure 4. The number of families having one, two, three, and so on, children, in a census of English families.

Figure 5. The relative number of persons having the indicated income in dollars per year in the United States in the year 1950. The theoretical curve (the so-called lognormal curve) that represents the multiplicative combination of random digits fits the points as well as the line can be drawn, though it can hardly have a deep meaning.

Figure 6. The beautifully normal distribution of IQ scores found for the several thousand young people in the standard stratified samples set up by Lewis Terman for the 1937 version of the Stanford-Binet tests, and adjusted.

tremes were squeezed for the test groups of ages two and a half and twelve, and spread out for the test group of twelve—which influences the IQ scores assigned by some five to eight points. (The designers call this "adjustment for a typical variability.")

One cannot deny that the IQ "instruments" are of a different order from the means we use to check the clouds overhead or the weight of a soldier or his blood pressure. The mind is a complicated animal, and the IQ "measures" it in a way no one can describe. The justifications are after the fact and profoundly statistical, and they stand under the heavy indictment of circularity. The normal curve is their banner, but why should we believe that curve measures anything beyond scores that have been adjusted to fit loosely?

History helps little. Modern psychometrics goes back now almost a century to Francis Galton. A convinced eugenicist, he saw in the best English families the evidence of genetic transmission of personal value. How else account for all those clergymen, generals, and parliamentarians in the better families?

Galton's more durable contribution, however, was the systematic measurement of human physical and sensory properties, many of which showed satisfying normal distributions. It was his hope that these tests—judging the pitch of sounds, lifting weights, matching colors, and the like—would lead to an assessment of mental abilities as well. But the relationship was weak; the American effort to apply Galton's tests to schoolchildren—actually widely practiced with missionary zeal by the psychologist James Cattell in the 1890s—did not work out. Test scores based on sensory abilities could not predict who might do well in school, and Galtonism floundered.

The Paris psychologist Alfred Binet was the first to succeed. He, too, was an enthusiastic measurer of children's diversity and abilities. But his insight was empirical. He found that retarded children failed to perform tasks that most pupils could easily manage. From this he elaborated a graduated series of items that could fix what he called "mental age."

Lewis Terman first introduced statistical sophistication, standard samples, the precise distribution of Gauss, and the rest, to the Binet-Simon test, elaborating over nearly fifty years his thrice-revised Stanford-Binet tests. The army's need for a group test that could be used with the millions of World War I draftees instead of the costly, individually administered Binet or its Stanford versions, was met by a student of Terman's, Arthur Otis, who developed the army Alpha test. To this day, one of the two most used group tests of intelligence (according to a 1973 survey of the hundred largest school districts in the nation) is the Otis-Lennon Mental Ability Test. All of these tests correlate strongly; all show—with some charity—the Gaussian form of distribution that they are constructed to show; and all correlate with school performance, not least because the schools and the tests have, like old married couples, a tendency to grow to resemble each other.

Here I become uneasy. From Binet until now, the volumes of results and their genuinely powerful treatment by the educational statisticians aim at one practical result, surely of value to the concerned school principal: will this student do well in school? The tests of correlation make a pretty strong case. But there seems to be very little case left for the name *intelligence quotient*. This ingeniously forced normal curve of test scores is good for something, all right, though it ought to be called by a more descriptive and modest name, say the *school success index*, or very optimistically, the *scholastic aptitude*—and indeed familiar tests bear the latter name.

There is little doubt that language—the fine distinctions of usage, paradox, and implication—plays the major role in IQ tests. Manual and visual items fade out of the tests at higher mental ages and correlate less well with overall score or with school success. Even the newer individual tests (such as the well-known Wechsler Intelligence Scale for Children, with its battery of nonverbal items) are still deeply linked to language. Schools, too, surround the student with the three Rs, whatever else they offer. It would be absurd to deny the primacy of language for human thought, but in a time when we recognize the complex nature of the two-sided brain, let alone the cultivated mind, it is at best premature and at worst dishonest to enthrone language and its nuances as the seat of human intelligence. Too many creative—and less articulate—artists, craftsmen, healers, farmers, experimenters, and musicians stand in the way.

•

A scientific critic cannot avoid looking behind the pragmatic results. Gauss showed that the normal curve, one precise kind of bell, resulted from the measurement of arbitrarily many independent, equal-chance units, which must add up arithmetically to give the total score. Tossing a hundred coins all at once is a near-perfect model. The number of heads per toss closely follows the normal curve.

Note the requirements: equal effect of each coin, all coins independent, and the score simply the head count, adding one after another. It is easy to change that model to obtain a wholly different distribution. For example, instead of *adding* random equal elements, merely *multiply* random numbers. The result is a very different curve that is equally elegant mathematically, but that gives different results. It is plain that when you add the elements, no particular one matters more than any other. But when you multiply, one small digit—even among many that are about average—drags down the product. A high product would imply a series of large numbers, not one of them low. Strangely enough, just such an idealized distribution fits very well to the socially determined curve of income per head. No one will think, I hope, that incomes are fixed by multiplication of random digits, but it is not implausible that high income "scores" result from a coincidence of favorable factors. (There is an old folk saying to describe it: them that has, gets.)

Most human abilities that we value—all save perhaps the IQ—seem to be based on a model that is closer to multiplication than to addition. Violinists, ballerinas, college presidents, machinists, pilots, and waiters, to name only a few, reflect training, improve with practice, and do better as they grow more. Their performance is not fixed by summing independent, small contributions, but by making first one and then another and then still another step along a path where success in each step makes the next one easier or more effective. One's height is something else again. I await not normal curves (no such bells ring for me!) but quite different evaluations that respect human interests and predilections, human specialties, human diversity, and human talent. IQ rings off key. If it is presently useful to schools, then that use is forced. Maybe we had better reform the whole. I am disturbed that the sophisticates of educational statistics have written so little about the other distributions, which are the basis of such modern statistics, and only here and there raised the issues that, it seems to me, are intrinsic to IQ. Until they have done so, I rest fearful that they have mistaken mere consistency for observation, and a circle for a clear line of argument.

This small study has given me one insight, at least. I now know how to answer the people who say, "If you're so smart, why aren't you rich?" Easy: in the United States, income has a multiplicative distribution and IQ only an additive one. The IQ bell tolls far too simply; it is past time for the American schools to demand something much better than the innumerable adjusted "normal" IQ scores of an elaborated Victorian eugenics.

A is to B as C is to Anything at All:

THE ILLOGIC OF IQ TESTS

JUDAH L. SCHWARTZ

Judah L. Schwartz is professor of engineering science and education at the Massachusetts Institute of Technology, Cambridge, Massachusetts. His research focuses on the development of mathematical and problem-solving competence in children.

For years group ability tests have been attacked. The tests' supporters have always managed to take refuge in the comfortable claim that the tests predict school achievement. That argument at first sight seems persuasive. Frequently, it is persuasive enough to put off additional critical inquiry. My purpose here is to press the inquiry further along in order to understand the reason that group ability tests predict school achievement.

In principle, we can distinguish between ability and achievement. Most people have little difficulty making a conceptual distinction between the two notions. Ability is thought of as an innate property of people, and achievement is seen as a measure of accomplishment in some field. This conceptual distinction between ability and achievement, however, is not easy to translate into operational terms. Let us examine why.

A child who is to be evaluated along any dimension, at any stage of his or her development, is clearly a very complicated mixture of ability and achievement. In general, no person is really ever a tabula rasa on any subject. In particular, no child of school age is a tabula rasa on the content of the school curriculum. Children possess knowledge, feelings, prejudices, and memories about many things. The notion that one can construct an ability test that will not be influenced by the child's experience is not a thoughtful notion.

The situation is, however, even more complicated. Not only is it true that experience is continually accumulating (it is therefore impossible to administer an "ability" test to a naive subject), but it is also true that ability and achievement interact. There is ample evidence, drawn from the observations of masters of all sorts of skills—from bricklaying to baking, from surgery to needlepoint, from topology to sculpture—that ability grows as experience is acquired. This simplistic distinction between ability and achievement is clearly inadequate.

The ability-achievement distinction is one that, in practice, cannot be made. I have offered some a priori, in principle arguments to support the assertion. There is, however, a further argument to be made: the evidence of the tests themselves reveals that the test makers have not been able to make the distinction apparent in their test instruments. Consider the following ten questions:

1. We see (children, plants, stars, houses, trees) only at night.

2. Bill bought two pads of paper at 25 cents each and four pens at 20 cents each. How much did he spend? ($1.30, 45¢, $1.05, none of these)

3. *Sob* means (prejudice, solemn, sigh, joy, kind).

4. When a new kind of machine is created it is called (an adoption, an invention, a fabrication, a novelty, a discovery).

5. Which term is missing in this series? 3, 5, 7, ?, 11, 13 (8, 9, 10, 14, 15)

6. Which term comes next in this series? 54, 45, 36, ? (31, 63, 25, 27)

7. Oxygen is a (compound, gas, solid, carbide).

8. To *prove* is to (agree, verify, see, mean).

9. Mary bought a comic book for 10 cents, some gum for 5 cents and a candy bar for 5 cents. How many cents did she spend in all? (15¢, 20¢, 25¢, 50¢, none of these)

10. The earth's crust is its (surface, energy, heat, poles).

Half of these questions are drawn from group ability tests and half from achievement tests, all designed for grades four to six.[1] The reader can decide for himself whether or not the point is made.

•

Now we are in a position to reinspect the question raised at the outset: why is it that group ability tests predict school achievement as well as they do? The answer is quite simple. Group achievement tests and group ability tests are sufficiently similar that without labels, one has difficulty telling which is which. If these group ability tests are used to predict, and group achievement tests are used to confirm those predictions, why should anyone be surprised?

Is this silly tautological situation anything more than a bad piece of logic that somehow slipped by us? Or do the ability-achievement test batteries cause damage? The answer depends on what the tests are useful for and used for—a subject that will be examined in more detail elsewhere in this issue.

Figure 1 shows four "creature cards" that were drawn from a set of fifteen developed by the Elementary Science

FIGURE 1

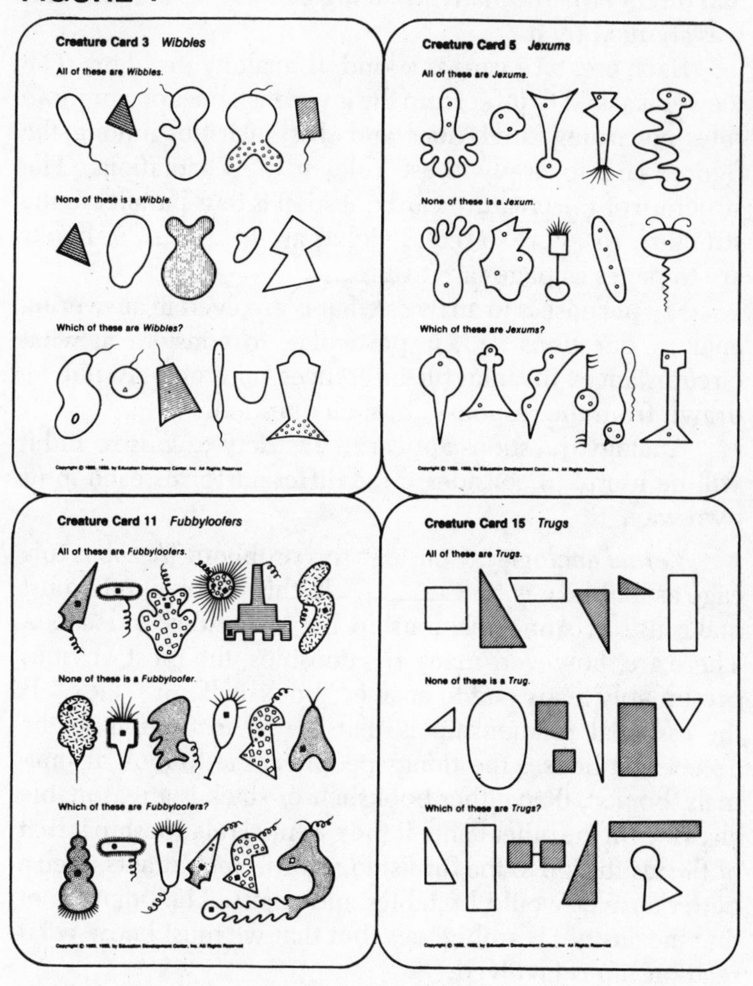

Study program of the Education Development Center. They have been in wide use for several years, and many people seem to enjoy their charming and lighthearted style. It came, therefore, as a shock to us about a year ago to encounter a bright nine-year-old girl who, after studying the cards carefully for a long time, said that she was unable to answer the question posed at the bottom of each card. She had discovered the inadvertent logical flaw on the card and was stymied by it.

Each creature card is a kind of analogy problem. The viewer is asked to infer from the given instances one or more rules governing similarities and dissimilarities among the figures and to apply those rules in new situations. The structure of the creature card question is thus parallel to the structure: roses are to red as violets are to ______; or books are to pages as pages are to ______.

My purpose is to analyze what is involved in answering analogy questions and, in particular, to consider in what circumstances meaningful inferences may or may not be drawn from the responses to such questions.

Analogy questions appear in a variety of guises, and it will be useful to consider these different forms each in its own way.

Verbal analogies. Consider this problem: "A zoo is to a cage as a library is to a ______." In this problem one must make use of some relationship between zoos and cages. There are, however, many relationships; the most obvious presumably leads one to answer "bookshelf" or "stack." If the essential relationship is that of the institution to the object that houses the things people come to look at (animals, books), then either bookshelf or stack is a reasonable answer. On the other hand, if the essential relationship is that of the institution to the furnishings for its inhabitants, then a better answer would be tables and chairs. The point is not that the answer is ambiguous, but that we must know what relationship is involved.

A second problem to consider is a sample analogy problem drawn from a booklet published by the devisors of a secondary level aptitude test:

Island: Water::
(a) Sand: Desert
(b) Mountains: Ocean
(c) City: Meadows

(d) Lake: Land
(e) River: Banks[2]

Choice (a) is acceptable if the relationship is Entity (Sand, grains of): Surround of Entity (Desert). Choice (b) is acceptable if one has in mind volcanoes, such as Surtsey in the North Atlantic, that are literally mountains in the ocean. Choice (c) is acceptable under the relationship—Relatively structured Entity (City): Relatively unstructured surround of Entity (Meadows). Choice (d) is acceptable if one has the topology in mind, and choice (e) is acceptable under the relationship—Entity (River): Boundary that defines the shape of the Entity (Banks).

These analogy questions are not particularly poor or good examples. They simply exhibit the logical flaw in analogy questions that precludes their use, as ordinarily administered, on examinations. Let me be very clear: *an analogy question never has a unique answer. The quality of any answer offered can only be judged in the light of the respondent's stated rationale for his or her answer.*

Visual analogies. The same situation exists in another common form of analogy question; that is, the visual analogy, as illustrated by the problem shown in Figure 2.

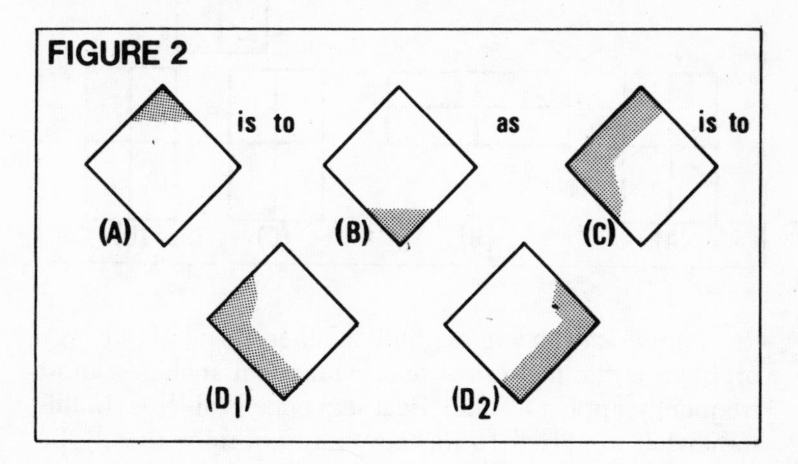

Choice (D^2) is acceptable if (A) is considered to be related to (B) by a rotation of 180° around an axis that passes through the center of the figure. Choice (D^1) is acceptable if (A) is considered to be related to (B) by a reflection in a horizontal line that passes through the center of the figure.

One further example, shown in Figure 3, may prove to underline the point and perhaps even amuse the reader. (A) is acceptable under the rule "Rotate clockwise 2 sectors." (B) is acceptable under the rule "Rotate clockwise 1 sector and reflect in a horizontal line." (C) is acceptable under the rule "Rotate counter-clockwise $4/n$ of a complete revolution, n being the number of sectors." (D) is acceptable under the rule "Rotate counterclockwise 2 sectors and reflect in a vertical line."

Once again it should be clear that unless the respondent is offered an opportunity to provide the rule used to generate the answer, as well as the answer, no judgment can be made.

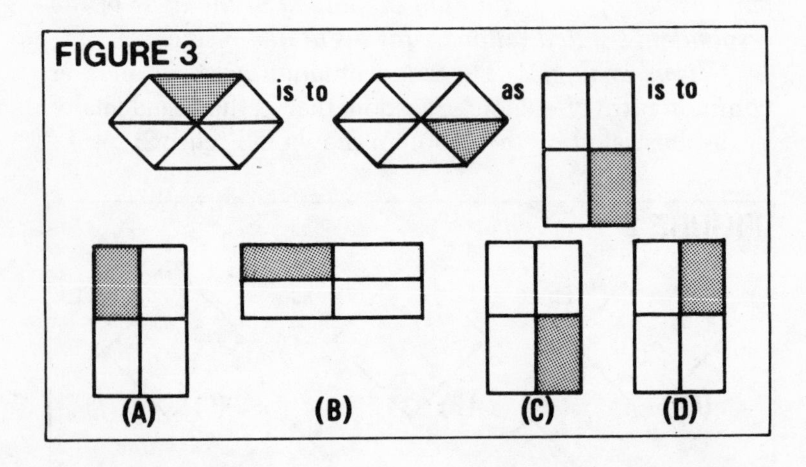

Numerical analogies. Still another form of analogy problem is the numerical one. Numerical analogies most frequently appear as numerical sequence problems. In this somewhat modified form, they may not immediately be recognized as analogy problems: "What is the next number in this sequence? 36, 45, 54, 63, □." This analogy problem simply asks, "36 is to 45 as 45 is to 54 as 54 is to 63 as 63 is to □." It is a string of analogy problems related to one another by the use of a common rule.

A procedure that absolutely guarantees a solution to such problems is based on the taking of differences:

(a) $45 - 36 = 9$
(b) $54 - 45 = 9$
(c) $63 - 54 = 9$

These differences are constant and suggest that if we set the next difference $\square - 63$ equal to 9, our problem is solved. Next consider this sequence: 1, 4, 9, 16, 25, □.

Differences between successive terms are:

(a) $4 - 1 = 3$
(b) $9 - 4 = 5$
(c) $16 - 9 = 7$
(d) $25 - 16 = 9$
(e) $\square - 25 =$ (call this difference $\triangle$)

These differences are not constant. Suppose we repeat the process and take the differences of the differences:

(a′) $5 - 3 = 2$
(b′) $7 - 5 = 2$
(c′) $9 - 7 = 2$

These differences are now constant and equal to 2. The next difference in this series is $\triangle - 9$, and let us set that equal to 2 as well:

If $\triangle - 9 = 2$
then $\triangle = 11$.
But since $\triangle = \square - 25$,

we now know that $11 = \square - 25$
or $36 = \square$.

The answer to our problem is that the next term in our sequence is 36, a result you will not find surprising.

•

You may convince yourself that this procedure will always work. It does and will always yield a "correct" next term in the sequence. At first blush one is tempted to say that we have found a counterexample to our contention that there is no unique way to solve analogy problems. We seem to have a well-defined rule that always works. It is, however, not the only rule. Consider the following problem: "What is the next number in this sequence? 1, 2, 4, 8, □." Suppress your urge to say 16 and join me in applying our procedure to the problem:

(a) $2 - 1 = 1$
(b) $4 - 2 = 2$
(c) $8 - 4 = 4$
(d) $\square - 8 = \triangle$ (say)

The differences are not constant, so we try again by taking differences of differences:

(a′) $2 - 1 = 1$
(b′) $4 - 2 = 2$
(c′) $\triangle - 4 = \bigcirc$ (say)

The differences are still not constant. Try again:

(a″) $2 - 1 = 1$
(b″) $\bigcirc - 2 = \triangle$(say)

These differences would be constant if we set:

⏢ = 1.
If ⏢ = 1
then ○ = ⏢ + 2 = 3
and △ = ○ + 4 = 7
and □ = △ + 8 = 15.

Our procedure yields the sequence:

1, 2, 4, 8, 15.

Would a student who completed the sequence this way receive credit for having employed a subtle problem-solving strategy, or is it more likely that he would not? I think the answer is both evident and shameful.

NOTES

1. Items 1, 3, and 9 are from: Irving Lorge et al., *Lorge-Thorndike Intelligence Tests, Level 4, Form A* (Boston: Houghton Mifflin Co., 1954-66), test 1, p. 2; test 4, p. 8; and test 3, p. 7; respectively.

Items 4 and 5 are from: A. S. Otis and R. T. Lennon, *Otis-Lennon Mental Ability Test, Elementary Level, Form J* (New York: Harcourt Brace and World, 1967), p. 2.

Items 2, 6, 7, 8, and 10 are from: Walter N. Durost et al., *Metropolitan Achievement Tests, Intermediate, Form F* (New York: Harcourt Brace Jovanovich, 1970), pp. 21, 18, 3, 3, and 2, respectively.

2. Attributed to the College Board Scholastic Aptitude Test in Banesh Hoffmann, "The College Boards Fail the Test," *New York Times Magazine*, 24 October 1965.

THE SCORE AGAINST IQ:

A Look at Some Test Items

Many of the articles in this book are illustrated with actual items from the intelligence tests. Lest you be tempted to conclude that the authors have deliberately selected the most outrageous examples from the tests, we urge you to take the time to examine the major tests in their entirety. Even with a generous selection of items, it is almost impossible to convey just how inadequate the tests are. To see them whole is to feel the full impact of the foolishness of trying to measure anything as complex as "intelligence" with such instruments.

However, for those readers who may not have easy access to the tests (and it is often needlessly difficult), we are including some additional selections here, with comment, both to provide a greater range of items and to cite some deficiencies of the tests not always mentioned elsewhere in this issue. It may be necessary to add that these items are neither the worst nor the best examples of the tests, but generally—and unfortunately—typify some of the basic flaws of the so-called intelligence tests.

THE EDITOR

•

Something you see in your sleep is a . . .

☐ dream ☐ fairy ☐ wish ☐ dread

Iowa Tests of Basic Skills,
Primary Battery, Level 7, Form 5,
Vocabulary Subtest

Dr. Freud might answer *wish* or *dread*, and a kid who's lost a tooth and put it under the pillow might answer *fairy*. And anyway, *see* is a poor choice of verbs. Did *you* see a dream last night?

hand beater : electric mixer : :
A broom : vacuum cleaner
B flashlight: light bulb
C sink : dish washer
D wrench : vise

Cooperative School and College Ability Tests, Series II, Form 3B, p. 3

If the relationship intended is that of a hand operated household item to an electrical household item that is used for the same purpose, then couldn't **B** and **C** also be acceptable answers?

You can't ____ him; he was just doing his job.
R annoy **S** help **T** blame **U** find **V** trust

Cognitive Abilities Test, Form 1, Levels A-H, Verbal Battery, p. 9

The answer wanted is *blame*, an excuse made famous by legions of low-level Nazis during the Nuremberg trials. In a Watergate government, the answer *trust* might be equally appropriate.

How tall is the average American man?
Any answer from 5′7″ to 5′11″.
(Do *not* give credit for 5′6½″ or 5′11½″.)

WISC-R, Manual, p. 68

It's hard to see how this question measures intelligence—or even intelligent guessing, if an answer that is off by half an inch is unacceptable.

Birds can fly.
Bats can fly.

Therefore, [1] a bat is a bird. [2] a bat is a mammal. [3] animals other than birds can fly.

California Test of Mental Maturity,
1963 Revision, Level 2, Test 9, p. 15

None of the answers are correct; without the additional statement that a bat is an animal, we cannot *logically* conclude that animals other than birds can fly.

When a dove begins to associate with crows, its feathers remain ____, but its heart grows black.

F black **G** white **H** dirty **J** spread **K** good

Lorge-Thorndike, Multi-Level Edition,
Level 3, Verbal Battery, p. 3

Not only is the statement itself erroneous, but think of the emotional impact of an item like this on a black child. (And, incidentally, not all doves are white.)

How the ____ roses flush up in the cheeks!

R white **S** pretty **T** small **U** yellow **V** red

Lorge-Thorndike, Multi-Level Edition,
Level 3, Verbal Battery, p. 3

The "correct" answer is *red*—but only if the cheek in question is white. Note also the quaint phrasing.

Grey hair is a sign of age, not of ____.

R color **S** youth **T** courage
U despair **V** wisdom

Lorge-Thorndike, Level 4, Form A,
Verbal Battery, p. 3

Youth and *wisdom* are equally valid answers for this ambiguous question.

Where there is ____, let me sow love.

R suspicion **S** friendliness **T** hatred
U love **V** hope

Cognitive Abilities Test, Form 1,
Levels A-H, Verbal Battery, p. 11

Another ambiguous question. Either *suspicion* or *hatred* would do, and—for those who need encouragement—so would *friendliness*.

dollar peso mark lira
F change **G** franc **H** foreign
J purchase **K** bank

Lorge-Thorndike, Level 4, Form A,
Verbal Battery, p. 6

This question might pose no difficulties for the well-traveled child, but it requires at least a smattering of global economics for the others.

kaiser emperor king czar
R senator **S** governor **T** pope
U sultan **V** general

Cognitive Abilities Test, Form 1,
Levels A-H, Verbal Battery, p. 17

If you've studied the Renaissance but not the history of the Middle East, *pope* might seem to be as good an answer as *sultan*.

tie cravat stock neckcloth
A bib **B** collar **C** scarf **D** kirtle **E** girdle

Lorge-Thorndike, Level 4, Form A,
Verbal Battery, p. 7

A, B, or **C**— and what, by the way, is a *kirtle*?

Find the drawing at the right that goes with the third drawing in the same way that the second goes with the first.

Lorge-Thorndike, Multi-Level Edition,
Level 3, Nonverbal Battery, p. 6

Ethnic stereotyping at its most unattractive, and outdated at that.

The pictures in the box go together in a certain way. We say: "Boy is to trousers as girl is to what?"

Otis-Lennon, Elementary I,
Form J, p. 5; Manual, p. 10

B

Most little girls wear blue jeans these days as often as they wear dresses.

In each row there is one picture that shows something which is the opposite *of the first picture. Find it and mark its number.*

California Test of Mental Maturity,
1963 Revision, Level 2, Test 1, p. 3

A "non-sense" question. What can the opposite of a pillow be, except a non-pillow? How can you tell from this drawing? What are 1 and 2? Is 4 a brick or a sponge?

TESTS CITED

California Test of Mental Maturity, 1963 Revision, Level 2. Elizabeth T. Sullivan, Willis W. Clark, and Ernest W. Tiegs (Monterey, Cal.: CTB/McGraw-Hill, 1963).

Cognitive Abilities Test, Multi-Level Booklet, Form 1, Levels A-H. Robert L. Thorndike and Elizabeth Hagan (Boston: Houghton Mifflin Co., 1971-72).

Cooperative School and College Ability Tests, Series II, Forms 1A-4B (Princeton, N.J.: Educational Testing Service, Cooperative Test Division, 1955-73).

Iowa Tests of Basic Skills, Primary Battery, Levels 7-8, Form 5. E. F. Lindquist and A. N. Hieronymous (Boston: Houghton Mifflin Co., 1972).

Lorge-Thorndike Intelligence Tests, Multi-Level Edition. Irving Lorge, Robert L. Thorndike, and Elizabeth Hagen (Boston: Houghton Mifflin Co., 1954-66).

Lorge-Thorndike Intelligence Tests, Level 4, Form A. Irving Lorge and Robert L. Thorndike (Boston: Houghton Mifflin Co., 1954).

Otis-Lennon Mental Ability Test, Elementary I Level, and *Manual for Administration*. Arthur S. Otis and Roger T. Lennon (New York: Harcourt, Brace, and World, 1967).

Wechsler Intelligence Scale for Children (WISC), and *Manual*. David Wechsler (New York: Psychological Corporation, 1949; revised edition 1974).

THE HIDDEN AGENDAS OF IQ

GEORGE PURVIN

George Purvin teaches social studies in a program of alternative education at Manhasset High School on Long Island. While studying child development at Harvard University, he was a member of the staff who planned the Brookline Early Education Program.

Mr. Purvin's article "Intro to Herrnstein 101" has been published in The New Assault on Equality: IQ and Social Stratification *(New York: Harper and Row, 1974).*

It is a well-known courtroom practice for lawyers to attack the reputation and character of hostile witnesses. Essentially, the tactic is to divert the attention of the jury from the substance of the charges and focus it on the unsavory reputation or unattractive behavior of the opposition.

The time has come for those of us in public schools, for the most part Caucasian teachers and administrators, to ask ourselves if we have been using this tactic to avoid responding to those who are bitterly critical of the widespread practice of testing for intelligence in public schools. Spokesmen for our critics include militants, the noisiest of whom would deny academic freedom and the academic platform to Dr. Schockley, while others argue the case for a social policy based on the proposition that 80 percent of an individual's intelligence is inherited. Along with the sticks and stones they aim at the bones of testing policy and procedure, they call us "racists," which—contrary to the saying about sticks, stones, and names—hurts some of us very much indeed.

Let us, for a moment, ignore the name calling and the quarter from which attacks are coming and concentrate entirely on the substance of the charges. Public school people, for good and valuable consideration, have contracted to teach skills and otherwise educate society's new arrivals. However, the claim is made that, hidden behind our rough red brick or smooth white stone walls, large numbers of young people are milling about unable to perform the tasks considered appropriate for the age. The fact that an inordinate percentage of these children are non-Caucasian suggests some failure on our part in relation to these children. But it is a failure we refuse to acknowledge. Instead, it is alleged, we breach our contract by simplistically categorizing them as failures.

While we have not yet been required formally to answer charges on a breach of contract suit, we have more or less defended ourselves by putting out the word that no one is at fault, neither teacher nor pupil; that the population that cannot master basic skills came to us without the intellectual equipment to learn; and that we do the best we can with what we are given. Our experience tells us that kids with high IQ scores do well in school and those with low IQ scores do poorly. Consequently, the widespread practice of administering these tests is not a devious scheme aimed at any population in particular, but rather it is valuable in helping us compare school performance with potential.

This defense of IQ tests is probably good enough for most living rooms, corner bars, and faculty lounges. But will it hold up in a court of scholarly inquiry? If we were to be brought into such a court, we would not be permitted to rest our case on the fact the IQ tests reliably predict school performance. At some time during the cross-examination, we would be obliged to acknowledge that it is one thing to predict school performance—that is, predict how well a student is likely to perform other tasks similar to the ones given on the test—and it is quite another thing to argue that we are measuring inborn, innate, or native intelligence. We seem to be hooked on the proposition that our test is measuring some predetermined intellectual capacity over which we have little or no control. We must also affirm that we believe the test to be "culture fair," that is to say that the test results have not been significantly distorted by the previous learning or experience of the test taker.

To continue the courtroom construct, we must be prepared for devastating testimony on this point. The plaintiffs will probably bring in Henry C. Dyer of Educational Testing Service, who will be identified as one of the nation's foremost authorities on intelligence and ability testing. On the issue of culture-fair testing, he will offer his opinion that there are only two conditions under which a test can be culture fair: 1) either the learning required to perform acceptably on the test is commonly and equally available to all people of all cultures, or 2) the stimulus material on the test is completely novel to all people of all cultures.[1]

Furthermore, he will contend that neither of these conditions is obtainable. After making these comments about culture-fair testing, Dyer will be asked directly to offer an expert opinion on the widely used Stanford-Binet Intelligence Scales and the Wechsler Intelligence Scale for Children as instruments for measuring genetic endowment for intelligence. He will inform the court that there are no tests for native intelligence:

> *. . . the concept of "native intelligence" is essentially meaningless. Every response to the stimulus material in intelligence tests is of necessity a learned response. The kind and amount of learning an individual acquires depends upon the experiences that come to him from the environment and upon his structural assets and liabilities. To some extent structural assets and liabilities are genetically determined; to some extent they are environmentally determined. Therefore, there is no way of determining from an intelligence test score how much of the learning that produced it has been affected by genetic factors.*[2]

In our defense we will call psychologists such as Arthur Jensen of Berkeley, who will state that the uncommon similarity in IQ scores of identical twins reared apart satisfies him that 80 percent of an individual's intellectual capacity is fixed at the moment of conception. The other side will call their psychologists, such as Leon Kamin of Princeton, who will attack the data that came out of the twin studies and make the case for environment and experience in determining intelligence. Essentially, however, the jury will be asked to decide if the IQ tests we use in school separate out the genetic component for intelligence from the components for environment and experience, and measure it. But before the jury goes out to reach a verdict, it will no doubt hear from Jerome Kagan of Harvard, a psychologist who has done a number of cross-cultural studies on cognitive development. Kagan will tell us that if the IQ tests were translated into various languages native to Latin America, Asia, and Africa and administered to the entire ten-year-old population of these continents, a majority of the scores would fall within the range of what we call mentally retarded.[3] It would indeed take a jury of twelve Archie Bunkers to believe that the majority of the world's non-Western ten-year-olds are mentally retarded.

When a case looks weak at best, lawyers generally advise clients to settle out of court. The question is whether we are prepared to lay the hidden agenda on the table. If we are genuinely serious about settling this IQ business at some negotiating table, we have to admit that we are using a test that included only Caucasian children in the standardization samples that psychologists used to create the test—a test that reflects the values and experiences of the white middle class. And furthermore, we have to admit that we do in fact use the test to label children. Regardless of what individual boards of education, superintendents, or principals might say about their stated policy on the use of IQ scores, faculty and administrators as functioning individuals do make inferences about the intelligence of children on the basis of these test scores. As a consequence, large numbers of non-

Caucasian children are labeled unintelligent. In our culture, to be identified as unintelligent not only handicaps children in the contest for the better things in life, but also makes it impossible for them to develop a sense of self-respect and a wholesome self-image.

Consider the synonyms for the word *unintelligent*. All of them, old synonyms as well as new slang, carry a derisive connotation, and anyone so identified becomes a target for ridicule or contempt. Moreover, like it or not, the identification of large groups of nonwhite children as inadequate, contemptible, or ridiculous is the essence of racism. Once we have permitted that word to surface and become part of our discussion, we have taken a giant step toward establishing good faith in the negotiation of testing policies.

But there remains still another difficult hurdle. At some point in the discussions, the more militant members of the other side will want to make a particularly scurrilous charge. They will allege that the white power structure is already preparing programs and policies involving massive repression for black, Puerto Rican, and Chicano minorities. In order to get the white American citizen to accept, if not support, social policies that are openly repressive, it is first necessary (the argument goes) that the American people view these non-Caucasian populations as a lower order of humanity. Our part in the conspiracy, it is charged, is to help in the process of dehumanizing "these people" by putting out the word that they are inferior as a consequence of a genetic blueprint. These charges, of course, may very well be untrue, but that does not mean that they are unworthy of scrutiny.

•

At least since Aristotle, the hereditarians have assured those in power that their right to rule and exploit their fellow-man was predetermined by God or nature. The nature-nurture controversy has had a way of surfacing to the advantage of the nature side when those in power feel threatened by lower class aspirations for social and economic mobility, or when they feel the need to engage in some form of ruthless exploitation. Would two hundred years of chattel slavery have been possible without the reassurance of those leaders, North and South, respected for their wisdom and righteousness, that the Negro was a different species, a different and lower order of humanity?

At the turn of the century, men with good academic credentials applied Darwin's biological thesis to social situations and provided the intellectual underpinnings for the brutal living and working conditions imposed on the immigrants from southern and eastern Europe who comprised the unskilled labor force. Historians are in substantial agreement that the naked oppression of nineteenth century colonialism would have been difficult, if not impossible, without the concept of Anglo-Saxon/Teutonic natural superiority. This concept was nourished by the late nineteenth century press, pulpit, and university. It will not do to wave away this history as unrelated in any way to the present situation. Is it mere coincidence that Richard Herrnstein's *Atlantic Monthly* article on IQ was so widely publicized and summarized in the media? The article, it will be remembered, argued that social status is predetermined to a large extent by inheritance of mental ability as measured by IQ tests. As we become a society that advances people on the basis of merit or ability, Herrnstein wrote,

> *. . . there will be precipitated out of the mass of humanity a low-capacity (intellectual or otherwise) residue that may be unable to master the common occupations, cannot compete for success and achievement, and are most likely to be born to parents who have similarly failed.*
>
> *. . . in times to come, as technology advances, the tendency to be unemployed may run in the genes of a family about as certainly as bad teeth do now.*[4]

Strangely, educators backed away from the outcry and polemic that followed the Herrnstein article. After all, what is education if it is not identifying and providing the environment and experience that nourish human development? Humanistic considerations aside, those who maintain that 80 percent of a person's intellectual equipment is fixed when the winning sperm makes contact with the egg are striking out at our educational rice bowl by implying that it makes no sense to throw good money after bad genes.

People in education are very much involved. What is debated on academic platforms at the university has a way of filtering down into legislative chambers and high school cafeterias, aborting educational appropriations and causing interracial fistfights. To permit open discussion of these matters is not to confess to being part of a racist conspiracy. But if the nonwhite population feels in any way threatened, we educators must be willing to actively oppose any resurrection of Social Darwinism and resist any attempt to use the schools to nourish it.

•

The question to consider now is where we are once we have cut away the inborn, innate, native intelligence mystique from the IQ test. Has it any educational value? Can we do anything with an instrument that appears to predict future performance? Some educators and psychologists argue that the tests are valueless because they are ethnocentric. Proponents of this position claim we have improperly used white middle class behavior as a yardstick with which to measure all behavior. We are ethnocentric, the argument goes, when we equate linguistic competence with standard English. I doubt, however, that this position would get much support from the groups these advocates claim to represent. It is difficult to conceive of a situation in which linguistic competence in English is disabling. But many witnesses would affirm that incompetence in English in this culture is at least economically disabling.

Can some two hundred million English-speaking Americans of all races coexist with a subculture that speaks broken English or no English at all, with both groups having equal access to the economic benefits and social mobility that they value in common? I seriously doubt it. The concept of cultural pluralism is rooted in the idea that parochial education, racial and ethnic pride, and bilingualism are compatible with literacy in English. It is fundamental and nonnegotiable that the American public school nourish in each and every individual the power to read, write, and speak his or her thoughts in English, and attend to the ideas and words of others who communicate in English.

If we are in agreement that acceptable performance during the school years is a worthy and high priority objective, then we can turn our attention to the instrument that measures the ingredients for future learning. Suppose all children performed adequately on the test? Would it not follow that they would also perform acceptably in subsequent schooling? Is it possible to systematically provide all children with those skills that will enable them to do well in schooling and, as a by-product, to perform acceptably on the test?

Psychologists who specialize in human development are in substantial agreement that intellectual growth occurs in stages as the organism is stimulated by and interacts with his environment. The developing infant consumes his experiences and ingests them for growth to higher and higher levels of intellectual sophistication. This concept of human development sees the child bringing with him on his first day of formal schooling all the learning he has accumulated in his preschool experience. His capacity to cope successfully with the demands of the school will be profoundly influenced by the preceding five years. The right amount of raw materials of experience will give one five-year-old child the capital he needs to perform the identified tasks and behavior appropriate for the age, while "missing parts" of early experience will put another child, of equal potential, under a severe handicap.

Burton White, of Harvard's Pre-School Project and the Brookline Early Education Project, believes that developmental deficits during the first three years of life are not necessarily outgrown, and that many, when undetected and untreated, multiply and set off chain reactions causing new problems that may defy solution. White theorizes that the period of a child's development between eight and thirty months is of particular importance. It is at this time that acquisition of language is taking place and increased mobility offers new opportunity for learning.[5]

This thinking implies that our IQ test is measuring, on the low end of the spectrum, what could be called intellectual malnutrition. Society deals with the problem of malnutrition by providing proper diet during the early stages of growth—not by diagnosing it after the damage is done, which is, in effect, what IQ testing does.

This brings us to the question of cost. In these days of austerity and taxpayers' revolts, where will the money come from to begin education at infancy? There are two arguments. The first is that when all segments of the population possess skills, dignity, and identification with society, added increments of productivity will not only repay the investment but will deliver all kinds of tangible and intangible dividends. American history gives us another possible argument. In the middle of the nineteenth century, a member of Congress proposed a solution to the slavery controversy by suggesting that the federal government appropriate funds to buy the slaves from the owners and set them free in the labor market. In response, another member of Congress chided his colleague and, to the amusement of the entire chamber, pointed out that the appropriation would come to the unheard of sum of $2 billion—more than the assessed valuation of the land of the entire State of Virginia. Ten years later the North alone found $22 billion to fight a war that killed or maimed three-quarters of a million Americans. When the social as well as economic costs of bad or inadequate education are honestly calculated, it might very well be that education, intervention, help, or whatever you wish to call it, is society's best if not *only* alternative.

But new programs involving education from infancy are hardly likely to get started next semester. What do we do about IQ tests right now? Is it possible to relabel them and take advantage of their reliability in predicting certain kinds of school performance?

I don't think it can be done. For the moment, at least, the situation is out of control. Psychologists such as Jensen, Herrnstein, and Eysenck persist in the proposition that "intelligence" is what IQ scores are measuring and that 80 percent of "it" is fixed at the moment of conception. Prestigious publications open their pages to these social scientists—the *New York Times Magazine* to Jensen, the *Atlantic Monthly* to Herrnstein. Summaries of their "findings" are ubiquitous. Some teachers and administrators use them to relieve the anxieties and blunt the sharp edges of the frustrations that teaching necessarily involves. Others seize them as a way of avoiding what is to them the bitter cup of racial equality. Any value the tests might have is totally obliterated by the pernicious and unscholarly inferences that are widely drawn from the test results. Los Angeles, New York, and Washington have already abandoned IQ testing in their city schools. Until such time as all toddlers and preschoolers are provided with those skills required for IQ tests, use of the tests should be generally abandoned.

NOTES

1. Henry C. Dyer, response, in *Race and Intelligence: An Examination of the Scientific Evidence by Four Authorities* (New York: B'nai B'rith Anti-Defamation League, 1963), p. 25.

2. Ibid.

3. Jerome Kagan, "What Is Intelligence?" in *The New Assault on Equality: IQ and Social Stratification,* ed. Alan Gartner, Colin Greer, and Frank Riessman (New York: Harper and Row, 1974), p. 117.

4. R. J. Herrnstein, "I.Q.," *Atlantic Monthly,* September 1971, pp. 43-64.

5. Burton L. White and Jean Carew Watts, *Experience and Environment: Major Influences on the Development of the Young Child* (Englewood Cliffs, N.J.: Prentice-Hall, 1973), pp. 20-22.

CULTURE, COGNITION, AND IQ TESTING

MICHAEL COLE

Michael Cole is associate professor of Ethnographic Psychology and Experimental Anthropology at the Rockefeller University in New York City. He is also director of the Laboratory of Comparative Human Cognition at Rockefeller.

Recent publications by Mr. Cole include The New Mathematics and an Old Culture, *coauthored with John Gay, published by Holt, Rinehart and Winston in 1967, and* Culture and Cognition, *coauthored with Sylvia Scribner, published by John Wiley and Sons in 1974.*

Among the many virtues of experiencing a different cultural setting is the opportunity it provides for learning about yourself. Like the proverbial fish that discovers water when taken out of it, a few social scientists, mostly anthropologists, have placed themselves in a position to learn about themselves and their culture through exposure to situations far removed from their ordinary experience.

A beautiful description of one such encounter can be found in Laura Bohannan's book about her life among the Tiv of Northern Nigeria. As an earnest young anthropologist, Bohannan set about trying to "learn" Tiv culture. One of the lessons set for her by the village elders was to master the names of plants important to the Tiv as sources of food and medicine:

> *The woman and the boy returned, each with an armful of leaves. Kako spread about a dozen out on the ground before me and named them one by one;*

then the next dozen, and on and on. Some he told me were edible. By pointing at the farms to the North . . . and then back to the South, he informed me which were cultivated. . . .

By nine o'clock that morning, I had several pages of words, and my tongue was limp from unaccustomed twisting. . . . Reluctantly I began to name [the leaves]. With every word Kako became more dour . . . my pronunciation couldn't be that bad . . . the woman seemed incredulous. The little boy could stand it no longer. He snatched from me the leaf I was naming and handed me another. The order had been mixed, and not once had I put the right name to the right plant.[1]

There are many lessons to be learned from this anecdote. In this paper, I would like to concentrate on the notion that a person's intellectual competence can be assessed by observing what he does when confronted with tasks that "any child can cope with."

To an American reading Bohannan's narrative, there is special irony in her plight. We know her to be an intelligent and accomplished woman because she was able to go to Tiv-land, obtain a Ph.D., and write her book. After extensive experience, the elders in the village where Bohannan lived also came to appreciate her intellectual competence, although they were often perplexed by her ineptness in particular situations.

The incident with the leaves left them aghast at her stupidity because the Tiv could not appreciate the enormous amount of information she had been asked to assimilate. It was a part of the fabric of their everyday lives. It was the water in which they swam.

•

I would like to suggest that many youngsters entering our schools are faced with problems at least as difficult as

Bohannan's. They enter school no less equipped intellectually to deal with the cultural environment from which they come, but by no means conversant with the fauna and flora of the classroom.

Unhappily, many do not enter an environment particularly well equipped to enculturate them. Part of the problem results from our failure to recognize that despite variations among them, by and large America's schools represent a culture that must be learned by all children. The systems of knowledge, belief, and value transmitted by American schools overlap to a very large extent with the home and neighborhood cultures of many children, often making it difficult to believe that anything like "culture learning" goes on at school. But it does. Because this is an article about testing, I want to consider problems that arise from a failure to appreciate cultural differences that influence performance on tests of both the achievement and ability varieties as these instruments are applied to measure children early in their school careers. But rather than repeat old arguments about biases in testing, I would like to describe one small area in which my colleagues and I have stumbled onto a hidden contribution of children's past experience in a test that presumes to measure a basic ability.

The example concerns tests of semantic development and those parts of IQ tests designed to assess the ability to classify, and this kind of example is quite familiar. For classification, the child is given a word pair (*plum-peach* is the first such item on the Wechsler Intelligence Scale for Children) and asked how they are alike. The scoring manual gives us explicit rules for allotting credit to different answers:

PLUM—PEACH

> *2 points*—A response stating they are both fruits.
> *1 point*—Both food . . . Both round (or similarly shaped) . . . Both have a skin (pits, juice, etc.) . . . Can them.
> *0 points*—Good for you . . . Taste alike . . . Both small . . . Same kind of skin.[2]

Why are answers like "good for you" allotted no score at all? There are two answers to the question. First, as an empirical observation, it has been found that older children are more likely than younger ones to give the answers that receive higher scores, and at a specified age, children who give the better answers are more likely to do well in school. Second, there are *theoretical* rationales deriving from studies of age related changes in children's verbal behavior. Many studies have shown that when children of different ages are told to "say the first word that comes to mind" in response to stimulus words like peach, there is a regular change in the nature of responses that is age dependent. Young children (five or six years of age) are likely to respond as if they were fitting the word into a phrase or sentence. For example, we might observe the following responses to stimulus words: peach-fuzzy, run-home, or red-balloon. To be sure, we might also encounter sequences such as dog-cat or cow-milk, but the preponderance of young children's responses are of the type identified as phrase constructions.

Older children (eleven or twelve years of age) engage in relatively little phrase constructing. They are much more likely to produce the following responses: peach-pear, run-skip, or red-black.

This shift in the nature of children's verbal responses is widely believed to reflect a more mature language processing capacity, which has many counterparts in other areas of the child's intellectual behavior. Such parallels have led developmental theorists to formulate a series of stages or milestones of intellectual development, such as Jerome Bruner's idea that children first represent information as part of an action, then as an image, and finally as a symbolic form. All of this seems so commonsensical that it is a little difficult to fault—until the fish comes out of the water.

This experience occurred for me when I read an article about "the production of childlike associates in adults" in a very respectable scientific journal. The experiments reported in the article were the essence of simplicity. Using standardized norms of word frequency (taken from a variety of printed sources), the authors constructed two lists of words. One list was made up entirely of synonyms of the words in the other list. The only difference between the two lists was their frequency of occurrence on the norms. The first list was made up of very high-frequency words, the second list of low-frequency synonyms. Some samples from the two lists are: many/myriad; neat/fastidious; and clever/ingenious.

One group of college students was presented the first list, another group the second in a standard "say the first word that comes to mind" experiment. From the title of the article and my brief description, it is probably easy to anticipate the results. When given the high-frequency words, the college students responded like adults. They produced words of the same grammatical form class as the stimulus word (for example, many-few). But the responses to the low-frequency words were preponderantly childlike. They were words appropriate to the use of the stimulus word in a phrase (for example, myriad opportunities).

This article stimulated me to reconsider the rationale for assuming that word association studies measure semantic development as a property of individual children's level of mental development. If frequency of encountering a word controls the nature of adults' responses, wouldn't the same apply to children? And if the frequency principle applies to children, how can we use such materials to test ideas about intellectual development independent of experience? One thing about children of different ages that we can be pretty sure about is that older children have heard any particular word more often than their younger friends. If we are only testing children's age by a circuitous route, the exercise is rather fruitless.

What about children of the same age but of different family backgrounds? The same principle applies. We know that children from different subcultural groups are exposed to different vocabulary. How children (or adults) respond to a problem (even one so simple as saying what comes to mind when we say "peach") depends in large measure on their familiarity with the content of the problem, and this familiarity varies in unknown ways with children's home culture.

Once we are sensitized to the way even simple mental operations depend on previous experience with the task, we are likely to be very skeptical when told that a test is "culture free" or "culture fair." The whole notion of culture free becomes very difficult to accept, because it means "independent of experience." It is extremely doubtful if we can discover any mental processes independent of experience.

Culture fair is an interesting notion to consider. A culture-fair test of semantic development would ensure that the materials used to elicit associative responses were equivalent in frequency of occurrence for each person being tested. No existing test of semantic development in particular or of mental ability in general has ever attempted to tailor its materials to major subcultural groups, let alone individuals.

Instead, the dominant strategy has been to attain culture fairness by making the test materials equally unfamiliar to everyone. The catch in this enterprise is in the word "equally." We simply have no way to determine if such equality has been achieved unless we know what the different groups know in the first place. But we don't know that or we could devise culture-fair tests. A pretty circle.

One of the distressing aspects of this problem is that it is difficult to identify. We have long known that asking inner-city children about gazebos and violin-cellos is absurd. But when we see that the same problem arises again in more subtle form with peaches and pears, we begin to seriously doubt the efficacy of ability tests as anything more than a measure of what children have learned to do at the time of testing. We certainly don't want to leap to conclusions about their educability.

Lest it be thought that I have picked a special case, let

me mention that virtually every time we look closely at a test, the same issues are almost certain to arise. Many recent studies have demonstrated the role of children's knowledge about words on tasks used to tap "higher order memory skills." Older children ordinarily recall more than younger ones, but not if we are careful to choose words that the younger children spontaneously organize in the way older children organize standard memory materials. Older children are unlikely to be fooled by changes in the configuration of a row of m & m's into thinking that the number of candies has changed. Young children are more easily misled, but not if we use few enough m & m's so that young children can count the smaller set as well as the older children can count the larger one.

As Laura Bohannan so aptly phrased the predicament of anyone facing an unfamiliar problem, "in each other's countries, where we do not understand, we become children again, who still have everything to learn."[3]

What implications can we draw from our predicament if we begin to operate on the assumption that for most children tests are largely or wholly measures of a child's past learning, not his or her general capacity?

First, we must acknowledge that no educational problems are solved by this decision. If Bohannan's future well-being had depended solely on her ability to learn about Nigerian plant life, she would have been in serious trouble. It is virtually certain that her past experience was an impediment to such learning; she "knew" she couldn't learn about leaves.

In a similar way, recognition that children are culturally different, not devoid of culture, can direct us toward new educational tasks, but such recognition provides no answers to the question of how to expedite second-culture learning.

The second implication of a decision to treat tests as measures of children's past experience should be to make us seek tests that will inform us more adequately about the children we want to teach. Based entirely on the culture of the school (because it is school performance that they are designed to predict), standardized tests tell us something about what part of the school culture children have learned that the teacher could build upon. Perhaps future test designers could aid teachers in their effort to understand their children by building as much cultural variability into their tests as possible. For the time being, however, teachers can expect little pedagogical help from standardized tests.

Everyone might be better off spending the time devising ways to discover what the children *do* know.

NOTES

1. Laura Bohannan, *Return to Laughter* (New York: American Museum of Natural History and Doubleday Publishing Co., 1964), pp. 15-16.
2. David Wechsler, *Wechsler Intelligence Scale for Children, Manual* (New York: Psychological Corporation, 1949), p. 67.
3. Bohannan, *Return to Laughter*, pp. 142-43.

IQ Tests:

A CASE OF CULTURAL MYOPIA

AMADO M. PADILLA
BLAS M. GARZA

Amado M. Padilla is associate professor of psychology at the University of California, Los Angeles. An experimental psychologist, Mr. Padilla was formerly the director of the Institute for Applied Behavioral Science at the University of California, Santa Barbara. He is the author of articles on topics ranging from learning theory to language acquisition in bilingual children and is coauthor of Latino Mental Health.

Blas M. Garza is principal of Adams Elementary School, Santa Barbara, California, and chairperson of the Equal Education Opportunity Committee of the Association of California School administrators. Mr. Garza was formerly the director of Intergroup Education for the Santa Barbara School District and is the author of numerous bilingual/bicultural educational guides for Santa Barbara teachers.

No test of intelligence can be divorced from the cultural frame in which the examinee is expected to perform. Nonetheless, test makers argue that IQ tests have been designed to measure general intelligence in such a way that subcultural differences are not significant factors. This notion, however, is increasingly challenged by significantly large economically and culturally different groups—Appalachian whites, blacks, native Americans, and the Spanish surnamed. One should seriously question the cultural bag of assumptions and attitudes that underlie intelligence tests, since they may be far removed from the realities that have molded the child being tested. We must search penetratingly for the influences that have shaped the composite of the child's world, and we must determine how an IQ test purports to measure these influences. Since tests are inventories of behavior, how well they evaluate what a child has been exposed to depends on how well they sample from the life experiences of the child.

Our contention is that IQ tests are inadequate for Spanish-surnamed children because they do not sample from their particular cultural and linguistic life experiences. (In order to avoid confusion, we will adhere to the Department of Health, Education, and Welfare definition of the term *Spanish surnamed*; that is, all persons considered by themselves, by the school, or by the community to be of Mexican, Puerto Rican, Central American, Cuban, Latin American, or other Spanish origin.[1])

Two findings of the Mexican-American Education Study Project of the U.S. Commission on Civil Rights are particularly relevant to the problems of using IQ tests with Spanish-surnamed children. First, the study project reported that Mexican-American children were two times as likely to be found in classes for slow learners in Texas, and two and a half times as likely in California. The major factor for this placement was poor performance on standard IQ tests.[2] This finding is significant since California and Texas schools enroll more than 80 percent of the total number of Mexican-American students in the Southwest.

Second, it was found in a study of school holding power that 40 percent of all Mexican-American students in the five Southwestern states (Arizona, California, Colorado, New Mexico, and Texas) leave school prior to graduation. The reasons for school dropout are complex, but one of the major factors is clearly under-achievement in reading.[3] Although these two findings pertain only to the Mexican-American subgroup, there is every reason to believe that other Spanish-surnamed students are also overrepresented in classes for slow learners and leave school earlier than majority group students do.

We are not reporting these findings to argue that IQ tests alone cause the high rate of placement in slow classes or the high dropout rate among Spanish-surnamed students. The point is, simply, that approximately one-tenth of the total school-age population is Spanish surnamed and that, for a number of reasons, these students are not receiving the same quality or even the same number of years of education as are children of the majority group. It is important that we recognize that the use of tests in school—including the standard IQ tests—is in part responsible for the undereducation of Spanish-surnamed children. To demonstrate this, we must ask ourselves four important questions.

•

The first question we should ask is, who do we test? This country is perhaps the most test oriented nation in the world, and testing here follows an orderly, assembly line model. Children are typically given a standard achievement test on admission to school and again, each fall and spring, until they graduate from high school. Let us focus on the child who enters school speaking little or no English. Admittedly, school administrators are becoming more sensitive to the needs of those who speak Spanish primarily, but there is still widespread resentment or neglect of the child whose presence demands so many departures from the regular curriculum. It should be noted that inability to speak English is only one of a multitude of significant variables found among the heterogenous groups of the Spanish surnamed and that generalizations about the group's characteristics are misleading.

Introduction to English is in itself a monumental achievement. Consider, for example, the English "uh" sound (or "schwa," as the linguists call it), which does not exist at all in the Spanish sound inventory. Consider also that in English the schwa sound can appear at the beginning of a word (*o*ther), in the middle (truck), or at the end (camer*a*). Now let's take a child whose sound inventory does not include "uh." Not only must he substitute whatever sound in his own inventory approximates that sound, but he must also decide whether "uh" is represented by *o*, *u*, or *a*. This is only one of many complexities that the dominant Spanish-speaking student must master before becoming proficient in English.

Many school personnel are becoming sensitive to the language problems of children whose spoken English is limited, and sometimes these students are excused from taking tests in English. There is, however, a similar problem with another segment of the Spanish-speaking group: those children who acquire early a working knowledge of English. These children have learned enough basic English to get along in day-to-day situations—"How much is that?" and so on—but their dominant mode of communication continues to be Spanish.

When teachers or other school personnel hear these children speaking English in practical situations, they assume that the children speak English well enough to be tested in that language. We have often heard teachers say something like, "She understands more English than she lets on. I've listened to her on the playground." When such observations are made, we should assess the child's knowledge of English before deciding what language he or she should be tested in. Ideally, this assessment should be carried out by a teacher who knows both Spanish and English.

Our second question is, when is the best time for testing? If Spanish-speaking children are going to be tested on standardized IQ tests, the best time for testing them can only be after they have mastered English at least as well as their peers have. It is difficult to specify a developmental clock here, but it is not satisfactory to conclude that because a child is in the second, third, or fourth grade, he has necessarily learned enough English to be tested for IQ—especially if the outcome of the test is to be used as the major criterion for deciding the student's educational future.

It is, in fact, a more complicated matter than simply

trying to decide when the child knows enough English to be tested. The student must also have become sufficiently acculturated to know what is being asked by such general information items as these, which appear on the Wechsler Intelligence Scale for Children (WISC): "Who wrote 'Romeo and Juliet'?" "What is celebrated on the Fourth of July?" "What does C.O.D. mean?" "How far is it from New York to Chicago?" "When is Labor Day?"[4] If these questions have no significance in the life of the Spanish-surnamed student, then they are invalid measures of intelligence, and it makes little difference whether the student can communicate in English or not. An analogous situation might be to ask a child who is not Mexican American what holiday is celebrated on the sixteenth of September or who Cantinflas is.

A third question we need to consider is, what conditions do we test for? A quick answer is that we test for cognitive or intellectual development. But unfortunately, a quick answer won't suffice, because we don't have any one measurement instrument that gives estimates across a broad range of constructs within cognitive development. In some respects, it is not wrong to say that it would take hours and hours to test a child properly for his level of cognitive development. What appears to be especially troublesome when trying to explain the performance of Spanish-surnamed children on tests of intelligence is the failure to locate the test designers' priorities in developing tests and their definition of what constitutes intelligence in the first place. All too often, psychometricians appear to be satisfied with the cliche that intelligence is what the test measures. Though this circular definition has appealed to many as a way to forestall any discussion of the essence of intelligence, it is hardly a satisfactory answer. If this were our only way of defining intelligence, then school authorities would be bound to accept the results of any pointless activity or test, so long as it were clearly labeled "intelligence test." And unfortunately, this is not too far from the present state of the art.

We believe that IQ tests in their present state of refinement do not measure intelligence—that is, the actual mental ability or capability of an individual—at all; rather, they measure a number of extraneous variables, all of which have important consequences for the student. Some of these variables are:

• *The skill of the test administrator.* He must use appropriate language systems and behavioral mechanisms for communicating to the child what is expected of him on the test and provide a valid interpretation of responses. A test examiner is not merely a neutral recorder of the child's intellectual ability as it is demonstrated in the test situation. On the contrary, the examiner is engaged in an extremely complex, two-person interaction. The examiner can maximize or minimize the child's performance by his or her actions. Similarly, by misinterpreting the child's responses, the examiner can significantly raise or lower the final IQ score. This aspect of IQ testing has usually been ignored, and we are particularly concerned about emphasizing it here. When a Spanish-surnamed child and a non-Spanish-surnamed examiner sit across from each other in a testing situation, there is often a wider gulf separating them than just the table. Typically, there is a linguistic, cultural, and socio-economic gap between them, associated with their different sets of life experiences. An examiner who is not sensitive to these differences will surely have a negative influence on the outcome of the child's performance.

• *The child's ability to perform under pressure.* It doesn't require any great amount of insight on the part of the Spanish-surnamed child to recognize that he or she is different from the other children in the classroom. He may have difficulty keeping up because he can't entirely understand what is being said around him. He is embarrassed at not being able to respond because he doesn't know what is asked of him, or, if he can reply, he fears that someone may laugh. Then comes the fateful day when he is referred for testing—and everyone knows it. How many adults are not apprehensive when they must perform under pressure? How many adults have not felt anxiety, hostility, and immobility under similar circumstances? How then is the child to feel when he hears the examiner say, "This is a test and I want to see how well you do"?

• *The child's motivation to identify success or failure in the testing situation.* A child who is being tested for giftedness and another child who is being tested for possible placement in a class for the educable mentally retarded will be motivated quite differently. Both children are aware of the process that brought them to the testing situation. The one who is being tested for giftedness will probably be highly motivated to perform well, but the other child is likely to see the test as just another step in a series of humiliations. These two children will be motivated to respond quite differently to a question that requires them to name as many different words as possible in one minute.[5] (This question, from the Stanford-Binet, is considered appropriate for ten-year-olds; our point here is not to argue the merit of the question, though it might well be argued.) What child can get excited by such a request if he suspects that the examiner only wants to determine how much he does not know?

• *The values underlying many of the test items, which are outside the life experiences of some children.* One item on the Stanford-Binet subtest for ten-year-olds requires that the child give two reasons why "children should not be too noisy in school" and why "most people would rather have an automobile than a bicycle."[6] Similarly, on the WISC General Comprehension subtest, we find such questions as, "Why are criminals locked up?" "Why is it better to pay bills by check than by cash?" "Why is it generally better to give money to an organized charity than it is a street beggar?" What do these questions measure? Many Mexican-American or Puerto Rican children may be unable to respond to such questions simply because their life experiences have contributed to the formation of a different set of values. Many of these children may have wondered why a friend or a member of their family has been sent to jail, and they may have arrived at quite a different answer than the one in the tester's manual, which requires some notion of protection for society and deterrence of future crimes.[7] In the same way, a child whose family lives on the fringe of poverty may have little idea of the values associated with checking accounts or donating to organized charities.

The last question we must ask ourselves is, how do we test for IQ? Just as there were no simple answers to the preceding questions, there is no simple answer to this one. It would certainly be convenient if we had a machine modeled after the airport metal detectors, which would pick up and register a person's cognitive or intellectual ability as he walked through it and then proceed to print out a sheet with the pertinent information. Unfortunately (or fortunately, depending on your point of view), such a machine does not exist. What we need to do is to consider what instruments are available and what our priorities for testing are.

How often an examiner is right or wrong in his assessment of a child's intellectual potential depends to a great degree on the state of the art of intelligence testing. If IQ tests are as far from perfect as we contend that they are, then we are forced to assume that many children are falsely and injuriously labeled mentally deficient. How many of them are placed in low-expectancy programs because of low test scores? And how many gifted children are overlooked by the testing instruments? Any child who is mislabeled and placed in a class for slow learners will not be educated up to his or her true ability. Such mislabeling creates anxiety for the child and for his family, and often lowers his self-esteem as well. And ultimately, society at large is deprived of the skills and contributions the child might have made if allowed to develop to his or her full potential.

There is an important difference, to use a medical analogy, between a psychometrician and a physician with respect to testing. If a child scores poorly on an IQ test, the psychologist often concludes on the basis of no further examination that he should be placed in a low-expectancy class. The physician, on the other hand, treats a screening instrument as only one indicator of a person's physical well-being, so that the screening process merely identifies those patients who need further evaluation.

If this procedure were followed by psychometricians and educators, the mislabeling of children as slow learners would not concern us unduly. But it is our contention that IQ testing instruments result in frequent mislabeling and mistaken diagnosis, especially among Spanish-surnamed children. We believe that any instrument that results in a high rate of misdiagnosed children is useless and should be outlawed. It is interesting to note, in this regard, the growing number of lawsuits involving school districts and Spanish-surnamed parents whose children have been placed in low-expectancy classes. In several cases these suits have forced legislation on the criteria necessary for the placement of children in special education classes.[8]

•

What, then, are the alternatives? Should Spanish-surnamed children be tested for IQ? Four major alternatives have been offered:

Culture-free tests. The difficulties of actually measuring whether a child's environment has been "normally favorable" have led test makers to try to circumvent environment altogether. The hope has been to salvage "general intelligence" as a personal attribute that determines what a child learns from his environment. The possibility of culture-free tests has figured importantly in the debate over black-white differences and has, understandably, surfaced a number of times with respect to testing Spanish-surnamed children, as well. Culture-free tests are supposed to measure performance in terms that are completely unrelated to any particular socioeconomic environment. Accordingly, an environment-free intelligence test could be taken to measure "true" intelligence.

Without reviewing the debate that has ensued from this approach, let us suggest that efforts to develop culture-free tests were doomed to failure from the beginning. All human experience is modulated by human society, and no test can be experience free. Experience, furthermore, cannot be separated from its social context. The materials used in the test, the language of the test, the manner of getting the testee to respond, the criteria for choosing which responses to record, the categories into which responses are classified, the test's validity criterion—all are culture bound.

Translated tests. Another alternative is translating either the WISC or the Stanford-Binet for use with Spanish-surnamed children. A review of some of the literature on translated tests, however, has shown that translation is not always the answer. Often the translated version of a test is no better than the original English version because the translator, though well intentioned, has paid little attention to the subtleties involved in translating materials from one language to another. The meaning of important phrases may be lost in translation; the level of difficulty of vocabulary items may change with translation; and translations may omit regionalisms and colloquialisms that communicate more effectively than do standard Spanish translations.[9]

A single example will suggest the difficulties encountered in translating between the two languages. Question 2 on the General Information subtest of the WISC indicates the thumb and asks, "What do you call this finger?" The formal word for thumb in Spanish is *pulgar*, but it is infrequently used. A Spanish-speaking child is more likely to reply with the common name for thumb, *dedo gordo*, which simply means fat finger. Is the child right or wrong in replying *dedo gordo*? The child is wrong if the examiner is not familiar with the colloquial phrase and merely follows the scoring manual.[10]

It would be misleading if we did not point out that Spanish versions of the WISC and Stanford-Binet tests have been standardized on children in both Puerto Rico and Mexico. Both of these Spanish-language versions of the tests have been adapted for use with different populations of Spanish-speaking children and do not correspond on an item-by-item comparison. Each version has been modified to best accommodate the particular subcultural variations that exist in Puerto Rican and Mexican children.

These versions of the tests offer no panacea in the United States, however. One complaint levied against the English versions of the WISC or Stanford-Binet is that Spanish-surnamed children in the United States were excluded from the standardization procedure. But the same is true of the Spanish versions of the tests, which were adapted and standardized with Puerto Rican and Mexican children, who may differ linguistically from the Spanish-surnamed children in the United States. A Spanish-surnamed child who grows up in the United States may not be as fluent in Spanish as is his counterpart in Mexico or Puerto Rico, partly because he has not been educated in Spanish. Accordingly, to test that child in Spanish would be to test him in a language that he does not completely understand, a subtle point that is sometimes overlooked by well-intentioned school personnel. The inability to adequately test a Spanish-surnamed child in either English or Spanish has led to a third alternative.

No testing at all. In recent years, an increasing number of parents and educators, minority and majority group alike, have spoken out against IQ tests or even advocated a total ban on them. The problem is, however, that school personnel will continue to need instruments and techniques for assessing the academic progress of children. What we advocate is the design of more valid tests for all children, including the Spanish surnamed. We also hope for the day when more enlightened use will be made of educational tests—when they are again used for the diagnostic purposes for which they were originally invented.

Culturally sensitive testing. The final alternative, and the one to which we subscribe, calls for a more sensible approach in the testing of culturally and linguistically different children. A program of culturally sensitive testing should include: 1) the assessment of noncognitive characteristics (for example, perceptual, psychomotor, affective, psychosocial, and behavioral), as well as cognitive abilities; 2) greater information sharing between the psychometrician, other school personnel, and the parents on the assessment instruments and outcomes in order to plan the best possible educational program for the child; and 3) the employment of psychometricians who have a good understanding of Spanish and an appreciation of the important sociocultural variables that may affect the outcomes of the testing of Spanish-surnamed children.

We recognize that these recommendations will be difficult to implement, yet they are important goals in meeting the equal educational needs of Spanish-speaking children. Because of present-day budgetary constraints and declining enrollments, however, it is unlikely that many school districts will consider these suggestions as high-priority items and employ people with the necessary skills and insights to carry out culturally sensitive testing. Accordingly, we see no alternative but to advocate a moratorium on the IQ testing of Spanish-surnamed and other minority students until culturally sensitive testing becomes a reality. We take this stance somewhat reluctantly, since we believe that certain tests can be useful instruments in guiding children's educational progress; nevertheless, too many students have been mislabeled and stigmatized to allow the process to continue until more adequate tests and testing procedures are devised.

NOTES

1. "Fall 1974, Elementary and Secondary School Civil Rights Survey," Form OS/CR 101 (Washington, D.C.: U.S. Department of Health, Education, and Welfare, Office for Civil Rights, 1974).

2. Report of the U.S. Commission on Civil Rights, Mexican-American Education Study Project, *Toward Quality Education for Mexican Americans* (Washington, D.C.: U.S. Government Printing Office, 1974).

3. Report of the U.S. Commission on Civil Rights, Mexican-American Education Study Project, *The Unfinished Education* (Washington, D.C.: U.S. Government Printing Office, 1971).

4. David Wechsler, *Wechsler Intelligence Scale for Children, Manual* (New York: Psychological Corporation, 1949), p. 62.

5. Lewis M. Terman and Maud A. Merrill, *Stanford-Binet Intelligence Scale: Manual for the Third Revision* (Boston: Houghton Mifflin Co., 1969), p. 96.

6. Ibid.

7. Wechsler, *Manual*, p. 63.

8. See note 2.

9. A. M. Padilla and R. A. Ruiz, *Latino Mental Health: A Review of Literature* (Washington, D.C.: U.S. Government Printing Office, 1973).

10. Wechsler, *Manual,* p. 61.

GOING UP, GOING DOWN

THOMAS J. COTTLE

Thomas J. Cottle is affiliated with the Children's Defense Fund of the Washington Research Project in Cambridge, Massachusetts. He is the author of Time's Children: Impressions of Youth, The Abandoners, the Voices of Schools, *and* Black Children, White Dreams.

This morning, I walked down the halls of a Boston area public school. The atmosphere in the school, that intangible quality that observers of education always mention, was difficult to describe. The children were in their classrooms running around or sitting at their desks. In one room there was utter chaos; in another room there was an uncanny sense of order and obedience. In still another room, a group of about ten children, perhaps eight or nine years old, huddled together on a green rug. They sat at the foot of a young man and looked up at him as though he were imparting the secrets of the world. The children obviously loved that teacher. Outside their classroom a small sign was taped to the blond oak door. It read, "Shh—we're testing in here."

It was pleasant enough in that room—unlike the atmosphere I usually find in the schoolrooms I visit. In one of Boston's city schools, where a sign also indicated that testing was going on in a classroom, I witnessed very different behavior. I watched a child sit for more than fifteen minutes—it seemed like a century—refusing to answer even one question the tester was asking. The tester, an older woman, seemed patient enough, but it was evident that this child wasn't going to speak. It was also clear that the child was terrified. She might not have been able to speak even if she had wanted to. The child stared at the tester, her eyes rarely blinking, and with each new question or request she swallowed, opened her eyes as wide as she could, and smiled—just slightly.

After fifteen minutes of this torturous routine, the tester gave in and excused the child. The girl stood up, opened her eyes wide, and walked slowly from the room. Outside in the hall she began to run, and disobeying the signs to walk at all times, she raced up the stairs at the end of the corridor and collided with a friend. She began at once to explain her testing session, and in an instant the two children were laughing hysterically and darting up the stairs together. That same day that same ten-year-old girl had the following statement entered in her official school record, "The child's IQ is so low she is not testable. Recommendation: special class work is required, probably not in this school."

Several months later the girl was out of school. Unable to find her a special class or special school, her parents let her drop out of school for a time. After several months, the child was readmitted to the same school, and a young psychologist was brought in to test the child. It was late spring, and the psychologist took the girl and the testing equipment out-of-doors. After talking together for almost an hour about all sorts of things, the psychologist explained the testing procedure and began to work with the little girl. The psychologists's final accounting showed an IQ of 115. The child's verbal ability was outstanding. Her weaknesses were in reading comprehension and arithmetic. A tutor was provided to work with the child in those weak areas. One year later she was tested by one of the school's guidance counselors, and her IQ tested 124. In the fall of the same year, the girl was admitted to a voluntary busing program, and she now attends the suburban school that I visited this morning. Her classmates say, "She's neat, except when she talks too much!"

The great advantage of IQ tests, in the opinion of many people who debate the value of IQ tests—all tests for that matter—is that the testers never have to know the children and young adults whose lives are affected by the tests. It is true that much research work *must* be done under isolated, even sanitized conditions; personal feelings and human interactions, it is said, spoil experimental results. But when people make bold pronouncements about what education should or shouldn't be, and how tests do this or that, or even proclaim that school doesn't matter, I wonder whether these people ever talk with the children in America's schools or stay associated with schools long enough to follow the lives of any students. After observing schools for ten years—most of them in poor urban areas operating under the worst possible conditions—I have come to know a group of young people and their families, and I have watched closely what tests and the whole testing procedure have done to these children.

Some three or four years ago, I recall speaking with a group of four black boys in the fourth grade of a Philadelphia school. Here is something of that conversation between Bernard and his friends.

"There ain't no fair test no black kid's ever going to get from no white man or white woman," Bernard said. "They put grades on those tests. We behave good, and they give us extra points. We bad mouth 'em, like if we did something to them once they didn't like, they take the points away from us. Only reason they give us those tests is so they can make us look bad to each other.

"Law says they got to give the test, so they give them. Man told my mother I couldn't read. He said the test showed I couldn't read. Test didn't have nothin' about reading in it so how'd he know I couldn't read? So my mother says, 'Bernard says the test wasn't on reading.' So the man says, 'You want to see the test?' So she says, 'Yes.' And here's this big part on the test about reading, you know—remembering what you're reading. But they never gave me that part 'cause I'd of remembered. Just 'cause your lips move when you read don't mean you don't remember.

"My older sister took this test with this other girl," Bernard went on. "All of 'em were supposed to be getting this test, whatever it was for—individual—but they made her take it with this other girl. So while the test is going on, my sister's trying to answer the questions, but the teacher ain't giving her a chance. She keeps telling my sister, 'You're next, you're next.' So my sister waits for the other girl to be done, keeps her mouth shut, being polite, but when the other girl is done, the teacher don't come back to my sister. She says, 'We're done.' So my sister thinks they didn't have no time and that she'll have to be tested another day, which kind of makes her nervous all over again. But there ain't no other day, man. She's had it. That was it. Hell, she'll be in the bottom track of this school 'til the day she dies."

"And you're going to be with her," his buddies teased him.

"That's what you think," Bernard retorted. "When they test me they're going to say, man, you're a genius, you got IQ points to give away."

"The day you got too many points, man, is the day I'm going to be the principal of this school," one of his buddies replied.

•

In a small industrial town in the western part of Massachusetts, I heard other accounts of the effects of testing on some white, middle class juniors who attended the town's main public high school and who met with me on several occasions. On one rainy afternoon at the front entrance of their school, a young woman told me a sad story.

"Georgia Willows," she began, "had been in my class ever since kindergarten. I never liked her too much, but I had to see her all the time 'cause our parents were friends. I remember she lived in this real large house. We used to play there. Georgia always thought she was the smartest girl in the world. God's gift, you know. By the time we were in grammar school, everybody considered her the smartest girl in the school.

"Then last year this other girl visited the school on one of these exchange programs—from Holland—and not only was she gorgeous, she was even smarter than Georgia. I think she spoke about six languages. She'd never even been in America before and she spoke better than I do. And she'd read a lot of books I hadn't even heard of, American books! So Georgia really had someone to compete with in school. She had thought she was going to be the queen all by herself, but then this Stephanie came and Georgia really got upset. One time at our house, when her parents were visiting, all of a sudden she started to cry. We were up in my room, and out of the clear blue, she began to cry. And she kept saying, 'If I'm not the smartest person in our class, if Stephanie's IQ is higher, I don't want to be alive.'

"I didn't think she was serious about it, but she was. Just before Easter she killed herself. Her mother told my mother that Georgia never got over not being the smartest. I think if IQ means that much to someone, something must be wrong. But maybe there's something wrong with testing people and making them think that how smart they are is the most important thing in their lives."

In that same school, the issue of testing was discussed by a young man who had just learned of his own performance on a set of standardized achievement tests.

"I try not to compare myself with anybody," he began, "but kids talk. Everybody says they aren't going to tell anybody what they got, but in about five minutes everybody knows. Some mystery. I was thinking about tests and all that the other day, and I decided that there's only one way to get rid of them—which they should 'cause they only make people anxious. If you eliminate money in our society, you could eliminate tests and all these test scores. See, to be

American means that you have to have a lot of money. No matter what you earn you aren't satisfied until you have more than the next guy. That's the same thing with tests. Giving us our score isn't enough. They have to give us the percentile reading as well. Nobody's supposed to get 690 and think they're really special. The guidance counselor tells them right away that 690 may sound good, but it's only the eightieth percentile. You got to have money and you got to have IQ points and PSAT points and SAT points. Americans love numbers, and quantities. Big's the name of the game. Produce and get bigger. Inches, pounds, dollars, points on tests, that's all anybody cares about—even the minority students in our school. Nobody asks them whether they're happy. All people want to know is whether their achievement scores have gone up, or how many points they scored in a basketball game."

•

I have experienced many pleasant incidents in grammar schools and high schools during the last few years. I remember how proud and excited a boy was as he bolted out of an assistant principal's office after being awarded an academic prize. I also remember the concerned faces of children as they were told that the results of some test indicated a problem that the school officials needed to discuss with their parents. Those children were crushed and afraid. They could barely hide their hurt from their classmates.

One of the most vivid school scenes, which usually occurred first thing on a school morning, was the look of anxiety and anticipation on the faces of students as they waited for their teacher to hand back a test. "Abrams, Adams, Briscoe, Coleman," the teacher calls out looking one last time at the test sheet as if memorizing the score. And Abrams, Adams, Briscoe, and Coleman—four children half sitting, half standing, waiting eagerly—bounce up or rise slowly and walk to the teacher to receive their grand accounting.

No one needs to announce their scores. Indeed, one doesn't even have to see their faces to know their scores; their bodies reveal everything. Abrams slinks away, careful not to touch anybody. Adams practically flies back to her seat and sits as if she rests on a cushion of clouds. Briscoe looks at the teacher and his body slouches; he actually seems to be several inches shorter than before he walked the few steps to his teacher. And Coleman seems to grow several inches as the teacher walks forward to bestow the good news on the slim girl whose eyes now seem to explode with excitement. Not only does she grow, but her step changes. She dances backward, showing the paper to her friends.

When the teacher returned last week's test to the third graders in that one class, the children were literally going up and going down in response to the numbers they read in the upper right hand corners of their papers. Going up and going down—in posture, in stature, and in spirit.

Throughout my life I have been troubled by the business of psychological and achievement testing. For years, the words *Princeton, New Jersey,* caused me to tremble with fright, for no matter how many people raved about that town and its renowned university, Princeton, New Jersey, meant the home office of school testing. I never questioned the use of testing. Few students in those days did. If adults had to reconcile themselves to death and taxes, then adolescents had to reconcile themselves to test results and acne, or something equally humiliating. It was a private and public response one had to the test-taking procedure. One might smile as if "who would care," like the girl I saw in that Boston school running out of the room and colliding with her friend. But inside, something was shattered. It is almost twenty years since I graduated from high school, and the nightmares of being tested and all that went with the testing procedures persist. They are dreams of terror that never fail to awake me.

How many billions of words have been written about education? How many thousands of articles have been written about the goals of schooling and the need for testing? But how many people know the financial aspects of testing? Do we pay close enough attention to what all this multimillion dollar testing business does to people? How many people know the reasons for testing that have nothing to do with diagnostic or intellectual inquiry? Are we aware of the hundreds of thousands of children who, on the basis of some test, will stop going to school and lead a life in which this early sense of incompetence, failure, and lack of grace will never be erased from their self-concept?

Children in this country are deeply affected for all of their lives by testing and the industry that underwrites it. They are going up and going down in a pattern that ought to frighten us. Some children do just fine. Others rise so quickly that they cannot comprehend the ascent, and they often never recover from the fall when they learn that test scores represent very little when hard work and disciplined ingenuity are required.

We ought to worry, too, about the child who goes home after learning that his test scores have earned him a place in the lowest academic track of his inadequate grammar school, and with tears in his eyes tells his parents: "They told me in school that I'm stupid. I didn't know what they were talking about. They told me there was no use talking back to them because they had it in their tests—everything they wanted to know about me. I said I should be in the other group because those kids were learning more and besides, they were getting all the best teachers in their classes. I didn't want them to put me in the class they put me in. But they said it wasn't what they *wanted* to do, it was what they *had* to do 'cause they don't decide what classes to put the student in, the tests decide that for them. People don't decide. . . ."

EVOLUTION AND LEARNING:

A Context for Evaluation

S. L. WASHBURN

S. L. Washburn is University Professor at the University of California at Berkeley. He is currently vice-president of the Society for the Study of Evolution and has been president of both the American Anthropological Association and the American Association of Physical Anthropologists.

Mr. Washburn presently holds a grant from the National Science Foundation for an ongoing research project on the analysis of primate behavior. The long-term objective of the program is the understanding of human evolution.

Among his recent publications is "Evolution and Education," which appeared in Daedalus. *His "Evolution and Human Nature" (with R. S. O. Harding) is in press.*

Today, living as we do in the United States, the necessity of schools seems so obvious that our efforts go into improvement of the curriculum or educational reform. It is easy to forget that through most of human history, people learned languages, complex social systems, and elaborate technology without schools. In preagricultural societies, people learned the local flora and fauna, geography, economic practices, social customs, religion, folklore—a whole complex way of life. It is not at all certain that the graduate of a modern high school has learned as much as an uncivilized, primitive hunter.

The high school graduate has learned different things than the hunter learned, but the modern student has the enormous handicap that what he has been asked to learn does not seem to fit into any easily visible way of life. In the folk society, learning is motivated by identification, emotion, and clear goals. From an evolutionary point of view, these motivations are seen as the necessary conditions of learning. What may be learned depends on biology, but what actually *is* learned depends on the social system.

The act of throwing may make the issues clear. It is easy for people to learn to enjoy throwing. Note the form of that statement: it is *easy* for people to *learn*. Many games include throwing, and skill requires an enormous amount of practice. From an evolutionary point of view, throwing has been an important skill in the survival of the species. It was important in hunting and in warfare, and practice in play ensured the development of the necessary skill.

Chimpanzees are one of the very few animals that also throw. They have the anatomy that permits throwing either underhand or overhand, anatomy shared only with the other apes and man. But chimpanzees do not practice. A chimpanzee does not make a pile of rocks and then throw them at a selected target. Other chimpanzees do not watch and call encouragement. In man, however, the act must be embedded in a social system of sports, so that the years of repetition necessary to develop a high level of skill are fun. Skills take years to develop, and the pleasure of play is the biological solution to the motivation of learning.

The learning of skills has been so important in human evolution that selection has incorporated the basis for skills in the structure of the brain. The part of the human brain most closely related to hand movements is very large. Proportionately, it is far larger in human beings than in any other primate. In other words, a much larger part of the human brain is related to skills—practiced, integrated movements. But just because there is a biological basis for learning skills does not mean that the skills will be learned. For learning to occur, there must also be a social system that puts the learning into an acceptable form and that clearly shows the learner the utility of the skill in adult life. In a folk society dependent on the spear in both hunting and war, the games of childhood were direct preparation for clearly perceived adult actions.

Learning of skills is affected by rewards, but the nature of the animal greatly affects the kind of reward that is appreciated. In the matter of hunting and fishing, human beings, especially males, will spend many hours and make great efforts for the most minimal success. For many people, catching a fish is a reward far beyond the possible economic value of the food. Many states have departments of fish and game that spent millions of dollars to provide fish and game for hunters long before lunches for hungry school children were even considered. Clearly, there is something about hunting that is remarkably rewarding to human beings. The importance of hunting in our evolutionary history has built a human biology that makes hunting *easy to learn,* and very little compensation is enough to motivate very substantial efforts. The pleasure of hunting makes people willing to work hard, practice the necessary skills, and devote much time and expense for a minimal reward.

The education of uncivilized people was successful without schools because learning was motivated by identification, emotion, and clear goals and because evolution (through natural selection) had produced a species for whom classes of learning were natural.

Clearly, the need for schools and the problems of the schools come from three quite different sources. First, there is no longer any folk society, any highly visible system of human behavior that can be easily appreciated by the participants. Second, many of the skills needed in modern complex society take years to acquire, and, so far, no one has succeeded in making the intermediate goals—the steps between elementary science and being a chemist, for example—exciting and adequately rewarding. Third, the necessary ways of life in complex society no longer bear any simple relation to human nature. For example, in all folk societies, basic learning is completed by maturity, and shortly thereafter people live as adults. But in our society, education may continue more than a dozen years after maturity. The institutional framework of the graduate school is merely an extension of the elementary school; there are still courses and marks, teachers and children. To live as an adult, a person must drop out of school.

Perhaps the most fundamental difference between folk learning and modern education is that under folk conditions, most people did the same things. There was a division of labor between men and women, but aside from that, there were not many different kinds of jobs. Boys played with spears because all men would use spears in hunting and warfare.

In marked contrast, very few students who take biology today become biologists. The situation in which most students do not think they are going to use what they learn is a new one. Lacking the fundamental human desire to learn what will be useful, students become bored, and the school resorts to discipline to maintain the process of education. But discipline is no substitute for play and internal motivation—and examinations are no substitute for life. A species that tries to substitute discipline for pleasure has given up its whole biological heritage, the whole relation of learning and life. Human beings are not pigeons who may be taught to peck out the solutions to futile problems. People are the most creative, imaginative, social, empathetic beings that exist. But schools may reduce youth to bored and alienated primates, people who have been educated out of their natural desires to learn and separated from the larger society in which they must ultimately live.

The distinction between learning and the schools is most clearly illustrated in the first few years of life. In monkeys, excellent observational and experimental studies show the importance of early learning. In a natural setting, the mother and infant are together constantly. The infant learns from its mother, or from other animals in close proximity. Long before the infant is weaned, for example, it has tried the kinds of foods its mother is eating, often spitting them out in distaste. But by the time it is weaned, the young monkey has learned what is edible and what is not. Separation of mother and infant leads to profound and lasting psychological disturbances. In extreme cases the infant may die, even though there is plenty of food easily available. These animal studies suggest the great importance of early experience, strong social bonds, and an enriched environment for learning. The emotional situation is a critical factor in learning, and a deprived infant ceases to learn.

If we turn to man with this kind of information in mind, we cannot say that early experience must be important simply because this is the case with our nearest relatives. Human behavior is not reduced to that of other primates, but there is, nevertheless, the strongest indication that events that take place before the nervous system has fully matured are somehow, incorporated in a way that is different from the incorporation of later events. What the animal studies do suggest is that learning in the first years of human life should be examined with the greatest care.

At birth, humans are far less mature than any of the nonhuman primates. After only a few days, an infant monkey can walk independently, and almost from the first day of life, it actively helps in the interaction with its mother. The human mother has a much greater responsibility, one that lasts over years, rather than months. Judging from the animal studies, we should expect to find that man is unique in the importance of early learning. A number of studies clearly show that this is the case. The most important events in human learning take place before formal schooling begins. In our culture almost no attention is paid to this critical period, and there is no education for effective mothering. Behavior in the family is regarded as a private concern; people may beat their children if they want to, and the state only intervenes if the child is battered to a degree considered criminal.

The schools receive the products of these critical early

years, and it is an illusion to suppose that a single teacher in a large class can overcome the deficits of each child's early experience. In both monkey and man, early learning takes place in an environment of few individuals and strong emotions. It takes place over many hours each day, and there is enormous pleasurable repetition. A few hours a day in a large class, well disciplined and without strong emotional bonds, cannot possibly provide the biosocial setting for effective early learning.

As a monkey grows older, much of its time is spent in a play group. Learning from peers gradually replaces learning from mother, although the attachment to mother may last for years. In the play group, the monkey learns social skills, the forms of adult behavior, and these are practiced every day. At a later stage, juvenile females play with infants and become skilled mothers before the birth of their own infants. With time, the play of juvenile males becomes much rougher, and they practice the aggressive behaviors that will be essential in later life. Both sexes learn the behaviors that are essential for life in the social group, and these behaviors may differ from one group to the next, especially with the kinds of food and dangers of predators.

From an evolutionary point of view, much of the behavior of human children is similar to that of other primates, but the time of maturation, learning, and practice is greatly prolonged. The slowing of maturation is costly from a biological point of view. Young primates are likely to be injured or killed, which suggests that prolonging youth must have been so important that it was favored by selection in spite of the risks involved. The delay of maturation took place long before the discovery of agriculture, so the explanation of the delay must lie in the life of the hunter-gatherers. These people led complicated lives that were quite different from those of the nonhuman primates. The biological delay of maturation appears to be directly related to the evolution of a nervous system that could learn the technical and social complexities of the uniquely human way of life. Both brain and way of life are evolved in a feedback relationship with each other. Learning lies at the core of being human, and this was the case many thousands of years before there were any schools. Peers played an essential role in that learning.

From a biological point of view, perhaps the most fundamental change that could be made in the schools is to give back the role of teacher to the peers. From a practical point of view, this would mean that slightly older children would do *some* of the teaching of the younger children. This would have three results. First, it would increase the number of teachers, so that much of the teaching could be done in the small, informal, emotionally supporting groups that are natural for man. Second, it would provide satisfactory social roles for many children, roles in which they could be proud of their accomplishments, work for which they could be praised. Third, to teach successfully, the peer teachers would have to really learn the subject matter.

I have tried peer teaching with college seniors teaching freshmen, and I have no doubt that the quality of college education could be greatly increased tomorrow by the careful use of student teachers. But the essential point is that the slightly older peer can have a very different relationship with the pupil. The point of teaching by peers is to restore the conditions of learning that are natural for man, the kind of situations in which the human brain evolved. Just as many sports continue natural situations of maturing and learning, situations that are pleasurable and socially rewarding even if one has to practice long and hard, so peer teaching could be used to create intellectual situations that would be pleasurable and rewarding even if one had to practice long and hard.

Peer teaching provides two kinds of motivations. First, the learner sees that someone just older than he can do the required tasks, and as a result, the tasks no longer seem impossible or irrelevant. Second, the peer teacher has an important social position in the life of the school, just as the successful athlete does. A peer teacher might spend up to one-fifth of his or her schooltime helping peers. Given the many different subject matters, most children might be teachers at least occasionally, and all would have the opportunity to be helped by peers. In the past, without schools, human beings were able to master complex social tasks in ways that were in accord with human nature. Surely, with modern knowledge, science, and a whole profession of educators, we should not do worse.

•

To summarize what we have been saying so far, the study of animal behavior and evolution suggests that early learning takes place primarily from the mother, closely associated people, or substitutes (as in the kibbutz). It involves countless repetitions in a warm, emotional environment. This early learning is critical in preparing the child for learning in school. In our society, there is no substitute for parents talking, reading, and playing with their children. As the child grows older, peers become more and more important, but the attitudes and actions of the home remain of great importance. Children play with peers, and this is a fundamental setting for learning, but their games reflect the actions and values of their adult community. It is only recently, for special reasons, that a separate institution (the school) has become necessary for teaching the young, and its problems arise from the loss of the traditional folk learning situation in which learning depends on identification, emotion, and clearly visible goals.

But even if early learning is successful, and even if peers help in creating a social situation for elementary learning, the problem of goals remains. How can the years in school be made to seem important to the developing human being? The answer is very simple: they have to be important in ways that a young person can understand. Many children do not enjoy learning, simply because they do not believe that what they are required to learn is practical and important. And many of us older people are skeptical of what is required because we, too, doubt that what is taught in the schools—beyond the basic skills—is necessary. Take Latin, for example. Latin was taught because it was the language of scholarship, international learning, and religion. But when it ceased to have these functions, it was still taught for "mind training," because of its supposed superior quality, and because it was required for college entrance. Latin is essential if one is to understand the classics and much of European history. Probably too few people master it today. But it is a lasting blot on the history of education that millions of hours were spent learning a language that was, for most people, useless; that was justified on the basis of spurious reasons; and that was used to prevent many from going to college.

The motivation of the older student requires support and understanding in the home and in the community. The student needs visible, important goals, as was the case in the folk society. As long as the school is considered a separate institution insisting on tasks that bear no relation to life, it will fail in its most important intellectual functions. Since the motivation for learning comes from family, peers, and society, the isolated school has minimized its chances to teach.

The ultimate aims of education should be to give the student some understanding of the nature of man, the world we live in, intellectual fun, and preparation for jobs. These matters have become technical problems, and so we need to have an institution designed to deal with them. The simple folk explanations of human nature are no longer enough. We are living in the world of DNA, modern biology, and complicated medicine of incredible possibility. The small, flat world, the center of the universe, has been replaced by a universe of temporal and spatial dimensions that would have been totally incomprehensible to our ancestors. Music, art, and literature are available in forms and quantity that the kings of years ago could not have commanded. Even as late as 1900, most of the jobs in the United States were on farms, and the sheer variety of careers now open to young people is something entirely new in human history.

If these technical problems were simple ones, they could be managed in the home, just as learning was for countless thousands of years. They are not simple, however, and they are changing all the time. But human beings are not changing. If we are still evolving, it is at a rate too slow to be of practical importance. The biology that evolved under the conditions of gathering and hunting—human biology—is the nature with which we must learn to live in the modern technical world. This is a new problem. On the one hand, the system of education must consider the nature of the youth being educated. And it must consider the social, emotional, and biological conditions of the system itself, as well. But the schools must also show how to deal with the new problems arising from the rapid change in the technical sciences.

Fortunately, many of the problems facing the world today do not fit into the traditional departments of educational categories. Population, energy, and crime, for example, involve many different sciences. Each has a history. Each involves trends. The daily newspaper provides numerous examples of problems whose solution will not come from any one branch of knowledge. The educated citizen in a democracy today should be able to see what kinds of information are actually useful in moving toward better solutions of the real problems that face us all. For example, the theory of continental drift provides understanding of earthquakes, mountains, volcanoes, and distributions of ancient life. Why the drift theory was opposed gives insights into the scientific enterprise and into some very human scientists. Studying carefully selected cases of this sort would make it possible for students to see the importance of what they are doing and the interrelations of different kinds of knowledge. And it could help them to develop intellectual habits that would last long after their formal education was over.

This is, after all, the fundamental issue. To live intelligently in a changing world, new information is necessary, and the purpose of the schools should be to help people learn how to live. The educated person should both have more fun and be more useful. Or, to put it more accurately, the educated person should be more likely to lead a satisfying, useful life.

The test for the schools comes in the actual behavior of their graduates. How do they approach problems? What resources do they bring? Are they innovative, cooperative? Do they know where to look for knowledge and how to ask for advice? It is not easy to test for these important abilities, and again, the biology suggests some of the complications. For example, those abilities that are measured by IQ tests are not changed by massive damage to the frontal lobes of the brain, a fact that was used as a defense of frontal brain operations. Yet this part of the brain is composed of billions of cells, both the number and complexity of which have increased in primate evolution, and especially in the later phases of human evolution. Since such increase is due to natural selection, we know that the frontal region must be important. Its probable functions are foresight, insight, planning, persistence, and originality—what are thought of as the higher mental functions. Not only is the so-called IQ greatly affected by the child's environment, but it does not measure the most important human abilities. Tests of performance clearly show the disastrous results of frontal brain operations, and the implications of this fact for testing are clear. Human beings are much too complicated to be evaluated by pencil-and-paper tests, which can be quickly administered to groups. People are more important than tests. What counts in life is performance, which is based on both biology and experience. For example, in modern science most projects are cooperative. In real life, the ability to work creatively with others is of the utmost importance. Yet the educational system minimizes cooperation and forces the student to work in isolation. The desire to grade a paper (how will we know who did the work?) forces immediate and trivial emphasis on individual work, which, in effect, discourages learning the complex personal and intellectual complications of cooperation. Yet performance in cooperative projects that lead toward problem solution is probably a far more useful measure of ability than the usual tests.

The problem of grading may be illustrated by writing and spelling. If the goal is the ability to express oneself in useful ways, the student needs to be encouraged to engage in the repetition necessary to master these skills. But if the student is penalized too much for misspelling, the whole task becomes distasteful. This is particularly the case if difficult words are introduced merely to find out who are the best spellers. Again, animal behavior clearly shows that creatures who are repeatedly discouraged give up the task. Conversely, success leads to repeated performance and to the development of skills. If the classroom, through frequent testing and grading, becomes the symbol of discouragement, students can only protect themselves by withdrawal in one form or another. From a biological point of view, the classroom should be a place of encouragement, and students should run into class as joyfully as they run out into the play yard.

In a recent issue of *Daedalus*, devoted to higher education, many authors mentioned the importance of discipline and the learning of a foreign language. As teachers, they seemed to feel no guilt that many of the problems are in the culture of the schools. Surely teachers should be among the first to urge the use of simplified spelling, the metric system, a rational typewriter keyboard, and the calculator. Children should not be blamed for difficulties that arise from the irrational behavior of adults. The issues can be most clearly seen in the problem of learning a foreign language. As noted earlier, mastery of a second language was not a problem when there was no school and the child was in a situation in which learning two languages was useful. Years of study in school may accomplish much less. Perhaps a minimum standard for evaluating a school might be that it not do worse than was easily achieved without a school. Certainly, experience shows that learning a language is easy if the process begins early; if it is done with a native speaker; and if it is perceived to be useful. A child may have a good start on a language but then forget it if he feels there is no reason to continue. Why it is useful to learn a language will depend on the time and place. For example, in California today, there are millions of Spanish-speaking people. This is the foreign language most likely to be useful to citizens of that state. Accordingly, many California schools should offer Spanish, not for magic or mind training, but because it is useful. Spanish-speaking children could be the peer teachers, and many hours would be devoted to games, texts, and tapes. This would change the position of the Spanish-speaking child in the school, and it might even prepare the way for better understanding between the cultures. Later, Spanish history would be studied, and the problems of Latin America would be contrasted with those of the United States. Finally, every effort would be made to show all the different kinds of careers in which it is an advantage to speak both Spanish and American English. The aim of such a program would be useful mastery of the language, and every aspect of it would be different from learning a soon-to-be-forgotten smattering of a scholarly language.

Of course, there will be problems in any changes in the schools. As Jerrold Zacharias has remarked, "Instant educational reform is wish fulfillment for the naive." But, as least occasionally, it is fun to be naive, to think how different it all might be. Perhaps evolution and animal behavior do give some hints for change. After all, as a recent presidential candidate orated, "Our future lies ahead of us," and that should give encouragement to those who see the schools as the place to start "the human use of human beings."

THE NUMBERS GAME:

How the Testing Industry Operates

SHERWOOD DAVIDSON KOHN

Sherwood Davidson Kohn is a Washington based journalist who frequently reports on the interaction of people and ideas.

This spring, in response to a growing feeling of unrest on the part of the educational community toward standardized testing, the National Association of Elementary School Principals and a research organization calling itself the North Dakota Study Group on Evaluation invited the country's major test publishers and some fifty concerned educators, adminstrators, scientists, and mathematicians to participate in a two-day symposium on educational testing.

The invitation was issued at a time when the press was reporting, on an almost daily basis, the fact that standardized test scores in both elementary and secondary schools had dropped significantly across the nation, and that an alarmingly large number of students were functional illiterates. In that context, and in the face of mounting public sentiment in favor of additional tests that would show what was wrong with our educational system, the symposium seemed oddly out of phase. But the sponsors were seeking more basic information. In effect, they called the meeting because many educators now feel that standardized tests do not accurately report the strengths and weaknesses of our educational system, and that they may actually be damaging students.

The group, which met in May in Rosslyn, Virginia, just across the Potomac River from Washington, D.C., where many educational associations are based, numbered among its attendants William W. Turnbull, president of the Educational Testing Service, the nation's largest testing firm, and Thomas J. Fitzgibbon, president of Harcourt Brace Jovanovich's Psychological Corporation, which ranks among the nation's three top-grossing test publishers. Vito Perrone, the innovative dean of North Dakota University's Center for Teaching and Learning, chaired the meeting.

Also on hand were Albert Sims, vice-president of the College Entrance Examination Board; Frank Snyder, director of McGraw-Hill's California Test Bureau (second among the three biggest money-makers in the test publishing and scoring business); Leo Munday, vice-president and general manager of Houghton Mifflin's Test Department, and Lyman Smith, director of assessment operations for IBM's Science Research Associates.

Among the educators were representatives of the National Education Association, the American Federation of Teachers, the National Association of School Psychologists, the Council for Exceptional Children, the American Council on Education, the American Association of School Administrators, and the American Psychological and Sociological Associations. Jerrold Zacharias, a noted nuclear physicist and head of the Education Development Center in Newton, Mass., and Banesh Hoffman, a former associate of Albert Einstein's and the author of *The Tyranny of Testing*—both men implacable foes of standardized, machine scored testing—were also in attendance.

All in all, the symposium participants represented more than two million people directly concerned with the evaluation of individual learning and aptitude, and they had come together to ask some very serious questions about the validity of standardized testing and, indeed, the moral and ethical responsibilities of the industry toward children and the public in general.

The first day-long sessions had been devoted to drawing up a list of queries for the test publishing executives to take home and study. Many of the questions contained a decidedly unfriendly note. Such queries as, "Do testers acknowledge that multiple choice tests penalize students who know too much?" and "Whose fault is it that tests are misused?" seemed aggressive and even hostile, but others clearly sought information that had long remained hidden, not only from the public, but from educators intimately involved with student assessment. For instance:

"What are the short- and long-range plans of the testing industry?"

"What are the testers doing about alternative forms of assessment?"

"Can statistical correlations really apply to individual children?"

"How can testers maintain standardization and still keep tests current with changing curriculum?"

"To what extent can tests be used to evaluate programs?"

"Have test companies researched the use of the tests and made the results of the research public?"

If the test publishers were to react in good faith, it would be clear that they would be doing some heavy homework.

The second session of the symposium was scheduled for the purpose of formally presenting the group's list of questions to the test publishers and for a verbal posing of additional queries in the hope that a constructive dialogue might be established.

However, it seemed apparent at the end of the second morning that while the test publishers had given their standard policy statements (Yes, they were men of good will with deep feelings of responsibility toward children. No, they did not view themselves as detached, scientific, "measurement specialists" without ethical involvement in test development, administration and scoring. Yes, the tests were sometimes misused, but in most cases by people who had not read and understood the accompanying manuals that carefully explained how to administer, score and interpret the instruments. No, it is not true that qualified persons cannot obtain sample copies of tests for examination and evaluation, etc.), and the assembled educators, psychologists, sociologists, and concerned humanists had posed their questions, that no new lines of communication had been clearly established. The lack of intercourse was frustrating, and finally, the representative of the Association for Childhood Education International, Monroe Cohen, burst out:

"I have been struggling, as perhaps others in the room have, with the concern of whether the purpose of this meeting, as a dialogue with publishers, was really being accomplished in a way that was not a confrontation, but a plaintive plea to power brokers to listen to people who represent many millions of children in this country.

"There are more than thirty major professional organizations represented by people in this room, and there are a lot of people with allied concerns who are not in this room, who are saying to you power brokers, 'Listen, or we won't buy. We'll help see that people don't buy, if by buying they're hurting children.' It's hard to say this without moving into what seems like a confrontation kind of situation, but in talking with some of you, you've acknowledged that many of the so-called achievement tests measure acculturation and not achievement. You've acknowledged that there is a racial and ethnic bias in some of the test items. You've acknowledged that there are fallacies in construction of some of the tests. And yet the dialogue comes back to, 'This is a competitive industry. We've got to protect what we have so we can sell the product.' But the product you're selling has to do with the lives of children, including your children. And that is what I hope you get as the message when you leave here. It seems to me that it would be a critical loss if you walk out of here without the major concern of this meeting: that it's really a plaintive call for communication, and hopefully for a form of collaboration.

"I don't think anybody dreams that ETS or Harcourt Brace or McGraw-Hill are going to fold up shop because some characters sitting around a table are shaking fingers at them, but the call came earlier here to have more responsibility, social responsibility. Ethics are what we're trying to set before you."

It seems odd that after approximately fifty years of standardized test publishing, that test users, or consumers, have never before confronted the industry with a joint demand for ethics or moral standards in the mass testing of individuals, but then most people had been used to thinking of testers as men of science, somehow divorced from subjective considerations or moral judgments. After all, we have only recently become aware of the responsibilites implied in the pursuit of physical science.

In fact, both the public and the testing industry have long accepted the premise that test designers and publishers are "measurement" specialists who try only to gauge an individual's probability of success in academic endeavors; that they are "scientists" who deal only with objective criteria: norms, percentiles, unambiguous data—numbers—and as everyone knows, numbers have no moral or ethical weight.

But another factor has been thrown into the balance. In our technologically oriented society, where many people place their faith solely in quantitative evidence of reality, and are unable to trust qualitative or subjective data, the individual who can support his contentions with numbers is infinitely more acceptable as an authority than the one who can only voice an opinion, no matter how well informed. The relationship of the testing industry to education is a clear case in point.

Americans spent about $119 billion on education last year, according to the U.S. Department of Health, Education, and Welfare. In contrast, the educational testing industry grossed about $200 million in 1975—two-tenths of one percent of the money we invest in public and private education.

A comparison of the dollar figures is deceptive. In this instance, money is not synonymous with power. The influence of the testing industry is measured in numbers of people and in mental attitudes; the more than twenty-five million elementary and secondary school students who take the dozen commonly used standardized achievement tests each year; the five million high school and college students who enroll annually in test preparation courses; the weight that numerical test scores are given as indices to student achievement, ability, aptitude and even capacity for learning; the influence that tests and testing have on school curriculums, public opinion about education, and the very lives of students who must take the tests and stand or fall on the basis of their results.

The key to much of this power is the computer, which enables technicians to test and score millions of students in a very short time, and the man who invented the test scoring computer and designed two of the industry's classic test batteries is E.F. Lindquist, professor emeritus of education at the University of Iowa, founder of the university's Measurement Research Center, and one of the founders of the American College Testing Program.

Lindquist is an important figure in the standardized educational testing business, and now, at seventy-four, his retirement years are warmed by the tributes of a grateful industry: a $3,545,000 "Center for Measurement" built in his name at the University of Iowa; a senior consultancy to the American College Testing Program, which has its headquarters in Iowa City; his portrait in the foyer of the MRC, which he helped sell to the Westinghouse Learning Corporation; awards and an honorary degree for significant contributions to the technology of testing, and a permanent niche in the numbers world as the reigning patriarch of measurement.

Although Lindquist was still in high school when such testing titans as Edward L. Thorndike, Henry Herbert Goddard, Lewis M. Terman and Arthur Otis were laying the groundwork for mental measurement during the first fifteen years of this century, Lindquist's work after the "boom" period of standardized test development (1915-1930) profoundly affected the field.

Before that, testing had been dominated by the Stanford-Binet intelligence test, adapted for use in this country by Terman, used by Goddard to weed out "undesirable" aliens at Ellis Island in 1912, and offering inspiration for the Army Alpha test and other IQ instruments, of which Walter Lippmann once wrote, "If the impression takes root that these tests really measure intelligence, that they constitute a sort of last judgment on the child's capacity, that they reveal scientifically his predestined ability, then it would be a thousand times better if all the intelligence testers and their questionnaires were sunk without warning in the Sargasso Sea."

"Unfortunately," wrote Paul Houts, the editor of the *National Elementary Principal* magazine, in the June, 1976, *Kappan*, "little attention was paid to Lippmann's warning . . . The development of achievement testing soon followed, and by 1929 more than five million tests were being administered annually."* Lindquist's two classic test batteries, the Iowa Tests of Educational Development (ITED) and the Iowa Tests of Basic Skills (ITBS) were natural outgrowths of the movement. Introduced in 1935 and 1942, repectively, and updated regularly since then, they are so much in demand that each is marketed by a separate and competing publisher. Science Research Associates distributes the ITED, and Houghton Mifflin sells the ITBS. Both standardized tests are produced by the Iowa Testing Program, which Lindquist founded and which he directed for forty years, and are scored by Westinghouse Learning's MRC, which houses the computerized scanners developed by Lindquist. Approximately ten million U.S. elementary and high school students take the two tests annually.

---

*Harcourt Brace Jovanovich still publishes the Stanford-Binet IQ test.

Lindquist's work with machine scoring, and his eventual development of a computerized scanner capable of scoring up to forty thousand tests an hour, are certainly major factors in an industry that deals more comfortably with quantitative than qualitative data. Without high-volume scoring, standardized testing would lose one of its principal premises: the concept of large-scale group testing. With it, the entire system of assigning test score numbers relative to a normative scale becomes not only feasible, but profitable. So profitable, indeed, that the Iowa Testing Programs were able to sell their lucrative MRC scoring business to Westinghouse and use the money to build a living monument, the E.F. Lindquist Center for Measurement.

The center, a stark, contemporary-style brick blockhouse with an indeterminate entrance brooded over by a story-deep marquee that is actually a structural wing on stilts, is located at the edge of the University of Iowa's campus in Iowa City. It houses the school's research and record-keeping computers and its computer-assisted instruction laboratory, along with the Iowa Center for Research in School Administration, the Division of School Administration, the Division of Educational Psychology, Measurement and Statistics, and the Iowa Testing Program. The MRC, which has its own building several miles away, near the American College Testing Program's campus, also has an office in the Lindquist Center. And the center has what must be one of the largest and slowest elevators in existence.

The elevator in the Lindquist Center for Measurement is reminiscent, at least in size, of the one that is used for hauling crowds up and down the Washington monument, and it was designed, not for people (although the building's human occupants are its most frequent passengers), but for transporting ponderous computers among the center's four levels.

Lindquist, a tall, dapper man with a neat brush moustache, explained that when he and his colleagues planned the center with its architects, the computer was a great, lumbering, vacuum-tube equipped brute, but that by the time the structure was finished, miniaturized circuits had reduced the size of the animal radically. Lindquist conducted me on a quick tour of the center and showed me the result of rapid technological advance: an expanse of empty space, glassed in from about half of the building's second floor. In one corner of this special room stood a Hewlett-Packard machine about the size of a Volkswagen bus. It was doing the statistical chores of all the machines that had originally been scheduled to fill the space.

In a way, the relationship of that compact computer, the nerve core of a research center, and the sizeable field of technical activity that it affects, is much like the relationship of the testing industry to education. Both the computer and the measurement business are almost exclusively concerned with quantitative analysis; both are tools no better or worse and no less fallible than the humans who manipulate them, and both exercise an influence on a domain of vastly greater proportions. And like the computer, the testing industry is inscrutible to those who lack the keys to its data banks and its logical processes. The layman, the outsider, encounters only scattered, incomplete information that merely hints at the scope of the instrument. But we do know the following:

• Approximately three million high school upperclassmen take the Educational Testing Service's Standard Achievement Test (SAT) or the American College Testing Program's ACT each year. Every student who elects to take one of the tests—and academic pressures make participation almost mandatory—pays $6.50 for the privilege. Those figures alone add up to a gross of $19.5 million.

• U.S. school systems, according to Eliot A. Minsker, president of Knowledge Sciences, Inc., a White Plains, New York, data-disseminating firm reporting on the education field, spend $24 million annually on testing elementary and secondary schoolchildren.

• The National Education Association estimates that U.S. educators administer more than 200 million standardized achievement tests each year, a figure that represents only about 65 percent of all standardized educational testing in this country.

•The Houghton Mifflin Company reported to the U.S. Securities and Exchange Commission that its 1974 sales of measurement and guidance services totaled $5,539,000. Houghton Mifflin publishes the Iowa Tests of Basic Skills.

• In 1961, the last year in which Science Research Associates filed an independent report with the SEC (SRA is now an IBM subsidiary), the firm's net sales totaled $9,436,000. Some six million elementary and secondary school children take SRA's achievement tests, among which are the Iowa Tests of Educational Development and the company's own achievement series.

• Harcourt Brace Jovanovich reported to the SEC in 1974 that its revenues from tests and testing services and sales totaled $20,814,978. More than four thousand of the country's approximately seventeen thousand school systems use HBJ's Stanford Achievement Test. HBJ also publishes the immensely popular and profitable Metropolitan Achievement Test and the Stanford-Binet IQ test.

• The American College Testing Program stated in its 1974 annual report that its net testing and reporting income was $11,290,874. About a million high school upperclassmen take the ACT each year.

• The Educational Testing Service reported in 1974 that its annual income was $53,901,717. About two million high school upperclassmen take the SAT each year, but ETS offers 134 other tests and services, including graduate school and professional certification tests, data retrieval, college placement and scholarship services, and audiovisual teaching materials.

- McGraw-Hill's California Test Bureau earned $30 million for the parent company in 1974, according to the Bank of New York's Research Division. CTB publishes three achievement test batteries.

- The Bank of New York's Research Division also reports that the Measurement Research Center, sold by the University of Iowa to Westinghouse Learning Corporation, grossed $50 million in 1974.

The testing industry is secretive, and data is sparse, but it is almost self-evident that the $200 million testing industry significantly affects the $1 billion-plus market in textbooks and educational materials. But even that influence is deceptively small. The testing industry also affects such costly items as curriculum development (many teachers who claim that they are not teaching to the tests are, at best, naive), equipment sales, administrative and instructional time and money, printing, and distribution expenditures.

Montgomery County, Maryland, for example, tests a minimum of sixty thousand third-, fifth-, seventh-, and ninth-grade students each year, employs a full-time test administration staff at the system level, and will spend more than $55,000 on tests, testing materials, and processing in 1976.

The industry, through such services as ETS's College Scholarship Service, a centralized system of scholarship application, evaluation, and dissemination, also influences the dispensation of millions of dollars of scholarship funds without the slightest gesture of accountability to students and parents who are asked in their applications to reveal all manner of confidential information, including income tax and liability statements.

Unhappily, there have been hints that ETS has consistently violated the confidentiality of its student clients' records. One congressional subcommittee is already looking into accusations that SAT scores, private financial data, and other confidential information has been leaked or is readily available to federal agencies without consent, and one government official I interviewed boasted that he could get my CSS file from ETS "in five minutes."*

There is little question that the influence of the testing industry is felt far beyond the traditional bounds of academic activity. The competitive pressure of standardized testing, the desperate struggle to place well in an all but inescapable environment of vitally important credentials, has also spawned a $5 million-plus ancillary industry that involves the design, publishing, and teaching of courses and instructional materials concerned exclusively with training students how to take achievement tests.

"It seems obvious," said Banesh Hoffmann, "that test publishing, despite its narrow technical domain, exerts an enormous bureaucratic tyranny. The activities of testers give rise to psychological trauma, contribute to dehumanization and bring to them a considerable measure of economic control over matters that should remain the province of scholars, rather than businessmen."

A closer look at the business reveals how concentrated its power is. ***Tests in Print II***, one of Oscar K. Buros's two definitive compendiums of tests reviews and available "measurement" tools (***Mental Measurements Yearbook*** is the other), lists 2,585 tests on the market, 1,678 of which are published by the industry's forty-five top firms. Of these, ETS, Harcourt Brace Jovanovich, Houghton Mifflin, Sci-

*In the process of supporting his son's application for a scholarship at Pratt Institute in 1975, the author was required to answer two pages of detailed questions on the ETS "Parent's Confidential Statement" concerning his most intimate financial affairs, and to give permission for examination of his state and federal income tax statements. When he requested that a copy of the CSS "analysis" of his application be sent to him, as well as to Pratt Institute, he was refused.

ence Research Associates, and the California Test Bureau publish the dominant number, both in quantity and influence.

"Test publishing," wrote Buros in *TIP II*, "is even more concentrated among a few publishers than [a list of all tests] indicates. There are two large conglomerates of jointly owned or interlocking publishing organizations. Although listed separately, Educational Testing Service includes the Cooperative Tests and Services and the Educational Records Bureau. Since ETS also constructs all CEEB [College Entrance Examination Board] tests, the ETS conglomerate is represented by 315 tests, 14.3 percent of the tests published in the United States. The other publishing giant, Harcourt Brace Jovanovich, with its subsidiaries, Grune and Stratton and the Psychological Corporation, has a total of 174 tests, 7.9 percent of the same total. Together these two publishing groups account for 22.2 percent of the domestic tests in *TIP II*. Their dominating positions are even greater than these statistics reflect. Their tests are among the most widely used in the country."

Test scoring is even more centralized. ETS and SRA score most of their own tests and some others, and CTB does part of its own scoring, but Westinghouse Learning's Measurement Research Center is probably the leading wholesaler in the scoring business. MRC does more wholesale, or contract machine scoring than any other firm in the world. Burdette Hansen, vice president of the firm and manager of the Iowa City facility, would not say how many test booklets are checked, placed in batches, split apart and scanned at the plant, but he did say that MRC scores tests for Harcourt Brace, Houghton Mifflin, the American College Testing Program, CTB and even ETS. The numbers must be impressive, considering the firm's gross earnings, and in view of the chances for misuse, they must be disturbing. MIT's Jerrold R. Zacharias, who led a sweeping reform of elementary school science teaching in the 1960s, is very upset at the industry's potential for wanton damage.

"I feel emotionally toward the testing industry," he said,

"as I would toward any other merchant of death. I feel that way because of what they do to the kids. I'm not saying that they murder every child—only 20 percent of them. Testing has distorted their ambitions, distorted their careers. Ninety-five percent of the American population has taken an ability test of some kind. It's not something that should be put into the hands of commercial enterprises."

A dedicated opponent of standardized, multiple-choice, norm referenced testing, the nuclear physicist is passionately against what he feels is a mindless, paranoid, stagnant, technology obsessed business that is hopelessly prone to all manner of abuses against the human spirit.

"I think the whole psychological test business should cease and desist," he said. "It's an outrage. Measurement is a very important thing to me. But it implies one-dimensionality. The mind is not one-dimensional.

"Secrecy. That's what the trouble is. It will become one of the big issues in testing within the next ten years. And there is only one way to keep the testing business honest: that is, keep it open."

Harold Hodgkinson, director of the National Institute of Education, feels much the same way. "Most aptitude tests are not in the public domain," he said. "That is, no intelligent layman can make any interpretation of an aptitude test score. I think it's time the American public had the right to understand what those tests mean and what they don't mean."

At the moment, test score interpretation is probably the most open aspect of the testing industry. In the weeks following my initial probes into its operations, I questioned key officials in the field's half-dozen dominant firms, and none was willing or able to estimate such elementary figures as the number of students tested annually in the United States, the number of tests sold each year by individual companies, or the economic boundaries of the industry. None would even reveal how many of his firm's tests were scored annually. Even Oscar Buros said he was unable to obtain the figures, despite his position as the testing industry's only bibliographer. However, I was able to learn, from several independent sources, how a major test battery is developed and how much it costs to do it.

The development of a test battery of the size and scope of the Stanford Achievement Test is a complex and painstaking process, sometimes taking as many as eight or ten years, involving a team of five or six experienced authors, thousands of sample-group children, many hours of computer time, the printing of tryout tests, manuals and guides, and the programming of scanners to score the tests. The process costs in the neighborhood of $1 million, 25 percent of which is spent on the task of writing a computerized scoring program.

Even before a test can be developed, though, there must be a need for it. In the case of nonprofit ETS, according to ETS President Turnbull, the initiative always comes from a school or a school system. Educators, said Turnbull, come to the Educational Testing Service with a need to know how a group of students stand relative to a norm—within a school, a school system, or nationwide. The result is a norm referenced test. That, in fact, was how ETS came into being. The company was formed in 1948, largely to administer the College Entrance Board's norm referenced Scholastic Aptitude Test, and although it is a separate entity, with its own manicured campus in Princeton, New Jersey, ETS to this day maintains several trustees (including Turnbull) in common with CEEB.

Proprietary, or profit-making publishers like Harcourt Brace, base their activities on the market. The market for a test may reveal itself through a publishing house's salespeople, who are sensitive to potential customers' needs. Publishers may also make a survey, from which they determine what educators can use and what they will buy. Or information may come from liaison with the firm's textbook division, although publishers hasten to deny that tests are ever designed to create a demand for textbooks. And sometimes—although very infrequently—an educator may draft a test and try to peddle it to a publisher, in much the same way as a novelist might write a book on speculation.

That was, in fact, the way Harcourt Brace entered the testing business. In the early 1920s, Arthur Otis came to the old World Book Company—the forerunner of Harcourt Brace—and convinced the publisher that a standardized test that would help teachers teach children better would find a ready market. To show the publisher what they had in mind, Otis and the other authors of the Stanford Achievement Test came to World with a complete battery, on plates and ready for the presses. All World had to do was print and distribute it. The test proved a success, put the publisher in the test business, and subsequently developed into one of the industry's most widely sold batteries (the others being the Metropolitan Achievement Test, the Iowa Tests of Basic Skills, the California Achievement Tests, and the SRA achievement series).

But such events are rare these days. The large publishers prefer to respond directly to their markets, to develop tests that answer needs, and to sell those services. ETS maintains that it does no selling, but simply responds to educational demands. "We think of ourselves as an educational agency," said Turnbull. But critics of the Princeton firm say that the conferences to which ETS regularly invites educators are actually subtle promotion sessions, wherein school administrators, counselors and teachers are made aware of the many services that ETS has to offer.

The proprietary publishers sell their products openly by maintaining sizeable sales and service forces in the field. HBJ, for instance, keeps twenty-nine "test representatives" or "test consultants"—salespeople—traveling around the country at an annual cost of about $30,000 apiece. These salespeople work with schools, conduct training workshops, help set up testing programs, keep their eyes and ears open for the needs of educators, parents and students, and of course, sell tests and test services. Houghton Mifflin keeps 180 salespeople in the field at all times, but they do not specialize. They sell the whole Houghton Mifflin line, books as well as tests.

Once the need for a test has been established and the authors chosen from the ranks of education specialists (in the case of established tests, teams may evolve one or two members at a time, over a period of several years, and perhaps even decades), the first real step in development is an analysis of existing and new programs.

Herbert C. Rudman, a professor of education at Michigan State University and the science specialist among the five educators who write HBJ's Stanford Achievement Test, the "Cadillac of the industry," outlined the development process:

1. The team of authors confers and each member estimates what the school curriculum content will be like in his field by the time the revised test is scheduled.

2. The authors develop educational specifications for the concepts to be tested at various grade levels, and draw up an outline.

3. The team decides how many batteries the test will have, how many grades will be covered with each battery, and how many forms will be drawn up for each. In addition to the several forms of test batteries, the team draws up a "secure form" which is held in reserve in case one of the test forms is invalidated through accident or theft.

4. The authors determine the number of subtests, according to the various ways it intends to test students on each subject.

5. Team members decide how many items (questions) they need in each subtest to obtain what they feel is a reliable measure of the students' achievement.

6. Authors write items on the basis of their knowledge of current curriculums, texts and teaching methods.

7. Authors test the practicability of the questions they have written on actual students from varying social and economic groups. Their samples, spread among several schools, may consist of three thousand to four thousand children.

8. The tests are scored and the items assessed on the basis of discrimination, difficulty, and reliability. Many questions are discarded or changed.

9. The authors rebuild their tests according to the degree of difficulty they have decided upon.

10. The team submits the test to the publisher for editorial review, refinement and a national tryout. The size of the tryout sample at this point may be as large as fifty-four thousand.

11. Publisher and authors examine the results of this tryout, rebuild the tests again, and adjust the separate forms until they are equivalent.

12. The publisher prints a test form, which is standardized nationally by geographic region, type of school, population size, etc., on a sample having a representative set of characteristics.

13. The results of the standardization form are analyzed and norms built.

14. The test authors and the publisher's staff write manuals for testgivers: instructions for giving the tests, setting out the norms, interpreting scores, administering the tests, and explaining the profile's characteristics.

Having undergone all of these processes over a period of perhaps ten years (NIE Director Hodgkinson questions the ability of the test developers to predict curriculum content that far ahead), a major standardized test is ready for the market. But tests, say the industry's representatives, are greatly misused, abused and maligned. Test scores, despite what publishers claim are herculean efforts to educate test users and givers, are sometimes misinterpreted. In the face of explicit instructions on how to apply test scores, educators, parents, and even students, say the publishers, may give too much weight to the scores, interpreting them as indices of intelligence or personal worth, employing them competitively, using them as labels or worse, failing to recognize their limitations, and accepting them as infallible predictors of success or failure in both academic and nonacademic worlds.

There is also considerable evidence that the tests are sometimes grossly misused by school administrators, who can shop among tests of varying difficulty for those that will provide higher or lower scores to bolster a specific policy or budgetary strategy, employ tests as political tools in support of their jobs, or apply them as levers in initiating or maintaining racial segregation. The latter-day instances of misuse have been publicized and protested by various ethnic groups, but the most classic case, the one that has shown the susceptibility of such tests from the very beginning, went almost unnoticed. It was Henry Goddard's use, in 1913, 1914, and for several years after that, of the Stanford-Binet IQ test to weed out undesirable aliens at Ellis Island on the basis of "feeblemindedness." Strikingly, Goddard's tests marked 83 percent of the Jewish immigrants, 80 percent of the Hungarians, 79 percent of the Italians and 87 percent of the Russians arriving at Ellis Island as "feebleminded" and therefore eligible for deportation. It is hardly coincidental that most immigrants during that time were Middle-Europeans, Italians, Russians, and Jews.

Unquestionably, it is difficult, if not impossible, for the test publishers to stamp out all the inequities attendant upon the widespread availability and use of their instruments. But there are other factors—perhaps even more crucial—operating within the complex machinery of educational testing.

Educators, as well as the general public, tend to be

overwhelmed by the sheer weight of numbers offered by the testing industry, the enormous influence that test publishers wield in the field of education, and the claims of "scientific measurement" that test publishers have made in the past.

"At present," wrote Buros in his *Mental Measurements Yearbook*, "no matter how poor a test may be, if it is nicely packaged and if it promises to do all sorts of things which no test can do, the test will find many gullible buyers. When we initiated critical test reviewing in the 1938 *Yearbook*, we had no idea how difficult it would be to discourage the use of poorly constructed tests of unknown validity. Even the better informed test users who finally become convinced that a widely used test has no validity after all are likely to rush to use a new instrument which promises far more than any good test can possibly deliver. Counselors, personnel directors, psychologists, and school adminstrators seem to have an unshakable will to believe the exaggerated claims of test authors and publishers. If these test users were better informed regarding the merits and limitations of their testing instruments, they would probably be less happy and successful in their work. The test user who has faith—however unjustified—can speak with confidence in interpreting test results and in making recommendations. The well-informed test user cannot do this; he knows that the best of our tests are still highly fallible instruments which are extremely difficult to interpret with assurance in individual cases. Consequently, he must interpret test results cautiously and with so many reservations that others wonder whether he really knows what he is talking about."

Apparently the standardized, multiple-choice, educational achievement test, along with the general acceptance of that tool's infallibility as an actual measure of individual ability, is a social phenomenon. The public has a tendency to believe in concepts festooned with numbers, and educators seem to be no exception. In fact, they may be among the most gullible, as Buros indicates, since many are psychologically unable, or are trained not to trust qualitative, subjective judgments. As a result, they are conditioned to accept, almost without question, quantitative, so-called objective data as reality, when the situation may well be just the reverse.

Unfortunately, the testing industry is subject only to the law of supply and demand. Despite its protestations to the contrary, it answers to no one but itself.

"That's a crock!" said Psychological Corporation President Fitzgibbon. "This area is rigorously inspected. It has more criticism than any I can think of. This is the only business I know of that has something like the Buros *Mental Measurements Yearbook*, *Tests in Print* and a proliferation of educational and psychological journals that review tests. . We have to answer to the critics in the critical reviews. We have to answer to our customers, particularly in a competitive situation. We're always listening to what school people say. We're not only listening, we're always asking what they think, because if we get away from what they really need, we've had it. There's no way that I can sit here, for example, and say 'All right, the Stanford Achievement Test in the early 80s is going to be like this, this, and this, and I don't care who says anything else, that's the way it's going to be.' If I were to do that, we would be dead.

"Furthermore, the American Psychological Association, the American Educational Research Association, and the National Council of Measurement and Education periodically issue standards for the building and use of psychological tests. We have to pay attention to those, as well."

Interestingly enough, Buros' published view of this is exactly opposed. "The non-observance of the APA, AERA, NCME and MMY (*Mental Measurement Yearbook*) standards by test authors, publishers and users is shocking," he wrote in *Tests in Print II*. "When will test users make it unprofitable for publishers to market tests without reporting even the barest essentials of the data which were considered minimal forty-nine years ago?"

I asked Fitzgibbon, in view of his feeling that the

industry was closely monitored and kept in line by users, customers and peers, what would happen if Harcourt Brace were to disregard everyone else and strike out on its own to design any kind of test that would sell.

"Deep trouble," he said. "In the first place, nine-tenths of the staff would quit. These people see themselves as pros who feel that it is important that their work be good. I'd probably be afraid to go to the meeting I'm going to tomorrow. [Fitzgibbon is president of the NCME] Those guys would be all over me. They would confront me and say, 'What the hell are you doing?' Then all kinds of denunciations would come in the journals. There would be motions passed by my own organization and the APA. These are monitoring groups. It is, in my opinion, not possible to survive by paying little or no attention to others who are affected by what you do."

John Sommer, manager of Houghton Mifflin's Department of Measurement and Guidance, agreed with Fitzgibbon. "All publishers, or at least all the major publishers," he said, "subscribe to and follow with great care the standards set by the American Psychological Association. They don't have any policemen, but if you didn't follow the standards, you'd simply be out of it by reason of the fact that the profession would drive you out. They wouldn't support your efforts because you would be in violation of what all in the profession has accepted as good practice—kind of like the AMA. . . "

"I wish it were true," said Willo White, administrative associate in the APA's Office of Scientific Affairs. "We set the standards for test construction and development and offer a lot of information on preparing test manuals. However, if a testing company does not wish to adhere to the standards, we have no clout . . . The only mechanism we have with which to reprimand our members is based on ethics. We've thought a lot about what we could do, but it is felt that the only action we could take is educational."

Action in other quarters is talked about, but with the exception of serious attempts within the testing industry to correct minority and sex bias, change is invariably a function of the marketplace. ETS's Turnbull offers the possibility of response to direct demands on the part of educators and other test publishers for more incisive techniques, but so far, that demand has not made itself felt in strength.

Other test publishers' research activities are even less fruitful. Buros complains in *Tests in Print II* about the unchanged character of twenty- to forty-year-old personality assessment tests, but the same might be said about achievement tests. Everyone, including the test publishers, admits that the most widely used batteries can be pernicious in the hands of untrained or uninformed users, but they continue to sell, unchanged and relatively unchallenged.

Lately, even E.F. Lindquist, the reigning patriarch of testing, has had serious reservations. "I have been rather disappointed in developments within the educational testing field," he said. "Tests seem to me to have gone farther away from higher and higher precision and more accuracy in measurement. There seems to be less of an effort to provide a really faithful, dependable picture of the abilities and aptitudes of the individual child, and more concern with group achievement along the lines that are of interest to school adminstrators who are out to make a record, more interested in average scores and how they may be used politically, and more interested, perhaps, in getting the information needed for those purposes at a lower price, in terms of both money and time . . . The standards of scholarly research seem to me to have gone down, too."

On the other hand, some educators are working on more satisfying alternatives to standardized norm reference testing. Zacharias feels that "the testing industry is not exploiting its size to develop new tests" and proposes the development of a completely different kind of battery. He estimates that such a project would cost $10 million a year over the next ten years.

Frank B. Womer, a professor of education at the University of Michigan and former head of the National Assessment of Educational Progress, has been instrumental in developing a Michigan State assessment program using criterion-referenced or diagnostic approach to testing. Of course, the Michigan State Board of Education's intent is not to differentiate among students, but to discover how well they are learning. I suggested to Womer that this might be the wave of the future in the testing industry, particularly if enough protest arose against norm referenced testing.

"If norm referenced testing were eliminated," he replied, "it would have to be reinvented under some other name. I have a feeling that comparisons between human beings are so ingrained in our society that we're going to make them one way or another. And there is so much evidence that human judgments about other humans are not terribly reliable and that if we did away with tests, we'd be seeking something objective—which would end up being another test—to do the same job. I suspect that a fair proportion of the criticisms that are leveled at tests should be criticisms of our educational system, because tests are reasonably accurate reflections of what goes on in the system. To change the tests without changing the system isn't going to do a lot. I'd like to see a good, thorough study of the use and nonuse of tests; a survey of the actual impact of tests."

Such a study might well confirm what many now suspect: that standardized testing is largely an administrative creature, an animal of rather limited use in managerial functions, and one that actually results in even fewer benefits—or worse, damage—at the classroom and individual student levels. There is already considerable sentiment against norm referenced tests, some talk of government regulation, and serious pressure for criterion referenced tools; a trend that could cause test publishers to invest substantial amounts of money in the development of diagnostic tests. NIE Director Hodgkinson hopes that they will:

"We're moving toward an increasing array of diagnostic tests that can tell you specifically what a student is doing wrong," he said. "Not wrong in relation to other students, but in relation to his own past performance. We need to develop evaluation devices that are specific to the job to be done, and that means for the most part less reliance on norm referenced tests and more reliance on criterion referenced tests. The only real function of testing that I can see as essential is that of improving peoples' performance."

Obviously, the impetus for criterion referenced test development does not originate solely in a desire to satisfy an emotional demand. It is a fact that test sales, affected by a reduction in the elementary and secondary school population, were dropping, at least before the recent flap over students' poor scores in national literacy surveys. The criterion referenced, or diagnostic test, has the potential of filling the sales gap, unless the panic caused by low reading and writing scores has already stampeded school systems into additional norm referenced testing.

Other trends include the development by scoring firms of narrative, rather than raw number reports—a move that will raise the price of testing, but help somewhat to counteract misinterpretation, misapplication, and perhaps total rejection of test scores by educators.

Also under consideration are greater individualization, more dependence on qualitative evaluation, development of tests as teaching devices, the use of working teachers as test authors or item writers, and even total abolition of standardized testing in favor of a return to subjective evaluation by the device that many test critics feel is the most effective and responsive of all: the teacher.

But opposition is strong. "Education," warned ETS President Turnbull, "will suffer if it abolishes standardized testing." And so, of course, will test publishers.

Perhaps there is another analogy to be made concerning the relationship between the computer's effect on the testing industry and technology's effect on society. It is that the tool eventually gains some sway over the activities of its user. In the Age of Technology, numbers, as well as money, are power.

COMING TO TERMS WITH TESTING

MITCHELL LAZARUS

Mitchell Lazarus is senior staff associate with Project ONE, a group at Education Development Center, Newton, Massachusetts, that is producing a television series about mathematics, primarily for minority children, with related hands-on activities.

A test can be objective, properly standardized, reliable, and valid—and still be a very bad test. A fish can fly. It all depends on how you use the words.

•

There were a few of us in the Student Union several years ago, and just after finishing dinner one evening, a fellow future psychologist rose to leave with the words, "Well, I'm off to reinforce my rats!" An engineer who had joined us watched him depart in disbelief at first, then realized what the phrase must have meant.

"For a minute there," said the engineer, "I thought he was going to install steel rods in his rats. Don't you psychologists know your technical terms mean something in ordinary English, too? This business of using old words for new meanings can confuse a lot of people. Why can't he say he's going to feed his rats?"

Although I sprang to my colleague's defense at the time, in some respects the engineer was right. Psychology does have a reputation among lay people for using unnecessarily technical terms, even though many of the words come from ordinary English. Some people even feel psychology is nothing but a restatement of the obvious, intentionally put in language so technical that no one but other psychologists can understand it. This, of course, is exaggerated; psychologists, in fact, use their vocabulary more precisely than many nonpsychologists realize. As theory construction and research lead to more refined concepts, each new idea needs a new word to express it.

In this situation, the hard sciences by and large meet their new needs by inventing new words. Sometimes these come from Greek and Latin roots, sometimes from acronyms, and sometimes from the coiner's imagination. But psychologists have taken on the lazy habit of using an existing word to mean something different. This is fine among specialists who understand the word in its technical sense, as well as among the public, who continue to use the word as before, unaware that the psychologists have coopted it. But problems can arise when specialists use their adopted vocabulary to communicate with the public. The specialist means one thing by the word; the listener understands something else when he hears it. This can cause real confusion.

Even worse—and this is true in the field of testing—the English meaning of the word and the technical meaning may be similar enough that neither party realizes that they are miscommunicating. And still more reprehensible, the double meanings of some words make it possible to intentionally mislead people who are not familiar with the technical usages.

FOUR TROUBLESOME WORDS

In testing, there are four words that often cause confusion: *objectivity, standardization, reliability,* and *validity*. Each of these words has at least two meanings; they mean one thing in English but something very different in testing. When a test maker says a test is "reliable," he does *not* mean it can be relied on; when he says it is "valid," he does *not* mean its results are meaningful. In both cases, the technical uses of the words are very different from what one might expect. The test makers have a language of their own. Unfortunately, their language consists of English words used differently.

A test is *objective* if everybody takes it under more or less the same conditions, and if the papers are all graded under more or less the same conditions. Essay exams, for example, usually lack objectivity; they are difficult to grade consistently because the grading criteria tend to waver and shift as the grader works down through the pile of papers. Multiple-choice tests, however, can be objective if administered under uniform conditions. This objectivity is probably the main selling point for multiple-choice tests, although the economics of machine scoring are likely to be just as important.

Note that any multiple-choice test, consistently administered and graded uniformly, can be objective—regardless of what defects it may have. The test may be ambiguous, wrongheaded, open to argument, even downright erroneous in the answers it counts as correct; it is an objective test nevertheless. For example:

How tall was Macbeth?
a) 4 gallons
b) 3 pounds
c) 6 acres
d) 2 hours

Even nonsensical items such as this are completely objective—using the word in its narrow, technical sense.

Moreover, objectivity in a test does not mean it is impartial or fair. Many objective tests discriminate against one group or another, and some discriminate against students who know the subject matter extremely well. In its technical sense, objectivity offers no protection against bias in the test.

Objectivity, in fact, is a minor virtue. It is necessary for reliability and validity, which *are* important (when these words are properly used), but objectivity in itself should not count for much, since an objective test can still be a bad test.

In one sense objectivity can even be a drawback. Some kinds of subject matter are much easier to test objectively than others. And since test makers value objectivity highly (at least in part because multiple-choice tests can be cheaply machine scored), their tests focus on certain skills and traits at the expense of others. This focus, in turn, leads educators to put an unnatural emphasis on teaching these particular skills, which can distort the whole educational process. Although imagination, creativity, a constructive sense of humor, and extremely high intelligence do not show up well on current tests, they are traits sorely needed in this society. These traits can even be a drawback in the testing situation; for example, when teachers must tell their better students before a test, "Don't think too much." That is a great loss, both for the individuals and for society.

Standardization has two very different technical meanings in testing. In one sense of the word, it can refer to making arrangements for all students to take the test under similar conditions. Typically, this includes making sure that all students receive the same instructions the same way, that they all have the same available time, and so forth.

The other meaning of standardization, which is the way we shall use the word here, concerns establishing norms for performance so that test scores come out as percentiles.* The test maker gives the test to a sample of students, finds their percentiles among their fellows in the sample, makes a table of their scores against their percentiles, and later uses

---

*The *percentile* is the percentage of students whose scores are below (or the same as) the student being reported on. The fiftieth percentile is average; percentiles ranging from twenty-five to seventy-five are roughly average. The higher the percentile, the better the score. Instead of percentiles, some tests report in stanines or other breakdowns, but the principles remain the same.

this table to translate scores into percentiles for other students.

The rationale for this practice is that a particular score in itself is not informative without information about scores from other students. For example, suppose two students receive scores of 200 and 300. Are these scores good or bad? We know one student did better. But did he do much better, or a little better? On the other hand, if we know that the percentiles corresponding to these scores are the thirtieth and the ninetieth, we are better able (supposedly) to evaluate the students: one did quite poorly, and one did very well. (Then one must add: compared with the sample group.) But the percentiles give no information at all on how each student actually performed; they report only on how he or she compared with the standardization group.

Standardization, then, has no bearing on the quality of a test; it affects only the reporting of scores. Furthermore, there is nothing standard (in the ordinary English sense) about a standardized test. The test is not necessarily a recognized authority or an established basis for comparison, even though the word tends to invoke this kind of image. In fact, the word *standard* in standardized does not refer to the test at all; it applies to the sample population.

The people in the standardization group must be picked very carefully. If the test is for national use, these students must represent a fair cross section of the national population. But, although we sometimes hear otherwise, this fair representation is not a guarantee against discrimination in the test. For example, even though a standardization sample has the right number of blacks, the test can still discriminate against black culture. The presence of, say, 11 percent blacks in the standardization group has only a small effect on the percentile rank of a particular black child taking the test years later.

In general, if a test has defects, standardizing it will not uncover or correct them. Standardizing in that case will merely allow one to report the defective scores in the form of percentiles.

RELIABILITY AND TEST ERROR

A reliability coefficient of .90 for an achievement test is very acceptable in the industry, and it sounds reassuringly high. But when it is translated into test error, the results are disquieting.

Suppose the scores of a particular test are adjusted to show a mean score of 500 points and a standard deviation of 100. (This is true of many Educational Testing Service products, including some of those most widely used.) And suppose the test has a reliability coefficient of .90. This means there is some error in the test, although it is acceptable by industry standards. A child receives a particular score, but his "true score"—the score he would receive on an error-free test—is probably different.

Suppose we establish a range of scores just broad enough to be "90 percent sure" that the child's true score falls inside it; that is, a range of test error that will include the true score for 90 percent of the students. Calculating with the numbers above, this range must be over *100 points wide!*

Thus if a child's score is 550, we can be "90 percent sure" that his true score is somewhere between 500 and 600. In percentile form, the score tells us only that the child probably falls somewhere between the fiftieth and the eighty-fourth percentile—anywhere from average to first-class performance! And for a full 10 percent of the students, their scores will lie outside this range altogether.

Even relatively high reliability co-efficients can lead to very wide margins of test error. Thus even the best tests available are suitable for only extremely broad and soft comparisons among students. Yet people who use test scores for making decisions routinely draw much finer distinctions. In a large fraction of cases, the decisions must rest on test error rather than on individual competence or ability.

Reliability turns up heavily in materials promoting tests. Test makers consider it to be very important. But again, this word has two meanings, and the technical meaning is not what one might expect from the meaning of the word in everyday English.

In its technical sense, reliability simply means how well a test agrees with itself. Suppose we administer a test today and again tomorrow, somehow compensating for what the child learned the first time. The results will probably not be identical, even though the child's knowledge remains the same, for any test has built-in error. For example, think of measuring with a rubber ruler; the instrument itself gives different answers at different times. But the closer the results are, the more "reliable" the test is considered. In other words, by correlating the scores from both sessions, we can estimate the test's reliability. A reliable test tends to agree with itself more than an unreliable test does; the rubber ruler is stiffer.

In practice, the test-retest technique has its problems. Today, companies usually test two forms of the same test—one against the other—relying on the forms being equivalent. Or they divide the test into two parts and test the parts against each other. There are other techniques, too. The result is usually given as a "reliability coefficient": in achievement tests, .95 is considered excellent, .90 pretty good, and .80 not so good. The aim is always to determine how much the test is likely to be in error for any particular child. (See the box above.)

Reliability, in its technical sense, is easy to measure, and there are established ways to make tests more reliable. (Some methods, such as shortening the time so that most students cannot finish, may artificially boost the reliability coefficient unless there are precautions in the analysis.) Test makers have good control over this kind of reliability, and they promote it as an important characteristic of their tests.

Because reliability has two very distinct meanings—technically and in ordinary English—the word lends itself to very misleading claims. Any test can be technically reliable but completely miss the mark in terms of its stated purpose.

Validity is the soul of a test; that is, the degree to which a test measures what it is supposed to measure. It is here that most discussions of testing run aground and most informed proponents of tests fall silent, because validity is extremely difficult to measure or establish. This point is crucial, because anyone who uses test results as a basis for making decisions is depending primarily on validity. To use a test score, one must believe that the score means something. Test makers claim to establish this, and they sometimes publish "validity coefficients." But their understanding of validity is unique and technical—very different from the way in which the majority of people ordinarily use the word.

Test makers assess technical validity in two ways: either by having an expert look at the test and pronounce it valid, or by comparing the test results with some other measure. (There are about ten variations on these two techniques.) The first approach, usually called "content validity" or "face validity," is validation by opinion. If a test looks like a test of addition and subtraction, then this approach makes sense; many other cases are less obvious. But when test makers say a test "possesses high content validity," they mean only that certain people have said that it looks like a good test.

The second approach is validation by comparison. For example, scores from an arithmethic achievement test are compared with actual performances in arithmetic, or scores from a French test are compared with the students' actual abilities to speak, understand, read, or write French. This approach looks more scientific on the surface, but it, too, has fundamental problems.

To validate by comparing, there must always be some second measure of the competence—some other way to measure ability that is sound enough to prove the test is working properly. The difficulty here is that this second criterion, whatever form it takes, is also a sort of test, and so it needs validation, too. It, in turn, must be validated either by opinion or by comparison; if it is validated by comparison, it will lead to a third measure that must also be validated, and so on.

For example, suppose I devise a multiple-choice test to measure creativity. To validate it, I might invent a number of problems, using real materials that students can handle, that give opportunities for creative solutions. I could have a sample of students try both the objective test and the hands-on problems. Suppose I find a good correlation—that students who do well in the hands-on situation also score high in the multiple-choice test. Does this validate the test? Not until I can establish that the hands-on problems are themselves good measures of creativity. To do that, I might take another sample of people, perhaps adults this time, and put them through the hands-on tryout. Then I could examine their life histories for evidence of creative accomplishment, trying to correlate this evidence with creative solutions in the hands-on situation. But this, in turn, assumes that the life histories are good indications of creativity, and there are several reasons to doubt this. Therefore, I must now show that my history technique is accurately identifying creative people, and so forth.

As well as being somewhat contrived, this scenario fails to mention many problems along the way. But it does show that in principle every validation points up the need for yet another validation.

There are only three ways in which such a chain of validations can end: 1) the validation may ultimately rest on an unvalidated measure; 2) the validation chain may terminate at an instrument having content validity or face validity; in other words, simply opinion; and 3) the validation chain may become circular, with the validation of A depending on B, the validation of B depending on C, and the validation of C depending on A. This may have happened to some extent in IQ testing.

In short, if we use the word *valid* in its usual dictionary sense, validation is a very uncertain business. Testing people make the problem seem less severe by redefining the word—by softening it to the point where a test can be called valid even though an informed user would put very little faith in it. The careless user, however, may take many tests far too seriously if he does not appreciate their major uncertainties and limitations. There is no way to assess validity in the sense that most people ordinarily use the word.

FURTHER TROUBLES

There are other defects in the test, which need to be pointed out in any discussion of standardized testing. These defects take several forms, and the list that follows is in no particular order of importance. Furthermore, not every defect in the list applies to every test, but nearly all the criticisms apply to nearly all the most widely used, standardized, norm referenced achievement tests.

- *Inappropriate content.* No test can examine "mathematics" or "reading" or any other subject area in general; a test can only sample particular content within the subject matter. Thus each test becomes a statement about what content the test maker thinks is important enough to sample. This is a matter of judgment, and sometimes the judgments are questionable. For example, mathematics tests put such a heavy stress on calculation that a child's "mathematics" score is mostly a calculation score. Yet longhand calculation is a nearly obsolete skill, far less important today than many other parts of mathematics.

• *Need for reading and linguistic skills.* Before a multiple-choice test is a test of mathematics or anything else, it is a reading test first—and beyond that, a reading test in a particular form of English, usually compact and stylized. A low score can mean low achievement in the subject under test, or it can mean poor reading. There is no way of telling which. Although indispensable in themselves, language skills are too unpredictable to become contaminating factors in tests of other subjects.

• *Frequent incorrectness.* Many existing tests, including some of the most respected, show serious mistakes in subject matter: both wrong answers counted right and perfectly good answers counted wrong. This impedes students who know the subject matter extremely well, because they must put aside their knowledge and instead figure out what the tester might want. Although it is unfair and inexcusable, this problem appears surprisingly often.

• *Ambiguity and lack of clarity.* Many items on current tests are unnecessarily obscure or frankly ambiguous, as examples quoted throughout this issue show.

• *Clerical emphasis.* Most large-scale tests are scored by machine. To accommodate the machine, students must usually mark their answers by shading in little squares on separate answer sheets. Finding the right square on the sheet is troublesome for some students, and it distracts them from the main purposes of the test. Children who are sloppy or careless in their answer sheet bookkeeping will receive low scores even if they know the answers to most of the questions.

• *Excessive time pressure.* By design, many tests are too long for most children to finish in the time allowed. This puts youngsters who tighten up under time pressure at a serious disadvantage, even though calmness under stress is not, supposedly, the trait that is being tested.

• *Inflexibility.* Different people think in different ways, but present tests make no allowances for individuality, no matter how effective. A creative answer is almost always a wrong answer, and an alert sense of humor can only lead the child into trouble. Tests force children into particular styles of thinking, styles that come more naturally to some youngsters than to others.

• *No credit for partial understanding.* On current large-scale achievement tests, answers are either right or wrong. There is no room for answers that are merely better or worse. A child will receive an item score of zero whether he or she has no idea what the question is about, or whether he or she eliminates all the wrong answers but two and then makes the wrong choice between those two. Guessing is a good tactic in the second case, but some children find it very hard to guess on a test, even if they are encouraged to.

• *Secrecy.* An atmosphere of military secrecy surrounds educational testing today. Parents have no access to the tests that play an important role in deciding their children's futures, and the public has no way of judging whether it is being well served. The testing industry has a tremendous advantage in defending itself, because only very dedicated and persistent critics can even gain access to the materials. Our society has become suspicious of secrecy lately, and this suspicion should extend to testing and to tests.

• *Lack of diagnostic value.* Standardized achievement tests are almost useless for classroom diagnosis, and so fail one of the most important testing needs altogether.

• *Cultural and linguistic bias.* In present achievement tests, the question itself, the available answers, and information the student might use almost always appear in printed form. This means that every test is in a particular language, and that it must take certain linguistic usages for granted. Children who grow up in the same cultural environment as the test makers may have little trouble, as they share the same nuances of language and unspoken values. But other children—including many minority children—carry a different set of implicit understandings. Thus many minority children have the extra task of "decoding" each question, trying to grasp what it might mean in somebody else's language and culture. This is probably part of the reason that minority children do less well on achievement tests than majority youngsters.

- *Norm referenced scores.* Comparing people to one another along a single scale of ability is fundamentally demeaning and unfair. The case is even stronger with tests that fail to measure the ability well. People are different; they have different kinds of skills, abilities, and styles. It is foolish to pretend otherwise, yet the concept of norm referenced tests assumes that people are very similar in certain kinds of ways.

This list can be broken down into two categories: those defects that arise in particular tests and can be fixed, and those that are basic to the test format and cannot be fixed. For example, incorrectness and ambiguity could be eliminated or greatly reduced through proper care in preparing the tests. Their occurrence need not reflect on the testing process as a whole. However, many of the other defects stem from the norm referenced, content validated, multiple-choice format itself. There is no way to correct these defects except by shifting to a different kind of test altogether.

The inescapable outcome is that we need alternative approaches to testing. The rather dry points above have been distilled from millions of youngsters sitting tensely at their school desks, shading in the little squares on which their futures depend. Competition and achievement are hard enough when the judging is fair, but when it is not, the joy of accomplishment—of proving oneself in the arena—can only turn into bitter frustration and apathy. We need tests that treat children equally, although not always identically; test that overlook race, culture, and language to discriminate mainly on the basis of capability instead.

•

Under analysis, much of the apparently solid foundation on which testing rests simply disintegrates, leaving the whole testing business largely unsupported. Had testing questions been current two thousand years ago, a cynical Roman might well have observed (along with *caveat emptor*, which never goes out of date), *quis custodiet ipsos custodes?* In the end, until better tests can be developed, it is up to those who use the present tests to guard themselves.

A CONVERSATION WITH BANESH HOFFMANN

PAUL L. HOUTS

Paul L. Houts is director of publications and editor of Principal.

On a quiet residential street in Flushing, New York, lives a quiet, scholarly professor of mathematics, who, since 1962, has come to be considered the doyen of American critics of standardized testing. The year 1962 marked the publication of Banesh Hoffmann's broadside attack on multiple-choice testing, *The Tyranny of Testing,* and those who have yet to read it will find that, in keeping with its author, it is penetrating in its criticism, incisive in its analysis, marvelously literate and witty in its style, and altogether a thoroughly engaging book. In fact, in spite of its considerable eloquence, the book may have been too engaging. Over the last several decades, the American public has become inured to all but the most strident of warnings, all but the most sensational of exposes. However, Hoffmann is anything but a muckraker. Rather, he is a man of considerable civility and, above all, a man of reason who not unreasonably expected that a well-reasoned critique of mass "objective" testing might stir some much needed reform. Even Jacques Barzun in his forword to *The Tyranny of Testing* was moved to observe that, "Now the tide has turned. As the present book shows, it is the testers who are on the defensive, fighting a rearguard action against the irresistible force of the argument which says that their questions are in practice often bad and in theory very dangerous."

But the tide did not turn; the revolution never came. Indeed, it is quite likely that standardized testing holds far greater sway today than it did in 1962. Nevertheless, although Hoffmann's book failed to bring about the immediate reform it should have, it may have started something important after all. *The Tyranny of Testing* is now a classic on the subject, and a necessary embarkation point for anyone seriously interested in studying the pros and cons of standardized testing. It has left thousands of readers with grave doubts about the validity of the tests, and so perhaps its most important impact is yet to come.

On a gray January afternoon last winter, when we met in his study, with its scholarly scattering of books and papers, Hoffmann commented on the impact of his book. "I was disappointed, of course, by subsequent events," he told me. "But I shouldn't have been surprised, should I, by the way ETS and the testing companies and the foundations responded, for it only bore out the point of my book—that testing holds great power in this country and that the power of the test makers is deeply entrenched. What perhaps was most amusing was that the testers' first response was to attack me on the basis of my lack of qualifications to criticize the tests, since I was not a so-called psychometrician. And that, you see, is a terribly common defense by the testing companies. It's a most predictable and, I might add, thoroughly fatuous line of reasoning. They want you to believe that test development is a very arcane science that even scholars in science are not capable of understanding."

In fact, the British-born, Oxford-educated Hoffmann is not a psychometrician. But even a few of the many highlights of his career offer an impressive testimony to his qualifications as both educator and critic of the tests. (Actually, John Winterbottom, special assistant to ETS President William Turnbull, later remarked to me that ETS considered Hoffmann "a most worthy adversary.")

Banesh Hoffmann began his career in this country at Princeton University, serving as a research associate to the noted mathematician O. Veblin. After a stay at the University of Rochester, he became a member of the Institute of Advanced Study in Princeton, where he collaborated with Albert Einstein and Leopold Infeld. Their research proved that the gravitational field equations automatically determine the motion of bodies, and it has become classic in the theory of relativity. In 1937, he became a charter member of the Queens College faculty.

Hoffmann's first book, *The Strange Story of the Quantum,* was widely acclaimed and has been translated into Spanish, Polish, French, Rumanian, and Japanese. His most recent book, *Albert Einstein: Creator and Rebel,* written in collaboration with Einstein's secretary, Helen Duclos, received the 1973 Science Writing Award of the American Institute of Physics and the United States Steel Foundation.

Among other accomplishments, Hoffmann was honored as Distinguished Teacher of the Year in 1963 by the Alumni Association of Queens College. He is also a Baker Street Irregular (his article, "Sherlock, Shakespeare and the Bomb" appeared in the *Ellery Queen Mystery Magazine),* the inventor of an Orthoepic Alphabet for the teaching of reading, a frequent lecturer on science and testing on both radio and television, and the author of numerous articles that have appeared in a wide range of popular and scientific magazines and journals.

However, it was neither the past nor the richness of his career that this splendid sixty-eight-year-old man was anxious to talk about, but rather the future reform of testing. "You know," he said, wagging a finger at me and speaking in clipped, precise tones, "I had almost begun to believe that nothing would ever really change very much in testing. But here the two of us are, aren't we, talking about concerns that surely must be on the minds of so many others. Your organization is doing two magazines on the subject, and I notice that others have begun to write again. So perhaps there is a chance. Perhaps something might just happen after all these years. And wouldn't that be marvelous?

HOUTS: *Tell me, Dr. Hoffmann, how did you become interested in testing?*

HOFFMANN: Many years ago, Westinghouse Corporation was funding a Science Talent Search, and Science Service was doing the actual administering. After the first year, there was an article in the *American Scientist* explaining how the talent had been selected. I read it, and I was horrified by the examples of the multiple-choice questions. And so I took a week off and wrote an article, which was published, and everything grew out of that. The Westinghouse people invited me and one or two other critics to lunch and said, "We want you to help us." I told them that I didn't believe in what they were doing. They said something like this: "We are committed to using multiple-choice tests. Of all people, Dr. Hoffmann, you have an obligation, a moral obligation, to help us make these tests as good as possible." I was over-awed and said that I'd do it.

They sent me the preliminary version of the next test, and I made extremely angry comments about it. To my surprise, they sent me another test the next year. I thought I had been more than rude enough to discourage them, but the tests kept coming and coming and coming, and I continued to criticize them—a service for which they paid me $25 a year. I'd like to mention that finally, after twenty-five years, the Science Talent Search stopped using multiple-choice questions and now uses only the sort of evaluation that the multiple-choice testers call "subjective."

When the National Merit Scholarship came into existence, I again raised objections, and the Ford Foundation urged me to speak to the people at ETS. This I did and, in fact, ETS asked me to become a consultant. I refused. Then they asked me not to publish any further criticisms of tests for the next few months, because they wanted to invite me to speak, not at the big annual public College Board meeting, but to the small inner group that ran things. I agreed not to make any further public statements or write anything about tests until after I had spoken to them. That was in June, and the meeting was scheduled for Thanksgiving time. I waited until a week before Thanksgiving, and still no invitation was extended. So I wrote to ETS and was told that someone had forgotten to follow through on the invitation. I then asked them to release me from my promise, and they said they would and that they would invite me again. Well, I was never invited, and it has gone on and on like that.

I call these episodes "The Tales of Hoffmann." But they are one of the reasons why I wonder whether we can ever accomplish any significant reform in testing. Another reason is that I think people in education, particularly superintendents, are going to be afraid.

HOUTS: *Why do you say that? What have they to be afraid of?*

HOFFMANN: I think that the educational establishment is afraid of making waves. Also, I feel that the establishment people—those who want an establishment and feel they are a part of it—are going to be leery of saying anything contrary to the testers. After all, they enjoy being invited to ETS. It can be quite pleasant, and it looks good on their vitae.

HOUTS: *But don't you think the average teacher and principal are anxious to see some testing reform? After all, given the current emphasis on accountability, they are increasingly being judged on the basis of their students' test scores.*

HOFFMANN: That may be. But I also think the average person is rather apathetic about everything. And yet, I must admit that the climate may be just right. The accountability movement, for example, has led teachers' organizations to protest—even though, I must add, they did not protest anything like as strongly when only the students were being evaluated by the tests. In addition, there have been some recent investigations that have been successful—I'm thinking particularly of Watergate—and so reform is very much on the public's mind. But reform is not easily come by.

That's why I think that the crucial first step is to have a powerful investigating committee examine the whole area of standardized testing.

HOUTS: *I assume that you believe the abuses are so great at the moment that there is fertile ground for this kind of investigation.*

HOFFMANN: Oh yes, indeed. It's a quite awful situation, as I believe my book *The Tyranny of Testing* explained. Multiple-choice tests penalize the deep student, dampen creativity, foster intellectual dishonesty, and undermine the very foundations of education. Although the test makers claim to be scientific, they drop their pose when cornered and resort instead to propaganda. And make no mistake about it, they were well and truly cornered by the evidence in my book.

HOUTS: *That book was published in 1962. Do you think educators have a greater understanding of the limitations of standardized tests today, or is the situation just the same as it was when your book came out?*

HOFFMANN: It's hard for me to answer that question. Every now and then, I'm surprised to hear that my book has had some influence, even at ETS. But unfortunately, that influence is not nearly great enough to bring about the sort of revolution that is needed.

HOUTS: *Were you surprised when the book was first published that it was strongly criticized by people in education?*

HOFFMANN: Not at all. Many people spoke highly of it. The ones who objected had vested interests, or believed what they were told about testing without realizing that it's all very unscientific—instead of scientific, as the testers claim.

However, to go back to your earlier question for a moment, I do believe that today there is a bit more of a balance than there was when the book first came out. Four or five months ago, for example, I was at a conference at which two people from ETS gave a talk on a certain test that they were developing. I was surprised when they said, "Please don't take our test scores seriously." They were very careful to say that. After the presentation, I introduced myself and told them that I was delighted to see how honest they were and that I would like to see their organization be just as honest. I think ETS does try harder than some other testing companies to persuade people that these tests are not magical cures for every problem pertaining to evaluation.

HOUTS: *But do you think the test instruments themselves have been improved?*

HOFFMANN: No, I don't. There may have been a slight increase in trying to correct some of the ambiguities, but I haven't seen a significant improvement. The multiple-choice format is the same, and that's what is so insidious.

HOUTS: *Why do you believe so few people have questioned the value of the tests?*

HOFFMANN: Look at what has happened with the nursing homes. It's an absolutely scandalous situation, and it took years to bring the deplorable conditions of the nursing homes to the attention of the general public. In the meantime, the scandal was covered up by the politicians. The same sort of thing is true with testing. The testing people have friends in high places. It will take a revolution to change testing in America.

HOUTS: *Let's assume for a moment that there were to be such a revolution. What form do you think it should take?*

HOFFMANN: I think it should be more of a counterrevolution—a return to the sort of testing we used when we didn't rely on the machines. Once you decide to let the machine do all the dirty work, the tests have to conform to the limited capabilities of the machine. I think that's putting the cart before the horse.

HOUTS: *But many people maintain that when you return testing to the teacher—to an individual—then you will get very subjective opinions. Human error, bias, prejudice, and so forth, will interfere.*

HOFFMANN: But every type of testing is subjective, isn't

it? Fore example, suppose a multiple-choice test is given to decide who should be awarded a particular scholarship. The person who obtains the scholarship gets it because a multiple-choice test was the type of test that was given. If it had been a different type of test—say an interview—and a more profound person received the scholarship, you could easily say that the second person got it on the basis of a subjective test—an interview. But didn't the first person get it because of the decision to use a multiple-choice test and thus to penalize profundity? And wasn't that decision a subjective one? So the first candidate also won for a subjective reason.

HOUTS: *Doesn't the whole concept of standardized testing rest on a lack of trust in the ability of the teacher to adequately evaluate pupil progress?*

HOFFMANN: No, I don't think so. The word "trust" suggests that you think the teacher is going to be dishonest. So let's put it a different way. The test makers have made experiments to show that in grading essays, different people will give different grades, depending on the circumstances; for example, whether an essay is the first or the last of a batch, or what the weather's like when they're doing the grading, and so forth. Furthermore, when one gives the same batch of essays to the same teacher two weeks later, he or she will often give different grades from before.

Unfortunately, the testers will not make converse experiments to show how bad the multiple-choice tests are. In my book, I suggested an experiment that they have never done—or if they have done it, they have kept singularly quiet about it. It is a very simple experiment: pick a multiple-choice test and administer it to a group of people; then ask them what their reasons were for their choices of answers to the test items. The variety of reasons they will give is incredible. Some people pick the wanted answer for the oddest reasons. Some people know too much and select an unwanted answer as a result. In effect, you might say they are too good for the test. But in any case, it is a thoroughly hair-raising experience. You realize that these tests are not doing what they're supposed to be doing at all.

HOUTS: *What kind of testing would you like to see?*

HOFFMANN: I would like to see any type of testing that allows the student to do something himself, and in which the concern is not just with the answer or with the choice, but with the reasoning process used to arrive at the answer. That is what teachers must be most concerned about.

HOUTS: *Should we take testing, then, out of the hands of the publishing companies entirely?*

HOFFMANN: Well, I think that as long as testing remains a matter of making money, it is going to be in the wrong hands. I think testing has to be the responsibility of scholars who know the subject, rather than of psychologists, technicians, and business people.

HOUTS: *But the publishing companies claim that they bring the scholars in to advise them and to help develop the tests. How do you answer that?*

HOFFMANN: Of course, one way of answering it is to look at the product, which has been my approach. You carefully analyze test items themselves and demonstrate that they are manifestly bad. Then you consider all the test makers' arguments and all their marvelous looking statistics in favor of the product, and you show that the arguments don't hold up and that the statistics are misleading. If after all this, the testers are still boastful about their methods and the quality of the product, then I think it's clear that a great deal is wrong with their procedures and their claims. That's one answer.

Another answer is that the role of the subject matter expert in test development is small; that is, he or she is dominated by the psychologist, or whoever is in charge of making the test.

HOUTS: *But how can the subject matter expert be dominated? How is it done?*

HOFFMANN: This sort of thing happens, for example: a newly recruited subject matter expert joins a group of holdovers. He is usually told by the psychologists—and the holdovers, of course, agree—that the test has to be of the multiple-choice type. If he objects, he is quietly tolerated and also quietly not reinvited. He has practically no chance of influencing basic policy. If he plays ball, however, he finds himself pleasantly rewarded in many ways that boost his ego. After all, psychologists are experts in the art of influencing people and rewarding them for desired responses.

HOUTS: *The fact remains that the test publishers have a multimillion dollar business. Obviously, they're not going to divest themselves willingly of that kind of power and money. How, then, does the profession begin to act?*

HOFFMANN: That indeed is the question! How *do* we begin to act? I would like to feel that I began something that might, with a little miraculous help, bring about reform. But as you pointed out, there is a tremendous vested interest. Testing is a huge industry.

In other countries, testing is still done by the universities. But in this country, testing has been turned into big business; and, therefore, it is much harder to attack it and to influence it. My strategy, after trying various other things, was to make a prima facie case against the testers by attacking a peripheral weakness. I simply took actual, sample questions, demonstrated that these sample questions were defective, and then publicly challenged the testers to defend the questions. I pointed out to the testers that if they were to defend a bad question by saying that their statistics showed it was good, they would only be showing that their *statistics* were not good. Interestingly, they were so wedded to their "statistics show" argument that in spite of my warning, they sometimes could only retort by saying, "But our statistics show it's a good question."

Challenging the testers in this way made an even stronger prima facie case than I had expected. It clearly demonstrated that there was something that should be investigated, and I called for a commission of inquiry to look into the whole enterprise of testing. Furthermore, I urged that the commission of inquiry not be dominated by professionals in the testing field. It should have outstanding, creative people on it who could take a new look at and bring a breath of fresh air to the whole business of evaluation; and it should have people with a judicious cast of mind who are experienced in evaluating evidence and who would not be fooled by the pseudoscientific claims of the testers.

HOUTS: *Do you mean people from the arts, the sciences, all the professions, as well as education?*

HOFFMANN: Yes, but not educators who have fallen hopeless victims to the testing propaganda. Most of the members of the commission ought to be creative people. I would love to have people on it who have demonstrated their creativity, and who never did score well on the tests. But they would have to know how to recognize talent, and recognition of talent is not easy.

HOUTS: *What happened to your proposal for a national board of inquiry? Did it ever get anywhere?*

HOFFMANN: No, I'm sorry to say.

HOUTS: *Do you think that's an indication the public isn't really concerned with testing?*

HOFFMANN: Even if they're not, that's irrelevant, isn't it? The public is misinformed, and it is up to the profession to educate them. It is up to the profession to see that they become concerned.

HOUTS: *But, in fact, as you mentioned, the profession itself has been passive.*

HOFFMANN: Again, they don't want to make waves. And look what a marvelous saving of energy it is not to have to grade papers. It's so nice, so easy.

HOUTS: *What do you think about the recent efforts to stop the use of group IQ tests? As you know, they have been discontinued in New York City, Washington, and Los Angeles.*

HOFFMANN: I think it's a step in the right direction to ban group IQ tests. I am not against individually administered tests that are administered with insight. That's another matter entirely. But when you test on a mass basis and have a machine grade the results, I'm firmly against it. It's discouraging, however, that it has taken us so long even to begin to limit group IQ tests. We shouldn't have to persuade anyone these days that IQ tests cannot possibly measure anything that can legitimately be called intelligence. The tests are clearly culturally biased, even when they try not to be.

But let me make another point here. I'm glad that some cities are not using IQ tests, but I suspect they're not using them for the wrong reason. I think that the inherent bias in the IQ test is a good reason for not using it. I also think that there is a sort of evil in the multiple-choice IQ tests, becasue they don't show the mental processes behind the choices of answers. But I believe IQ testing in the cities you mentioned was given up solely for political reasons.

HOUTS: *Do you mean they were under great pressure from minority groups?*

HOFFMANN: Exactly. But if you give up IQ tests in certain cities solely because the tests are culturally biased, you ignore their more fundamental defects; you don't get to the bottom of the problem.

HOUTS: *In fact, it's given rise to another problem—at least in New York City, where the reading tests seem to have simply replaced IQ tests.*

HOFFMANN: Ah, yes. But, you see, the trouble always is that people want to try to measure, and they will sacrifice almost anything in order to measure.

It's interesting that our legal system, to a large extent, hasn't fallen into that trap. After all, if we really wanted to make things scientific, why couldn't we just dispense with cross-examination and juries and judges and just make everyone take a lie detector test? It's so nice and scientific. Statistics show that 70 percent of the time it works. Of course, it's true that some people who are innocent will mess up the lie detector test, and they will go to jail. But look at the money saved. We won't have to pay lawyers; we won't have to pay juries; it will all be automatic and scientific.

If we really want to argue along those lines, we could easily be carried away by modern technology. The fact that we can do it more cheaply encourages us to ignore the harm that's being done. And the harm is all-pervasive in education. For example, if anyone wants to introduce a new educational program of some sort, no one is going to buy it unless it has been evaluated. If you apply for a grant, you have got to say how you are going to evaluate your program. Now, ETS will be happy to evaluate it for you, but how will they do it? The chances are they will do it by using multiple-choice tests.

There used to be a theory that in order to teach kids music appreciation, you should take the themes of the various symphonies and put asinine words to them and make the children sing the themes with the asinine words. For many years that practice effectively ruined those symphonies for those children for the rest of their lives. But if you gave an objective test on matching themes with symphonies, the kids would do marvelously well. I think that rather shockingly shows how stupid it is to teach with that sort of evaluation as the arbiter of success.

You see, if we want to select people, we ought to select them not so much on the basis of what they don't know, as on the basis of what they do know. If we have people of great talent in certain areas—for instance, painters or poets—we must not hold it against them if they can't do geometry well or if they have a language problem. Let's look at the good qualities and let them stand out.

HOUTS: *How do we find those good qualities? Can we identify them trhough standardized tests?*

HOFFMANN: In the first place, there is no such thing as a standardized test that is the same test for everyone. To believe otherwise is to be taken in by a cruel fallacy. Suppose the same so-called standardized test in physics is given to everyone, and it happens to be written in Chinese.

How well would you make out? Would you want to abide by the score and agree that since you and the person whose native tongue was Chinese were given exactly the same test, graded objectively in exactly the same way, you were far inferior to that person in physics? Of course not! Yet, it's a "standardized" test. So you see, any standardized test is standardized only in the sense that it's the test itself that's standardized. If you give a so-called standardized test to middle-class whites and then to underprivileged blacks, it is not really a standardized test: you are not giving the same test to both, even though the wording is identical.

HOUTS: *What do you think of people like Jensen who are using IQ scores as a basis for making judgments about minority groups?*

HOFFMANN: When Jensen wrote his paper, I read about it in the *New York Times* and I was highly incensed. I was ready to go out on the hustings, write a letter to the *Times*, and all that. Then I thought, before I do that I had better read his paper. I did so and was surprised to find that it was really a serious, honest paper. I think, however, that Jensen has not realized one important thing that is very hard to measure, and that is the effect environment has on a person. For instance, if you are a black child, you can sense the hatred that is focused on you; you realize that if you do anything good, no one is going to like it coming from a black kid. So you have children growing up in an atmosphere of oppression and hatred. I don't think that Jensen realized how terrible that is, how it can stunt the intellectual and emotional growth of a person.

HOUTS: *Is there a way, in fact, that we can separate the individual from his milieu?*

HOFFMANN: No, I don't believe there is.

HOUTS: *It seems to me that they're hopelessly interwoven.*

HOFFMANN: Exactly. But let me give you an example involving what happened in Poland between the First and Second World Wars. In the First World War, Poland gained freedom. In the Second World War, it lost freedom. Now in that short-lived period of freedom, there was a sudden gorgeous, marvelous flowering of intellect, especially in mathematics. There grew up a Polish School of Mathematics that was one of the glories of that period in mathematics. Why did it come about? Where did it come from? Surely just from the taste of freedom.

Similarly, the prejudice against blacks is terribly pervasive, terribly oppressive. I think they have had very little chance to develop, and I think that this negates Jensen's conclusions.

HOUTS: *Let me ask another question. Do you think that it's morally defensible even to inquire into such things as racial characteristics?*

HOFFMANN: Yes, I think so. I believe that all sorts of things should be inquired into. I don't think that you should set limits on inquiry, although I shouldn't say I don't think you should *ever* set limits. There are some things that we should be careful about. For example, we don't want to explode a lot of atomic bombs simply in order to see what they would do to the atmosphere. But in the matter of racial characteristics, I think that we have to investigate it very, very carefully.

Now, I will add a qualification to that statement: that any such investigation should also depend on what the motivation is. The motivation might very well be that you want to kill everybody off, or eliminate a group of people, and if that is your motivation, then I would say that we would all be better off if you didn't make your experiment. But if your motivation is honestly and seriously scientific, I think that the more we know, on the whole, the better off we are.

HOUTS: *How do we answer parents who want to know where their child stands in class compared to other children?*

HOFFMANN: I think you have to rely, as far as possible, on the opinion of the teacher. A lot of teachers are afraid to have an opinion because they have all been told by the testing people that they're being subjective.

HOUTS: *But the public is also increasingly demanding that the profession be held accountable. How can we satisfy that need without test scores?*

HOFFMANN: Can we sensibly satisfy it if we *do* have test scores? The scores are extremely misleading and superficial, and they ignore the crucial intangibles of education. Do they really give us worthwhile measures of educational accomplishment in depth? Also, consider the distorting effect of accountability (at least as it is currently defined) on education. Isn't it bound to be analogous to the effect of rating police officers by the number of traffic tickets they give out? We all know the effect of that sort of rating.

Accountability in education is a misguided attempt to apply the methods of cost accounting to an activity to which they are alien. Luckily, the teachers are getting increasingly up in arms about it, and I hope the current and popular notion of accountability turns out to be just another passing fad.

HOUTS: *Assuming that the testing companies are not going to give up their monopoly on testing and the money that accrues to them as a result, is there a way that the education profession can work with the testing companies to develop better tests?*

HOFFMANN: Again, I must go back to my proposal for a national inquiry. We need an authoritative statement from such a commission saying that this is an extremely serious situation; that not only do these tests not do very well what they claim to do in the way of evaluation, but they are failing to identify important types of people that we should be encouraging; and that, in fact, they're polluting the whole atmosphere of education.

Now, if you could get a conclusion like that from a highly respected commission of inquiry, you might be able to make a dent in the present power structure. I don't know, though, whether the test makers would go along with it; it's against their instinct, against the whole way they earn their money. Of course I would be delighted if they would go along, but I would also be a little wary that they might go along in order to use their power in high places to deflect the onslaught.

HOUTS: *Do you see the government as having a role in this? For example, should a regulatory agency be set up?*

HOFFMANN: The government could get into it, of course, but I wonder whether that would lead to reform. The testers have the ear of the government agencies. Remember, ETS evaluates a number of government projects. In fact, the testers seem to be everywhere important. It's frightening to see the extent to which they have infiltrated the power structure of education. They are trusted advisers to major foundations, for instance. And working for ETS is a stepping-stone to college presidencies and other influential positions.

Suppose you approached a foundation and presented powerful, unrefuted—in fact, irrefutable—evidence that all is not well in testing. Furthermore, suppose you then proposed the formation of a distinguished commission of inquiry to look into all aspects of the matter. What would happen? Well, the foundation would consult its advisers on tests and then turn you down.

HOUTS: *But can you really be sure of that? How do you know they would turn you down?*

HOFFMANN: How do I know? I know because it has happened to me—twice. In fact, one foundation told me that there was no need for such a commission of inquiry because I had already proved my case.

HOUTS: *Is there, then, absolutely no hope of reform?*

HOFFMANN: Well, as I said earlier, attitudes are changing encouragingly. The very fact that your journal is so powerfully pressing for a new look is real cause for encouragement. Other groups are also taking up the cause. So certainly the time is ripe for action. And furthermore, I don't believe in giving up hope.

HOUTS: *I agree that there is a great need for the kind of*

inquiry you propose. We certainly need to bring to the attention of the public and the profession the flaws in the standardized tests, to show them that something is terribly wrong. But I think we also have to go on and answer the question, what then do we do about it? What are our alternatives?

HOFFMANN: I don't agree. "What do you do instead?" is not necessarily the right question. And I'd like to answer it with a parable: suppose a man comes to a doctor and says, "I have these painful symptoms; my chest hurts . . . " and so on. And the doctor tries out everything, and he can't determine what the problem is. In the end the patient says, "Do you think I should perhaps give up taking strychnine after breakfast every day?" And the doctor says, "Well, for goodness' sake, yes, give it up." "Well," the patient asks, "then what will I take instead?"

HOUTS: *Granted that some of the tests are pretty strong poison, do you think most parents really know what a detrimental effect they can have on their children?*

HOFFMANN: All that parents know is that the child gets such and such a score. And if it's low, then they put grade pressures on the child.

HOUTS: *The problem of what we are doing to children seems to get lost in our zeal to measure them.*

HOFFMANN: Ah, that is the key point. What are we doing to children? It's not whether we are measuring well or not; it's what we are doing to the children and what we are doing to education.

HOUTS: *Yet I'm troubled by your earlier statement that we don't need to have alternatives. Would you really advocate that we do nothing?*

HOFFMANN: To do nothing could very well be better, because if you did nothing, then in the end you would start doing something. If it were forbidden that you should use machines to score tests, you would have to do it by hand and you might, therefore, be forced to do something that was better.

You see, my general feeling about evaluation is that most students fall somewhere in the middle. What we have to do is try to identify unusual people, and in order to do that, we have to look at what it is that makes them unusual. If they are one-sided, we must let them be one-sided instead of saying, "No, that person has to fit the machine mold." Therefore, we have to rely on the skill of the teacher in spotting the unusual. That's an uncommon skill in teachers. Few possess it. But we must train the rest the best we can. It's not going to be easy, for it's well known that original, creative students are very often found to be quite annoying to their teachers.

HOUTS: *I think you're suggesting something very important—that we must start taking evaluation into account in our teacher training programs to a much greater degree and consider a wider diversity of evaluation techniques.*

HOFFMANN: Well, there are courses on evaluation if you want to get a teacher's certificate. But they primarily concentrate on mechanized testing; and while the textbooks do sometimes have a few kind words in passing for essays, by the time you have finished the chapter on essays, you are persuaded that essays are stupid. So the evaluation courses are basically just propaganda.

HOUTS: *We've talked about IQ and achievement testing. But what do you think of the National Assessment of Educational Progress?*

HOFFMANN: The National Assessment was hatched by people in and close to government, but foisted on us rather surreptitiously by being deliberately financed initially not by government agencies but by a nongovernment foundation. This was done to allay fears that it would become a government accountability program and bring undue federal influence to bear on the schools. It was viewed with great alarm by the school superintendents—the American Association of School Administrators—and strong pressure was brought to bear to bring them into line. It had the earmarks of an ugly power play.

I was very worried when it began, and I'm still not happy about it. But at least they seem to have wised up somewhat. They are not relying totally on multiple-choice tests, although they still use a lot of them. Frankly, some of their questions are pretty awful. But the trouble with National Assessment is that it began in a simple way, and its developers swore that it was never going to be used for comparing. It was just going to give research information for regions. But now, the National Assessment is becoming almost as important an institution as the National Merit Scholarship Corporation, and so I worry a bit. But I must say that their procedures strike me as much better than the procedures of the National Merit Scholarship Corporation.

HOUTS: *What about the College Boards? It's often maintained that College Boards generally predict "success" in college—that is, of course, good grades.*

HOFFMANN: But when you say they predict, the prediction is not a good one. So far as I can make out, the claim is that there is a correlation of .5 or so. But a correlation of .5, roughly speaking, means the factor of goodness is the square of that, which is .25—that's one-fourth. Would you say that's wonderful? In my book, I point out that in the relation between height and weight, the correlation is about .5. Suppose you wanted to form a basketball team, and you didn't know the heights of the players, so you picked them by their weight. You wouldn't get much of a basketball team. Several members would be roly-poly. If that's the way you want to do education, I say that you're quite welcome to it.

HOUTS: *There are an increasing number of reports across the nation that test scores are declining. Some of the reports from the National Assessment are also alarming. How should the public interpret these low test scores and pessimistic reports of how little our children and young people know? Do you think they're valid indications that children are actually learning less and that the quality of teaching is declining?*

HOFFMANN: You're asking a very difficult question. If

we look on the tests as giving us meaningful information so far as averages are concerned—even though not for individuals—we can conclude that standards have gone down on the whole. I'm not entirely sure what this implies. I'm inclined to accept it, however, not because the test scores tell me it is true but because it agrees with my own impression of the preparation of my own students.

As for whether I think that the test scores show the quality of teaching is declining, that, too, is a very complicated matter. For instance, one has to try to weigh the effects of the various new education programs, such as the so-called new math (of which, by the way, I am not an admirer); the effects of television, both good and bad, on such things as reading; and the effects on test scores of new styles of teaching that place greater emphasis on encouraging and using the innate curiosity of the child. So it could be that what is actually lowering the test scores is *good* teaching rather than bad. But as I said, it's a very complicated question and one that needs to be studied a great deal more.

HOUTS: *Would you say that the standardized tests that we're using today are not in any way useful and should be abolished?*

HOFFMANN: That is putting it too strongly. Multiple-choice tests can be useful for limited purposes, such as checking whether someone applying for a driver's license knows purely factual things like the speed limit, the rules for passing, and the meaning of STOP. But they are not useful for more serious evaluation. The inherent weaknesses of machine-gradable tests and their harmful effects on education far outweigh any advantages they might have, and we would be better off without them. For example, is it good that teachers actually urge their brightest students not to think too deeply when taking multiple-choice tests?

Furthermore, one serious disadvantage of the present widespread use of these tests is that they let the wrong sort of people take control of testing. It's time that the control was returned to better qualified people—to scholars and humanists instead of mere technicians of evaluation.

A TALE OF TESTING IN TWO CITIES

BERNARD H. McKENNA

Bernard H. McKenna is professional associate, National Education Association, Washington, D.C. Formerly associate dean of education at the State University of California, San Francisco, and executive director of a Columbia University research and study unit, Mr. McKenna has had long involvement in program, teacher, and student evaluation. He recently coordinated the work of a national task force on testing sponsored by the NEA and is author of several works on evaluation.

They're far apart geographically, and they're not much alike as cities. Royal Oak, Michigan, is mostly white middle class, a suburb of Detroit. The minority population of Royal Oak is less than 2 percent. The other city—Bakersfield, California—might be called an independent city. It stands alone, surrounded for miles by farmland. Bakersfield has a minority population of around 48 percent.

As different as these two cities are, they have a common problem in their public schools: testing. (I was a member of two separate evaluating panels that examined the testing programs in the Royal Oak and Bakersfield school systems. Full published reports of the findings and recommendations of these panels are available from the Michigan and California state education associations.)

The testing problem reached its height in these two cities in similar ways. New school superintendents came on the scene in both communities at a time when the public's faith in the schools was at a low ebb. An alleged reason given in both cities for the low level of community support was the poor showing students were making on standardized tests, particularly in the basic skills of reading and mathematics.*

In both school systems, the new superintendents came in with promises, implied or stated. They came in with ideas for getting local test scores up to or beyond national averages and vowed that students would show "a year's growth in a year" in reading and mathematics.

Such promises were made, or implied, despite the widespread findings of test and measurement specialists, who caution that neither educators nor anyone else know specific techniques for bringing about large gains in student learning. In addition, the idea of a year's growth in a year has come to be considered a faulty concept by reputable researchers.[1]

In one school system, a whole new reading program was implemented, accompanied by hundreds of performance objectives, numerous tests, and "treatment books" for identifying teaching strategies to accomplish each of the objectives. In the other, a national standardized test was introduced on top of already mandated state assessment tests, locally developed criterion referenced tests in the language arts, and other miscellaneous aptitude tests.

With this as general background, let us examine what happened as the testing programs in Royal Oak and Bakersfield progressed through several stages.

•

In both school systems, it was either explicitly predicted or implied to the boards of education that the new testing programs would show pupil gains that would restore public confidence in the local schools. In one city, there was

---

*I say "alleged" because surveys in recent years show that large percentages of the public have high confidence in their schools. Some believe poor faith is often a rationalization for freezing or withdrawing funding in times of economic reverses.

at least some rationale for such a prediction, since the new tests were accompanied by some new instructional programs. In the other, where a nationally normed test in the basic skills was introduced, there appears to have been no rationale for expecting gains, since the test had not been selected for its consistency with or attention to local goals and objectives, instructional content, and processes. It may have been that someone's experience somewhere else indicated that the test was one on which gain was likely to be shown no matter what the nature of instruction. If this is true, then attributing whatever student progress might be shown on the tests to the effects of local schools would be incorrect and misleading at the very least, if not fraudulent—even if it served the urgent political need of gaining public support.

As the implementation got under way in Bakersfield it was implied by central office staff—some said it was "made explicit"—that at the end of the year test scores from individual school buildings would be compared and that judgments about the building principals' futures might be at least partially based on the test results.

One can almost imagine how the scenario proceeded as the programs started up in the school buildings. Some principals suggested that individual classrooms would be compared in the same way that buildings were to be compared. (Later on, this became a reality.) And while classroom performace on the tests didn't appear to be used much for the purpose of evaluating teachers, the threat was there from the very beginning. In fact, the Bakersfield superintendent admitted that "that's part of it—tests are a part of the evaluation of teachers and principals."

Under the threat of being evaluated on post-test scores, Bakersfield teachers reacted in various ways. Some began to make plans to teach to the tests. Some found it easy to go beyond teaching to the tests and ended up actually *teaching* the tests, because parts of actual tests were provided for the teachers with the advice that they change them "slightly" in use. Others went on using their own professional expertise and judgment on content and process to accomplish instructional objectives as best they could. The variation in teacher response was probably related to the variation in both principals' security and behavior and teachers' security. How the test results might be used, and teachers' and principals' beliefs about the implications of how they might be used, had a definite influence on their behaviors.

One reason central office staff in both Royal Oak and Bakersfield gave for implementing programs based on highly specific performance objectives and tests was that it would make the curriculum "teacher proof." It is likely, however, that the time and effort would have been better spent on inservice programs and decision-making opportunities for teachers to assure that they themselves became "curriculum proof" through the use of their highest professional expertise and best judgment.

In both communities, decisions to use some of the tests and plans for their use were made by the central office with little or no involvement of teachers and counselors. And in both places, there was a broader issue that underlay this lack of involvement: communication in both school systems was generally acknowledged by teachers and administrators to be poor.

Besides not being meaningfully involved in decisions about the testing program and related matters, teachers and counselors—and in some cases, the principals themselves—were not even informed of the purposes of some parts of the program. What's more, few parents knew much about the testing program either. Many expressed interest in receiving a wide variety of information on their children's progress, which they had not been getting.

In both cities, the process of setting objectives became a problem itself, as well as the tests. It was far from clear that the objectives were acceptable to large numbers of teachers, let alone that the objectives being taught to in many classrooms were the same ones on which the students would be tested. In one city, the national standardized test chosen was not well matched to local objectives, instructional procedures, texts, and other materials in use. And while some locally created, criterion referenced tests were in use in both cities, there had been varying degrees of teacher involvement in their development.

Then there were problems with the numbers and manageability of performance objectives. In one system, over 200 objectives were mandated for one subject area alone. And in both systems, the promise of things to come in terms of the number of learning objectives was frightening. The idea that performance objectives were scheduled to be developed for a large number of subject areas (in one city, ten), and that each subject area might be accompanied by its own tests, caused teachers and counselors great consternation—particularly when they were having difficulty managing what had already been mandated. As someone once said about the total state assessment program in a Midwestern state, it had the promise of a snowball rolling downhill—no one knew how large it would become or where it would come to rest.

The scenario becomes even more macabre when we look at the testing programs as they went into full operation.

In one city, the combination of state mandated and local tests at the fourth- and seventh-grade levels caused teachers to spend the greater part of the first several weeks of school in testing—a time when they needed to work intensively to get new instructional programs underway and to take advantage of the students' beginning-of-the-year enthusiasm. In a secondary school in one system, it was estimated that administering a nationally standardized test cost more than $150,000 in terms of staff time alone.

In both school systems, the opportunity for teachers and counselors to receive inservice education in order to understand the nature of the tests and to learn the most appropriate means for their administration ranged from minimal to none. Consequently, the testing programs were poorly administered in both places. From the standpoint of those administering the tests, there were a host of problems:

- Social studies teachers were required to administer reading tests with which they had little or no familiarity.

- Some tests were mass administered over public-address equipment; instructions were difficult to understand and communication between the test administrator and the many room monitors was impossible, so monitors responded to student confusion and questions in varied and inconsistent ways.

- In the course of administration, some teachers and counselors answered questions, gave clues, and repeated instructions, while others did not, making for potential unreliability of results.

- In some schools, teachers were required to administer tests to special education students and to those for whom English was a second language, tests from which, in the teachers' judgment, these students should have been exempt.

- Some of the teachers who were most threatened by the veiled warnings of being evaluated on the basis of test results gave the tests rapidly and with little precision in the fall, hoping that, with more time and care, an appropriate amount of progress could be shown in the spring.

- Because tests were not well matched to the curriculum, items in some tests given to fourth graders covered materials not dealt with until fifth or sixth grades, and high school students with only general mathematics backgrounds were given tests requiring understanding of algebraic and geometric concepts to which they had not been introduced.

- In one community, teachers judged that the standardized social studies test was more a test of reading ability than of understanding of social studies concepts and issues.

- In some schools, teachers were told that if scores were inordinately poor, they should not be turned in.

How did the students react to all the testing? Because many students were involved and because students are all different, they obviously reacted in many different ways. Some students took the tests seriously and did their best. But teachers and others who administered and monitored the tests noted that many students reacted negatively to the testing programs. Some early elementary children cringed and cried when they entered the room and saw that it was arranged for testing again. Some developed nosebleeds. At upper elementary and high school levels, students shared answers, rushed through the tests or made no effort to complete them, marked the same answer columns throughout the whole test, and generally expressed the attitudes that the tests were stupid and did no good and that they were sick of tests.

After the administration of the tests in both communities came the inevitable scoring, profile building, and report making and filing. Even though these activities varied with the different tests, depending on how the tests were designed for mechanization, some teachers estimated that for certain tests they spent as many as forty hours in scoring, profiling, filing, and similar activities—the equivalent of more than a full week of instructional time. Hardly any of the teachers found that amount of time justifiable in terms of the amount of help the test results gave them in improving the diagnosis of individual learning problems and planning for instruction.

Many of the tests were delivered to outside agencies for scoring. Clearly, if the test results were to be useful, they had to be returned to the teachers soon enough for them to diagnose learning difficulties and plan and conduct instruction between pretest and post-test. And yet results were returned so late that there were only two or three months of instructional time left to act on them before the post-tests. In other cases, particularly at the secondary level, results arrived near the end of the semester, when class rosters were about to be shifted, which meant that teachers would no longer have in their classes the students for whom the data was reported. In another instance, students were identified for learning disability programs on the basis of tests, but no such programs were available for them. Surely, the valuable time of psychologists and others in making these test related determinations might have been better used.

However, even when results were available early, and when teachers found the results useful for diagnosis and planning for instruction (and there were a few such instances), little or no time was provided for planning effective programs to respond to the findings, nor was there time to work individually with those children whose diagnoses indicated that they required special attention.

For example, some teachers in Bakersfield were told by their principals (who got the word from the central office) that, in order to show appropriate growth on the tests over a year, they should give more attention to those children whose scores they believed would be easiest to raise. The obvious implication of such a practice is that children with the most severe learning difficulties will be neglected.

The heavy emphasis on testing for only quantitatively measurable objects also worked in subtle ways to affect curriculum priorities. Since the name of the game became to produce results on these objectives that could be quantified on tests, other goals got little or no attention. Prominent examples of neglected areas in both school systems were speaking and listening skills.

Once the program was implemented, the tests had been given, and the results reported, what were the effects of all these activities on student learning, staff behavior and morale, and community understanding and support?

In both school systems, there was little evidence overall that the testing programs had contributed much to improved student learning through diagnosis of individual learning problems and planning for instruction. An exception was certain components of criterion referenced tests in the areas of language arts and mathematics. But even in these cases, many teachers found that the test results only confirmed what they already knew.

Large numbers of students took the results no more seriously than they did the test taking itself. This is hardly surprising, since there was little concerted effort to enlighten students about the purposes and meaning of the tests or the ways the results would be used. Part of this lack of effort seemed to be due to the school administration's failure to mount orientation programs, and part of the lack of time provided for teachers and counselors to confer with individual students on test results. But even if there had been adequate opportunity for consultation, many teachers didn't understand the purposes of the testing program or weren't committed to it, and so they had little inclination to spend much time and effort with the results. In addition, test booklets, manuals, and other materials for some tests in one school system were unavailable to teachers for reporting-out sessions. As a result, they were able to describe the test results and their implications only in broad generalities.

As for the parents, their reactions to the outcomes of the testing programs and their uses were mixed. Some were almost totally unaware that the program existed at all. Some believed the tests were unimportant and wanted to receive other kinds of information about their children's progress. Some received the results with apathy. Some were confused and disturbed. A few were pleased, particularly those whose children came out well on the tests.

In one system, test results were mailed home to parents in terms of norms, with little accompanying explanatory information. Both parents and teachers found this a highly unsatisfactory reporting arrangement. The parents were confused and in some cases frightened by it. At the secondary level, parents were apparently apathetic. In one high school, where 2,200 mailings were made to parents inviting them to contact the school about the results, there were only 20 replies.

So what did it all come to? In both Royal Oak and Bakersfield, the teachers found the programs so onerous, so counterproductive to the improvement of instruction, that they called for outside evaluations of the programs. The scenario that has been presented here describes the findings of two separate and differently constituted panels of professionals, all highly knowledgeable in pedagogy in general and in evaluation in particular.

While it is not the main purpose of this article to provide broad and deep proposals for correcting the improprieties just described, I would be remiss if I did not cite some of the major recommendations of both investigating panels. The list that follows does not reflect all or even most of the recommendations made to correct the testing problems of Bakersfield and Royal Oak. It contains what I believe are the major common considerations for both school systems. I also believe that a number of these recommendations apply to thousands of school systems across the country, as well:

- Reduce the number of tests given and the priority in time and effort placed on testing generally.

- Adopt, develop, or adapt a broad range of supplementary and alternative measures to tests for evaluating school progress.

- From the beginning, and at all stages, involve the entire professional staff in broadly representative ways in planning and executing evaluation programs; in addition, get some advice from the community.

- Provide opportunity for in-depth inservice education on the evaluation systems for all those who will be involved in planning and administering them.

- Assure that whatever evaluation systems are used will reflect the goals and objectives of the schools.

• Provide for an annual review of the school district evaluation system, involving all those who are affected by it.

•

Some will say this story illustrates that it's not the tests that are at fault, but the uses they are put to. Actually, it's both. In my judgment, the irrelevance of much of the content of the tests, their lack of validity and reliability, their cultural and racial bias, and their ambiguities all operated in Royal Oak and Bakersfield to further intensify the dismal tale I have told here.

On the matter of the tests themselves, the warning of Jerrold Zacharias "that we not retreat to catch phrases like 'I know these tests are not very good, but they are all we have'"[2] merits serious and profound consideration. The tale of these two cities (which is probably much more common across the country than many suppose) strongly suggests that, as Zacharias recommends for intelligence tests, the administration of standardized achievement tests "as they now exist should cease and desist."

If the public requires some sort of precise evidence of the success of the schools, and it seems to, and if the profession has oversold the public on the usefulness of standardized tests for this purpose or any other, and it probably has, then there is an urgent need for educational researchers and the testing industry, in conjunction with practitioners (particularly principals and teachers) to get busy immediately at developing sound and tough-minded alternatives to standardized tests for evaluating the success of schools generally and student progress specifically.

This doesn't mean just other kinds of tests—criterion referenced, domain referenced, or whatever. As promising as the concept of criterion referencing seems for correcting some of the problems of standardized measurement, criterion referenced tests are not only complex and time consuming to develop, but they often retain many of the deficiencies of standardized tests: poor attention to instructional objectives; irrelevant and misleading items; and continued use for sorting, categorizing, and predicting success rather than for diagnosing learning difficulties and improving instruction. Even if and when criterion referenced tests are highly perfected, they will need to be accompanied with many other means of evaluating student progress, among them student performances, student products, self-evaluation, peer evaluation, in-depth interviews by teachers and other professionals, simulation, and role playing.

When a variety of such alternatives have been developed, when those responsible for implementing them are generally in accord on their usefulness and have had an opportunity for intensive inservice in their application, interpretation, and use and when such alternatives have been broadly disseminated, thoroughly evaluated, and judged successful, then—and only then—will there be an end to the kind of stories related in this article.

NOTES

1. Robert S. Soar and Ruth M. Soar, "Problems in Using Pupil Outcomes for Teacher Evaluation," mimeographed (Washington: National Education Association, 1975).

2. Jerrold R. Zacharias, "The Trouble with IQ Tests," *National Elementary Principal* 54 (March/April 1975): 29.

EVALUATION, THE ENGLISH EXPERIENCE

PHILIP SHERWOOD

Philip Sherwood is headmaster of the County Junior School in Leicestershire, England, where he has served since 1956. He collaborated with Z. P. Dienes in efforts to humanize the teaching of classroom mathematics, and he edits a publication dedicated to that end.

Mr. Sherwood has assisted with summer workshops at Cambridge, Massachusetts; Brooklyn, New York; Ghana and Tanzania.

In 1861 Queen Victoria required her well-beloved George William Frederick Villers, Earl of Clarendon, Lord Lyttleton, the Earl of Devon, Sir Henry Stafford Northcote, and others "to enquire into the revenues and management of certain colleges and public schools and the studies pursued and the instruction given therein. "The public schools examined were the nine great schools of England—Eton, Winchester, Westminster, Harrow, and so forth. It seemed reasonable to these Royal Commissioners that a written examination of the fifth forms of the schools would enable them to draw conclusions about the studies pursued. Accordingly, they wrote to each of the nine headmasters. The replies were terse and hostile:

> *Your letter appears to me so seriously objectionable that I must beg to decline to entertain the proposal. The Dean of Westminster concurs with me.*
>
> Reverend Charles R. Scott, Westminster.

Objectionable both in principle and detail.

Dr. Elwyn, Charterhouse.

We should be deeply and unnecessarily wounded by having it put on record that we had passed a bad one.

Dr. Moberly, Winchester.

This interference with the authority of the headmaster is calculated to cause evil.

Dr. Balston, Eton.*

The principals of these great schools would not entertain evaluation. It was in their best tradition; seventeenth century Dr. Busby would not uncover his head when King Charles II visited his school lest such action should be misconstrued by the boys and diminish his authority. More recently, Walter Hamilton, former headmaster of Rugby School, defined the ideal headmaster as someone "resembling the Archangel Gabriel—godly, wise, and a bit fierce."

Such were the principals of our independent schools; they would have no truck with evaluation, and Her Majesty's Commissioners had to accept their view. It is a view they maintain, though in perhaps less forthright language, to this day. The elementary school principals were less fortunate. Unlike America, England has no long-standing tradition of compulsory education and common schools. Education was left to charity, church, and Sunday school until just over a

---

*The historical quotes are taken from the official reports of the Royal Commission Appointed to Enquire into the Revenues and Management of Certain Colleges and Schools (Clarendon Commission), 1864, and the Royal Commission Appointed to Enquire into the Working of the Elementary Education Acts (Cross Commission), 1886. Other material came from J. Hurt's *Education in Evolution* (London, 1971).

century ago. State intervention, begun in 1838, took the form of grants to parochial schools. Although the word "accountability" was not used, the spirit of the word was familiar to the Committee of the Privy Council appointed to "superintend the application of any sums voted by Parliament for the purpose of promoting education." The committee recruited inspectors, "Her Majesty's Inspectors" (HMIs), so that they could examine and report on the efficiency of schools receiving government grants. The reports were generally subjective, each inspector applying his own standards but rarely denying grants to the school.

However, as the cost of education increased and the national income decreased after the futile Crimean War, the question of efficiency—value for money—became more critical; and in 1862 the era of "payment by results" (performance contracting) began. The annual treasury grant paid to any school would depend on attendance and success; for example, "every scholar attending [class]. more than 200 times in the morning or afternoon, for whom 8 shillings is claimed, forfeits 2s. 8d. for failure to satisfy the inspector in reading, 2s. 8d. in writing, and 2s. 8d. in arithmetic."

This example shows the spirit and intent of the Code of 1862. It was revised, amended, and extended, but it was always explicit that the teachers' salaries depended on how their children performed. At first, since we had no other schools, the code applied only to grants paid to denominational schools. In 1870, we wisely emulated the school board system in the United States—not to replace parochial schools but to supplement them. The new school boards were born into this era of payment by results.

It was undoubtedly a pernicious system, and it is easy to catalogue its baneful influence on education. If you are to put a teacher's livelihood at risk by evaluating his or her work by the crudest of measures, then in self-defense the teacher will seek means to outwit the evaluator—in our case, Her Majesty's Inspector. The reports of the Victorian inspectors still survive, and at least two wrote their biographies, HMI Sneyd Kinnersley and HMI Holmes. Sneyd Kinnersley catalogues some of the defensive machanisms adopted by teachers, the most outrageous of which was used at one school where bright pupils were borrowed from a neighboring school and presented for inspection so that the school's examination prospects might be improved. Unfortunately, the inspector recognized some of the faces from a previous examination.

The inspectors relied on printed cards for the evaluation of arithmetic. In his 1870 Education Act Commemorative Lecture, Sir Alec Clegg described the recollections of a miner's son who was in school during that era: "At exam times these cards were handed out to the pupils to be solved. In some way the schoolmasters would get possession of these cards in advance of the exams. By exchange of information, they could work on the answers along with the scholars to be examined, so they usually passed the exams."

The result of each examination was entered on the teacher's "parchment," which was a record of his success or failure in outwitting inspectors. It was not unknown for retiring, successful teachers to sell their parchments so that, with a little forgery, they could be used to further the prospects of less successful colleagues.

Teachers developed techniques of signaling information at examination time. For example: hands in pockets = multiplication, hands behind back = subtraction. Where reading was concerned, nonreaders were coerced into learning the primer by heart, and inspectors occasionally noted apparently fluent readers holding the book upside down. What had begun as a national educational venture tended to degenerate into a battle between inspector and inspected. In the inspectors' reports can be found such petulant complaints of dishonesty as, "A child in appearance about ten may in the day school be presented as under six or in the night school as over twelve." (HMI Stokes).

The inspectors had their moments of triumph. The

teachers could present the near ineducable for exemption from the examination, but the exemption was rarely given. The dialogue went thus: "If you put a boy down and say that he is dull, the inspector comes in and says to the boy, 'How old are you?' The boy answers, 'Nine, sir.' And the inspector comments, 'Oh, nine. An intelligent boy this. As you came along to school this morning, did you see any grass?' The boy replies, 'Yes, sir.' 'What color was it?' queries the inspector. 'Green, sir,' says the boy. 'Very intelligent boy this,' concludes the inspector, 'What did you put him on the exemption list for?' " (Miss E.M. Castle, evidence to the Cross Commisssion, 1886).

Education degenerated into a year of slaving to cover every possible permutation on the inspector's ragbag of questions. His stock essay questions were carefully prepared. HMI Brookfield preserved one essay written by a boy whose spirit rose up against the indoctrination and preparation of his teacher. The subject was horse racing, and the teacher had prepared his pupils to approach this topic with Victorian virtue. "The race horse," wrote the boy, "is a nobel animal used very cruel by gentlemen. Races are very bad places. None but wicked people know anything about races. The last Derby was won by Mr. Anson's Blinkbonny, a beautiful filly rising four. The odds were twenty-to-one against her, thirty started, and she won only by a neck." At least one small soul would not let his creative spirit be crushed by the dreary examination treadmill.

In time, however, there came to be recognized a physical and psychological effect on the children that was diagnosed as "overpressure," and the London School Board set up a committee to investigate this phenomenon. Dr. Creighton Brown, Her Majesty's Commissioner in Lunacy, chairman of the committee, claimed that "46.1 percent of the children attending elementary schools in London, suffer from habitual headaches," and he drew a lurid picture of "knots of children standing in the playground, neglecting hopscotch and skipping rope and speculating like precocious gamesters on their chances of passing and the questions that are most likely to be asked them. The infantile lip that would curl with contempt at any reference to a witch or a ghost, quivers with anxiety at the name of a government inspector and the examination day has appropriated to itself much of the foreboding which used to be reserved for the day of judgment."

Teachers had little love for the system, and at the conference of the National Union of Elementary Teachers at Leicester in 1884, a resolution was passed stating that "payment by results is unsound in theory and injurious in practice." The system had little public support. Thomas Smythe, a representative of the working classes, assured the Cross Commission in 1886 that he had been educated before the days of payment by results, but he always found that his teachers "had an honest aspiration to turn out the best work they could."

The major and progressive school boards like the London School Board had scant admiration for inspection, and the London School Board assured its teachers that "the Board does not pay so much attention to the percentage of passes at the Government Inspection." Even the inspectors themselves doubted the value of their work. HMI Matthew Arnold, poet and son of the great headmaster of Rugby, despaired and described the whole system as "a game of mechanical contrivance in which the teacher will, and must more and more, learn how to beat us." By the turn of the century "performance contractings" and "evaluation" were so discredited that they passed from our educational history, leaving a teaching profession hostile to anything vaguely suggestive of testing to national standards.

•

You may say that teachers today in America would never stoop to the game of "mechanical contrivances" as did

Victorian teachers. But was there not some evidence in the Texarkana project that children had been coached for the test? My own brief and happy encounter with American teachers and principals has led me to suspect that "their honest aspiration to turn out the best work they could" is somewhat hindered by the threat of tests like the Metropolitan Achievement Test, which has its own unhappy history of teachers "teaching to the tests."

Although payment by results disappeared from English education, some degree of monitoring was introduced by the tests set for scholarship to the grammar school. In 1944, these tests became the Eleven Plus examination, to which all children were subjected. Brian Simon is prepared to argue that the English predilection for tracking (streaming) can be traced to the need for elementary schools to aquit themselves well in getting children through to the grammar school. Certainly, public esteem was earned by those schools with good "track records" in the grammar school entrance stakes.

What is even more certain is that the pressures of that examination distorted educational aims within schools and resurrected some of the malpractice of payment by results—that is, copying tests and coaching for tests to the exclusion of wider educational objectives. When Stewart Mason, director of education for Leicestershire, wished to introduce comprehensive education to the county in 1957, he cited the effect of the examination on the primary schools. Mason said, "At one time only the very worst, it seemed, were prepared to allow it to distort the curriculum. Every year I grow a little more uneasy. It seems that increasingly we are reaching a point as a result of social pressure where this can only be said of the very best, where the head is a person of very strong character as well as of very liberal outlook." The Eleven Plus, a bizarre examination by educational standards, has now gone the way of payment by results.

Without evaluation, how is it possible to monitor national norms? It seems that we must accept some degree of evaluation. We have no evaluation based industry, but since the war the National Foundation for Educational Research (NFER) has attempted some modest research. In 1972, NFER was assigned the task of evaluating national standards in mathematics. It is interesting to note how cautiously the director, A. Yates, approaches the task. There will be no wholesale or nationwide testing; only light sampling will be employed. As Yates puts it, "Lightly scraping the surface, given time, can have the same effect as digging a dirty great hole." Even with this promise the project is viewed with suspicion, however, and I know at least one headmaster who would have no part in trials of the item bank. I think that the NFER has placed its priorities correctly:

> *If we were to issue periodic scores, that purported to represent the levels of attainment of the nation's children, which would be announced in the six o'clock news along with the Financial Times Index and the exchange rate, we might well do a profound disservice to the educational system and all who serve.*

As for those whose lives are devoted to testing and evaluating, Queen Victoria's Inspector Sneyd Kinnersley has this to say: "It is a pleasant profession for a peacably minded man. If I were asked to state its principal charm, I should say it is *irresponsibility*." He admitted that the task involved work but wisely pointed out that work does not kill, whereas worry does. And there is no worry or responsibility to the testing industry. Testing and evaluating create no ulcers; those are reserved for the tested.

There is little for American principals to learn from our experience, except perhaps to reach for that archangel status and remember that once there were principals who, finding testing objectionable in principle and detail, rejected it. Where testing can be seen to serve no real educational purpose, it deserves rejection.

Whether we are principals or headmasters, we are accountable, not to some external authority to be placated with percentage passes, but only to those we teach, so that they may one day say of us—as Thomas Smythe said of his teachers—that we had "an honest aspiration to turn out the best work we could." That endeavor, of course, cannot be measured by norms, standardized tests, or percentile ranks.

POWER AND THE NATIONAL ASSESSMENT OF EDUCATIONAL PROGRESS

PAUL A. OLSON

Paul A. Olson is director of the Study Commission on Undergraduate Education and the Education of Teachers at the Nebraska Curriculum Development Center, University of Nebraska at Lincoln. The Study Commission, which works with school based teacher education, has published two reports of particular interest to school administrators: The University Can't Train Teachers *and* What Is School-Community Based Teacher Education?

Mr. Olson is also a medievalist and gardener.

I have been asked to write about the National Assessment of Educational Progress. Though I am not a specialist in assessing educational progress, I am a citizen. I have children. I have taught in schools and colleges in all kinds of cultural contexts, and I have an interest in how people, communities, and school systems are valued by other people or institutions. In particular, I am interested in how the powerless or different in America are valued, and encouraged to value themselves, by the powerful and "well-respected" people of our world.* My thesis is that the National Assessment represents:

*I share with contemporary ethnomethodology the assumption that a society is characterized by its own accounting and describing procedures and that "social order is precarious, having no existence apart from those accounting and describing procedures." A national assessment is not just an assessment, but an assessment by *someone* and, therefore, to others a social interaction. Compare Nicholas and Carolyn Mullins, *Theories and Theory Groups in Sociology* (New York, 1973), pp. 194-96.

- An assessment based on national norms in a period when the courts are saying that local norms and parent or community concerns are crucial

- An assessment that offers the appearance of a national consensus with respect to what education should do only by virtue of leaving out many of the concerned parties

- An assessment that, at best, asks powerless communities to assess themselves in terms provided by the powerful.

The notion of a National Assessment of Educational Progress is not a new notion. It is at least a century old, and should perhaps be celebrated in the Bicentennial. The original Department of Education bill, prepared as part of the Reconstruction legislation in 1867, included a plan "to enforce education, without regard to race or color, upon the population of all such states as shall fall below a standard to be established by Congress."[1] This language was rejected; had it been passed at the time of the creation of the Department of Education, the National Assessment would now be over a hundred years old, and we would have a clearer understanding of its effects. Instead, however, Congress chose much milder language calling for a Department of Education that would be a service organization to the people of the United States:

> *Be it enacted by the Senate and House of Representatives of the United States of America in Congress assembled, that there shall be established, at the city of Washington, a Department of Education, for the purpose of collecting such statistics and facts as shall show the condition and progress of education in the several States and Territories, and of diffusing such information respecting the organization and management of schools and school systems, and methods of teaching, as shall aid the*

> *people of the United States in the establishment and maintenance of efficient school systems, and otherwise promote the cause of education throughout the country.*[2]

It is clear from the debate record that "the people of the United States" means "the people in their natural local communities" and not the nation-state.

The thinking that led the Congress to reject a national standard and its enforcement is still alive. It is alive in the Supreme Court's statement in the recent Detroit desegregation decision, which, for better or for worse, affirms that community control of education is not only an old tradition in this country but confers significant educational benefits in that it permits the development of an organic relation between school and home and the creation of experiment, competition, and new directions that improve education:

> *No single tradition in public education is more deeply rooted than local control over the operation of schools; local autonomy has long been thought essential both to the maintenance of community concern and support for public schools and to quality of the educational process. . . . Thus, in San Antonio School District v. Rodriguez, 411 U.S., 1, 50, we observed that local control over the educational process affords citizens an opportunity to participate in decision-making, permits the structuring of school programs to fit local needs, and encourages experimentation, innovation and a healthy competition for educational excellence."*[3]

This thinking also comes prominently into the various federal and circuit cases that interpret education as an extension of child rearing, such as *Pierce v. Society of Sisters, Meyer v. Nebraska, Farrington v. Tokushige,* and *Wisconsin v. Yoder.*[4]

Respect for the local, unique culture as the prime determinant in the construction of educational processes is also alive in the several recent court decisions giving people the right to education in their own language (*Aspira, Lau,* and *Portales*). It speaks through the various decisions that require that teachers be educated and licensed to fit local conditions and job conditions and job descriptions (*Mercado and Chance v. New York City Board of Examiners; Walston v. Nansemond County*). And I feel that something of the spirit of the original effort to avoid a national standard speaks in Justice William O. Douglas's opinion in *DeFunis v. Odegaard*, a case that the rest of the Court regarded as moot. Douglas wrote of the Law School Admissions Tests:

> *Insofar as the LSAT tests reflect the dimensions and orientation of the Organization Man, they do a disservice to minorities. I personally know that admissions tests were once used to eliminate Jews. How many other minorities they aim at I do not know. . . . The invention of substitute tests might be made to get a measure of an applicant's cultural background, perception, ability to analyze, and* his or her relation to groups.[5] (Emphasis added)

In looking at the LSATs, Douglas affirms that the candidate's relation in his local group *is* important in norm construction and that different groups may look to different thinkers: the Native American of Washington state to Chief Seattle or Chief Joseph rather than Adam Smith or Marx; black groups to Sekou Torae or Senghor rather than to Smith or Marx; and so on. In short, in a variety of cases and given a variety of problems, the courts have fairly consistently seen education as a local matter, an extension of child rearing, requiring different approaches, norms, and works for different people.

There is, I think, an alternative to the Court view which for the want of a better word, I shall call the "professional" view. By "professional" in this context, I do not mean the competent view, or the view that helps children learn most and best. Rather, I mean the view that has come into fashion as defining what spokesmen for professional education agencies are expected to defend when they address the public—the view to which the person entering the profession tends to be tribalized. This view is formulated well by Stephen Bailey of the American Council on Education:

> *The language [of local control] falls pleasingly on the ears of local school board members, superintendents, teachers and parents; and it may well be a barrier to arbitrariness at higher levels. But the term "local-control"—powerful as it is as a political shibboleth—flies in the face of the fiscal and administrative realities of state and federal grants in aid and the standardizing effect of professionalism upon public education across the land. This struggle between shibboleth and reality is one of the political anomalies of educational finance. Part of the political tension which surrounds and infuses contemporary educational finance controversies derives from the fact that in a highly interdependent, technological world, the myth of local control of educational policy is increasingly unrealistic.*[6]

I wish to argue that the National Assessment of Educational Progress, in its power base, conception, creation, and execution, runs against what I have described as the Court view and supports what I have called the professional view. Fundamental to the professional view, I think, is that education is an entity and that it is the function of national programs to clarify what that entity is, to develop a "delivery system" to deliver that entity to children, and to certify that the delivery has, in fact, been made.

One history of the origin of the National Assessment of Educational Progress appears in a study of testing by the Youth Project, a group related to Ralph Nader's organization.[7] According to that study, the NAEP program was itself the product of no local educational impulse or public debate. It had its source in a committee established by the Carnegie Corporation in 1964 to examine the feasibility of developing some mechanism for assessing the educational programs and learning levels in the United States.

By 1965, when it was provided a grant of $260,000, the committee had already developed descriptions of necessary and allegedly unique testing instruments and had got the Psychological Corporation, Science Research Associates, the American Institute for Research, and Educational Testing Service to help develop the instruments. The Ford Foundation put $496,000 into the effort in 1966, and Carnegie put in $640,000 more the following year. Commissioner Harold Howe first involved the Office of Education directly in 1968, and with a grant of $1 million. Opposition developed from the American Association of School Administrators, and then a former president of AASA was made chairman of the National Assessment Committee. An "independent" supervisor of the committee—the Education Commission of the States, a Carnegie supported coalition—took over supervision of the National Assessment for the Carnegie Corporation. The executive director of ECS, Wendell Pierce, had in turn served on the ETS Board of Directors from 1965 to 1968.* In testimony before the Mondale Committee in 1972, Francis Keppel, after giving a

---

*This information all comes from the Youth Project study (pp. 123-29); it also shows that eight of eleven members of the original exploratory committee (Ralph Tyler, John J. Corson, Devereux C. Josephs, Roy E. Larsen, Lloyd W. Morrisett, Katherine McBride, Melvin Barnes, and Paul Reinert) had had close relationships—many of them long standing—with both the Carnegie Corporation and ETS. In 1967, the AASA recommended that its members refuse to cooperate. The Carnegie Corporation expanded the committee to include several new organizations; named George Brain, former head of AASA, chairman of the new Committee on Assessing the Progress of Education, to succeed Ralph Tyler; and placed the committee with the Education Commission of the States. The Youth Project argues that "the organization which had criticized the program in 1966 had been co-opted" by the end of 1968.

very attractive account of the disappearance of opposition among school adminstrators and state people, remarked on the NAEP as follows:

> *There is an extraordinary hopeful possibility that out of this movement we can develop measures by the school—the program within the school building—which will make it possible . . . to rifle-shoot direct funds to improve the performance within a school building.*
>
> *I am making a contrast here between the school system as a whole—all the primary, junior high, and high schools, treated as a unit—because the important data on equal educational opportunity gets lost in that aggregate. It would seem to me essential that we disaggregate it; get the unit of measure down to the school itself, the place where the individual in charge can be held more responsible, in my judgment, than the superintendent.*
>
> *On the other hand, we would not, by these techniques, be overburdening the individual children with a whale of a lot of measures. A pretty good case can be made that too much testing is not good for children. By sampling technique, it is, as far as I can see, possible to reduce the amount of testing and still give the responsible authorities like yourself the data that you need for public policy. . . .*
>
> *. . . When the Congress and the executive branch are satisfied that the technical problems are under control, the Office of Education could then both collect data on such a basis and make public reports. Neither is possible today.*
>
> *You will have noted that this testimony puts special emphasis on the need of assessing what the institution, the particular school, is accomplishing, rather than on a school system as a whole or on how the individual learner is performing. Presumably, in*

> *years to come, this committee and the Congress will want to have aggregate data in order to understand the extent of variation from the goal of equal educational opportunity as expressed in measures of what pupils have learned. A child who cannot read or cipher up to a minimum standard cannot take advantage of educational opportunities. But for the national purpose, if remedial action is to be effective, this information has to be applied to the basic management unit—the individual school—where something can be done and where responsibility can be lodged.*[8]

Thus Keppel argued for the usefulness of the National Assessment not only as a kind of graph of where we are educationally in the nation, but as a different kind of local control and local management. Keppel also argued for the Office of Education's using NAEP nationally to "both collect data" and "make public reports"—that is, in national management. (Keppel's father was president of Carnegie from 1923 to 1942, and Keppel himself became a trustee of the corporation in 1970. Carnegie has, furthermore, pushed fairly consistently for national and a standardized management of education.) If I understand Mr. Keppel's testimony correctly, local judgments would be made using national tools. Once an outside group has established what the "accounting and describing" procedures are to be, the social order has been changed, no matter what the judgments are that emerge from examining the accounts.[9]

•

If the National Assessment originally came out of a fairly limited circle of consultation, its development was designed to make it have a wider, more persuasive clientele.

After the "exercises" (the National Assessment's substitute for "test items") were developed, they were reviewed by the following "lay" groups: AAUW, AFL-CIO, students in colleges of education, NAACP, National Citizens Committee of Christians and Jews, National Congress of Parents and Teachers, state PTAs, a range of school board associates, and the U.S. Chamber of Commerce Education Committee.[10]

These lay groups were asked three questions: 1) would you object to having the exercise used with your child? 2) would any important group object to the use of the exercise? and 3) is the exercise "sufficiently important to risk offending certain segments of the population?"[11] Lay people were *not* asked whether the items measured the goals of education as conceptualized in their local community or whether they measured, in any sense, the capacity to function in an expressive or vocational or any other competent, adult role in their community. Lay participants were apparently asked only if they found something offensive in the exercises, or if they thought that some other competent group in their community would. (How the lay participants were to find out if other people would find an item offensive is difficult to know.)

The lay participation group appears to have been predominantly middle class and predominantly white. It seems not to have included those stubborn, brilliant, determined cultural groups that have, year after year in the last decade, raised the right questions in the courts about their right to have education conducted according to the norms of their own community and assessed in terms of them: the Mennonites in Wisconsin; the Nation of Islam; the Puerto Ricans in the Aspira organization; the sorts of organizations that were the plaintiffs in the *Lau, Portales,* and *San Fepile del Rio* cases; and the Appalachian groups that have tried to achieve culture based education in Appalachia.

National Assessment items were later assessed for "subject matter" validity by people nominated by the International Reading Association, the National Council of

Teachers of English, the National Council of Teachers of Mathematics, the National Association of Industrial Teacher Educators, the National Science Teachers Association, the American Industrial Arts Association, the American Vocational Association, the National Art Education Association, the National Council for the Social Sciences, the American Historical Association, the Music Educators National Conference, and the National Association of Schools of Music.[12] The professional societies' nominated reviewers were asked to find out if the item: 1) sampled the objective indicated; 2) indicated the correct answer to an exercise; and 3) had any ambiguities or other flaws. Reviewers were also asked to estimate how many people of various ages would answer the items correctly.

Again it is clear that the picture of "professionalism" represented by the professional societies asked to nominate reviewers is not catholic. Why only the predominantly white educational associations and not other groups, such as the College English Association, the Indian Historical Society, or the educators who publish in Quinto Sol publications or in the *Black Scholar*? Why the "applied" professional societies and not the theory oriented ones, such as the American Institute for the Biological Sciences, the Linguistic Society of America, the American Physical Association, or the Mathematical Association of America? It is, I think, because a "national assessment" almost by definition seeks to homogenize things. Unique culture bearers do not get in, nor do the uniquely gifted. One doubts that the Noam Chomskys of the world were asked to review items having a linguistic or psycholinguistic content (writing, reading, literature).

The court decisions in *Lau*, *Portales*, and *Aspira*, which assert the right to be educated in one's own language, are particularly significant to the National Assessment efforts. All the NAEP schedules that I have reviewed use English as their only idiom. Perhaps significant to the reading examination is recent research showing that English-speaking children read best that material which used the idiom, landscape, iconography, and stories that are used in their own area and culture.*

The "exercise" construction process that this sort of administrative arrangement leads to may be characterized by Lawrence Freeman's description of the National Assessment of Musical Performance,[13] which was written for a preliminary version of our Study Commission's final report:

> *This assessment—supported by a USOE grant—was constructed in the following way. Exercises "were developed to measure the extent to which young people are achieving the objectives compiled by music professionals in 1965." The resultant test exercises include singing familiar songs, e.g., "America" and "Are You Sleeping"; repeating unfamiliar musical material; improvising; perfoming from notation; and perfoming a prepared piece. Precise criteria for judging performance were then developed. For example, in singing "America," "pitch" was judged unacceptable if a pitch was closer to the next half step than to the right original pitch; four or more pitch errors led to classifying a response as unacceptable. In improvising melody, an acceptable response had to begin "within two measures of the end of the stimulus, must not have deviated in tempo by more than 10 per cent and must have not contained more than two unidentifiable pitches."*

*This was first suggested by Paulo Freire and has been confirmed by Yetta and Ken Goodman in their researches on Appalachia. I am at a loss to know what earthly use is served by reporting reading scores by race, unless genetic assumptions are involved. Present linguistic research might suggest classification of reading scores in terms of first language of child or school; regional or socio-economic dialect (e.g., children who speak Gullah dialect); literacy and primary vocabulary of parents; and availability of books in the home.

And in sight-singing "a pitch was considered to be incorrect if it was closer to the next half step than to the right pitch. Three pitch errors and one change of key were allowed in an acceptable performance. However, if one of the major second intervals were maintained consistently, the other interval may have been sung at a minor second interval without causing the responses to be scored unacceptable."

. . . Nowhere in the materials that have been examined is there an explicit statement about the social and cultural function of music. In the performance test referred to, performance of music is apparently viewed as an individual, not a group act; performance was required apparently in a situation in which the individual was isolated from situations which might inspire enjoyable or effective exercises in music. Music performance is apparently thought of as a solo performance in Carnegie Hall before silent, critical strangers. The instances of familiar music, "America" and "Are You Sleeping," are familiar "school" pieces, not pieces that students would enjoy spontaneously rendering. And finally the performance of music is seen as an extremely technical process with the standards derived almost exclusively from Western European "high culture" music and Western European conceptions of pitch, tonality, harmony, and performance-timing. . . .

. . . And the notion of "music" implicit in the assessment is apparently non-American, with little recognition that the local sources of inspiration for American "classical" music—extensions of Western European music—have been primarily indigenous black and regional cultural music. If the notions of music implicit in the assessment are those out of which teaching is supposed to arise, one can hypothesize the decimation of those indigenous sources of inspiration.[14]

Freeman's rhetoric may be a little flamboyant, but his perception is, I think, essentially accurate. Somewhere in *Notes Toward a Definition of Culture,* T. S. Eliot remarks on the importance to English life of the survival of Welsh language and culture: "For the transmission of a culture—a peculiar way of thinking, feeling, and behaving—and for its maintenance, there is no significant safeguard more reliable than a language." And to survive, Eliot maintains, it must be an artistic language; "otherwise the spread of education will extinguish it."

Part of the unique artistic language of a culture is its musical language. Part of the function of fostering distinct cultures is to preserve unique regional modes of adapting to various nonhuman ecological systems. A multitude of cultures is a unique resource in a time in which, because of slim environmental resources, we are required to learn less standardized ways of habituating ourselves to extreme environments. To require extremely refined performance in one idiom as a measure of "educational progress" and to ignore quality performance in another idiom—say Sioux flute scales, which use non-Western scales—is not only to take away an expressive part of a culture. It is to leave a void that may have extreme effects on other aspects of a culture's adaptive or constructive capacities.

•

It is possible to see how much meaningful educational progress can be measured by looking at what, as the National Assessment was constructed, was deemed offensive: for example, questions touching family financing, references to specific minority groups, literary passages with sexual references, and questions dealing with birth control or religion. Exercises dealing with human rights were deemed offensive unless more exercises were added "dealing with . . . responsibilities in a free society." Deleted also were references to sex, unwed mothers, divorce, whisky, the FBI, the president, communism, and specific organizations such as the Ku Klux Klan and labor unions; references to violence or cruelty; exercises with "inappropriate" words or phrases, such as "sportive ladies leave their doors ajar"; exercises that might be interpreted as putting national heroes or the police and other authorities in an unfavorable light; and exercises about the Civil War that suggest the North was better than the South. Senator Joe McCarthy, that demagogue and hate maker of the 50s, is to be presented, according to the National Assessment, in a light that is neither too critical nor too favorable.[15]

Consider, if you will, a national assessment of educational progress that removes all of these areas of reality as "improper for questioning." What do you have left of the tough adult realities for which children must be educated, which they must learn to think about and deal with? In *The Changing Nature of Man*, Jan Van den Berg describes an inoffensive sex education lesson and asks, "What is left out of the picture of adult sexuality? Everything! The desire, the pain, the ecstasy—everything that makes adult sexuality meaningful." So it is here. The strictures against offensive material force the test to leave out everything—everything that makes education for competent adulthood worth struggling for in any specific culture or given any specific intellectual paradigm.

To measure national educational progress in terms that are tangential to survival in a specific community may not seem problematic so long as the assessment is only an assessment—something that somehow floats above the world of local decision making and action in child rearing, above the pictures of "what is" and "how to live" that we give the young.

But National Assessment is not that in most areas. Systemwide curriculum decisions (and not at the local building level, as Keppel expected) are often based on the assessment. Keppel himself saw NAEP as a tool of national management. The "Summer Institute" report to the Office of Education by B. O. Smith and others, which was connected to program development envisaged in connection with educational revenue sharing ("Renewal") and to follow-ups to the Renewal effort, proposed using the National Assessment to determine priorities in schools using discretionary funds—for curriculum reform, teacher training, and management reform.* Representative Albert Quie's proposal for Title I, in many ways a humane proposal, would have allocated Title I funds on the basis of nationwide criterion referenced tests in math and reading, tests that almost surely would have come to be the National Assessment. As Guthrie and Emrick remark in their follow-up study on the Quie proposal, no "curriculum neutral" tests can be created. Therefore, a national criterion referenced test implies a national "course of study":

> *Similarly, in defining a domain, considerations of curricula are important. If the domain definition were (or attempted to be) inclusive of all current curricula, it probably would resemble current standardized achievement tests. If the definition were curriculum-free, it might resemble an IQ test. If the definition were restricted to "dominant" curricula, it might be invalid for use with pupils whose educational experience is based on quite different curricula. This is to say, we do not yet fully understand the relative impacts of variations in curricula on educational attainment. It is most likely that these curricular variations produce corresponding differences in performance. . . . It should be noted that a characteristic shared by most currently used domain-referenced and other criterion-referenced systems of measurement is that they were developed in conjunction with specific methods and materials of instruction (e.g., Hively et al., 1973). For this reason*

---

*The "Summer Institute" on "Improvement and Reform of American Education" was an LTI-like effort mounted at the time "Renewal" was proposed. It continued after Renewal was rejected. The proposal to which I refer was included in a draft report of the institute, by Smith and others, which was circulated in the Office of Education.

they are imbedded within particular curricula. Any nationwide application which attempts to take into account variations in curricula, therefore, appears fraught with problems, given the current state of the art. . . . The creation of a National Commission on Educational Disadvantage, as suggested by Quie, for the purpose of determining the standard and developing a test would not alleviate any of the above developmental problems.[16]

Guthrie and Emrick also note that the Quie formula as proposed in HR 5163 would represent a sharp break with American legal and congressional traditions.

•

It may be useful to ask of any National Assessment proposed in the future, "Were the Navajos asked? Did the Mennonites approve of it as representing their view of educational progress? What did the people of Harlem Prep, or any of the other successful black or Chicano academies, say about it? In view of the overwhelming evidence that people learn to read and cipher, as well as to sing or draw or build, best in the idiom of their immediate environment and the educational problems it poses for their own unique cognitive frames, and in view of the evidence that moving into the ecumenical world meaningfully requires that one first be at home in one's own world, it appears that the national interest would best be served by putting intense pressure on relating the evaluative process to:

- local language and family or clan life
- local social structures and employment situations
- local natural environmental constraints
- the cognitive folk structures of the particular district and school in which the education is done.

If assessments are to be a tool at the building level, they have to permit principals, staff, and parents to relate the assessment to an area's unique culture, resources, problems, environment, and plans for the future. And no assessment by itself can do that. That takes thought, and a quality too little appreciated in the language of present management—wisdom.

NOTES

1. Compare Donald R. Warren, *To Enforce Education: A History of the Founding Years of the United States Office of Education* (Detroit: Wayne State University Press, 1974), pp. 78, 204-05, and 58-97 passim.
2. Warren, *To Enforce Education*, pp. 204-05.
3. *Milliken v. Bradley*, July 1974.
4. *Pierce v. Society of Sisters*, 268 U.S. 510, 534-35; *Meyer v. Nebraska*, 262 U.S. 390, 401-02; *Farrington v. Tokushige*, 273 U.S. 284, 293-94; and *Wisconsin v. Yoder*, 406 U.S. 205.
5. William O. Douglas, opinion in *DeFunis v. Odegaard*, reproduced in *Study Commission* (May 1974), supplement.
6. Joel S. Berke and Michael W. Kirst, *Federal Aid to Education: Who Benefits? Who Governs?* (Lexington: Lexington Books, 1972), pp. 22-23.
7. Youth Project, *The Project on Educational Testing: Interim Report*, pp. 123-29.
8. Francis Keppel, "Statement," *Hearings Before the Select Committee on Equal Opportunity, Part 22: Education Information*, pp. 10950-52.
9. Warren, *To Enforce Education.*
10. Carmen J. Finley, *The National Assessment Approach to Exercise Development* (Denver: National Assessment of Educational Progress, 1970), p. 38. This is an official NAEP publication.
11. Ibid., p. 36.
12. Ibid., pp. 47-48.
13. Frank Rivas, *The First National Assessment of Musical Performance* (Denver: National Assessment of Educational Progress, 1974).
14. *Teacher Education in America* (Lincoln: Study Commission on Undergraduate Education and the Education of Teachers, in press), chap. 4. This publication, the final report of the Study Commission, will be available by writing the Study Commission, Andrews 338, University of Nebraska, Lincoln, Nebraska 68508.
15. The list of exercises deemed offensive is from Finley, *National Assessment Approach*, pp. 42-46. Finley summarizes these items as "types of material considered offensive" by "lay reviewers."
16. John A. Emrick, James W. Guthrie, and others, *The Use of Performance Criteria to Allocate Compensatory Education Funds* (Menlo Park: Stanford Research Institute, 1974), vol. 1, p. 22.

SOME COMMENTS ON POWER AND THE NAEP

RALPH W. TYLER

Ralph W. Tyler is director emeritus of the Center for Advanced Study in the Behavioral Sciences, Stanford, California. Earlier he was chairman of the Department of Education and dean of the Division of Social Sciences at the University of Chicago.

Since his retirement in 1967 from the directorship of the Center for Advanced Study in the Behavioral Sciences, he has engaged in a number of educational activities, including serving as consultant to Science Research Associates, the Hebrew University of Jerusalem, and University College, Dublin.

From 1969 to 1972 Mr. Tyler was the consultant to Neighborhood Education Center, a project of four elementary schools in Detroit that developed an effective program for educating disadvantaged children. He is currently in Ghana as one of the staff of the African Regional Seminar on Curriculum Development.

Since I served as chairman of the Exploratory Committee to Assess the Progress of Education and thus know how the National Assessment of Educational Progress was developed, I have been asked to comment on Paul Olson's article "Power and the National Assessment of Educational Progress" (see page 239).

Olson's article appears to be based on the same misunderstanding that led the Executive Committee of the American Association of School Administrators (AASA) in 1967 to oppose the program. The opposition, however, was withdrawn when the program was studied carefully by a committee of AASA, which then appointed a committee to work with the National Assessment to help it serve as fully as possible the needs of the schools.

The National Assessment is not "based on national norms"; it is not a test taken by individuals; and no scores are obtained, either for individuals or for schools. It reports the percentage of American children, youth, and young adults who have learned some of the important things that schools are teaching that will help us to identify the progress we are making and the problems we still face in becoming a literate population.

The National Assessment does not "offer the appearance of a national consensus with respect to what education should do only by virtue of leaving out many of the concerned parties." Our nation is both a multicultural society and a highly interdependent one. Constructive participation in a democracy requires certain knowledge, skills, and attitudes that are common to all. These commonalities include such things as understanding the rights guaranteed by the Constitution; recognizing the responsibilities of citizenship; the ability to read and write; basic arithmetic concepts and skills; understanding natural phenomena; understanding the operation of common technological devices; the development of employable skills; and the ability to enjoy music and art. Our national policy seeks to encourage diversity of cultural expression as well as the abilities and dispositions that make possible our common life.

The identification of the kinds of things that are important for full participation in our society (which are being taught in our schools) was not casually arrived at in the development of the National Assessment. Every educational objective was submitted to scholars and other experts for criticism and authenticity and to teachers and other school personnel to make certain that the objective was being taught in the schools. Each objective was submitted to panels of parents and other concerned citizens for their answers to two questions: 1) Is this something you believe important for American children to learn? and 2) Is this something you want your children to learn?*

Only those objectives that survived these three critical reviews are included in the assessment. For each new assessment, since the first one in 1969-70, the objectives are thoroughly reviewed by the same procedure before any new assessment exercises are developed.

The National Assessment is not asking "powerless communities to assess themselves in terms provided by the powerful." No community is asked to assess itself. The National Assessment used representative samples of people just as do the opinion polls. No geographic area smaller than a region is sampled. For example, in the field of reading, the National Assessment reports the percent of individuals nine years old, thirteen years old, seventeen years old, and those twenty-six to thirty-five years old who read and comprehended simple newspaper paragraphs, instructions for assembling household appliances, and other common reading selections. In reporting results to the public, the actual exercise is shown together with the percent that did it successfully. In this way, the readers of the report can see for themselves what these educational accomplishments are and so do not have to rely on "scores" and other abstract numbers.

The National Assessment reports for each exercise the percent that did it successfully in each age group in the nation as a whole, and in the Northeast, Southeast, Central,

---

*Olson is misinformed when he states the questions that he thought were asked of laymen. The questions asked were not whether or not an exercise was offensive, objectionable, or trivial.

and Western Regions. It also reports results for each exercise by size of city, by inner city, remainder of city, suburbia, and rural areas. The purpose of the assessment is to help us all to understand what progress is being made in developing these significant aspects of an educated citizenry and what the problems are that need to be given thoughtful attention. Until the beginning of the National Assessment, the public had no dependable information on most of these matters. For example, some years ago, a book called *Why Johnny Can't Read* became a best-seller, and many people were led to believe that most children were not learning to read.

Actually, the first assessment of reading showed that approximately 75 percent of the nation's thirteen-year-olds could read and comprehend materials similar to newspaper articles. It also revealed that a majority of thirteen-year-olds in the inner cities and the extreme rural areas could not. This information furnished a better basis for concerted efforts to be made that would increase literacy in the nation.

The Olson article devotes a good deal of space to the lack of assessment of bicultural, bilingual, and other similar educational programs. I believe that all educational programs benefit by valid and unbiased evaluation, and I have been working with other consultants to help schools develop such evaluation programs. In doing so, however, we must not lose sight of the larger community. Minority group isolation is incompatible with a democratic society. No minority group members should be barred from participating in our national life because they lack the necessary means of communciation, confidence, respect, and understanding of their rights and responsibilities as citizens. The National Assessment is helping the American people to identify the areas where many people are still isolated because of the limitations of their education and to seek ways of improving educational opportunities and effectiveness.

The instruments of the National Assessment are not ideal, and they require continuous study and development. For their purposes, however, they are better than any other instruments now in existence. Paul Olson's article may have a constructive effect if it calls attention to the National Assessment program and enlists thoughful educators in an effort to improve it.*

---

*Reports of the current and earlier assessments may be obtained from the National Assessment of Educational Progress, Education Commission of the States, 1860 Lincoln, Denver, Colorado 80203.

THE CURRENT TESTS

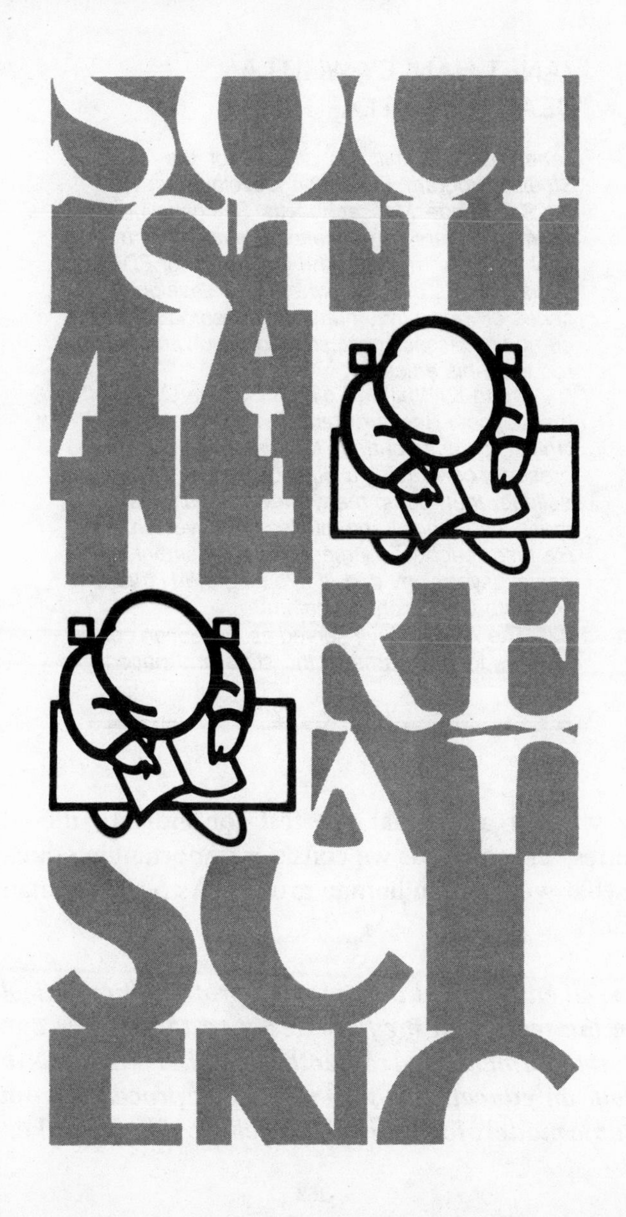

SOCIAL STUDIES TESTS

JANET HANLEY WHITLA
DEAN K. WHITLA

Janet Hanley Whitla is director of the Social Studies Program, Education Development Center, Cambridge, Massachusetts. She has worked for many years in educational evaluation and, until last year, directed the evaluation of EDC's social studies projects, where she developed a series of innovative, humanistic approaches to curriculum assessment, some of which are referred to in this article.

Dean K. Whitla is director of the Office of Instructional Research and Evaluation, Harvard University, Cambridge, Massachusetts. He is presently conducting a study of student growth in college that uses many new techniques for measuring ethical and intellectual development. He also teaches courses in measurement and social psychology and is directing the Harvard-Danforth Center on Teaching.

The Whitlas have served as evaluation consultants for programs at the state and national levels.

How we test and what we test for indicate the ideas, attitudes, and methods we consider important in education and what we value in human growth. As Neil Postman has put it:

> *. . . all educational practices are profoundly political in the sense that they are designed to produce one sort of human being rather than another—which is to say, an educational system always proceeds from some model of what a human being ought to be like.*[1]

One of the dilemmas facing us as we began this article was the perceived role of social education in the elementary school. While the importance of the social and emotional growth of the child is never questioned, the subject area where values about self and society are naturally formed and informed—social studies—does not receive much attention in the elementary school curriculum. In a 1972 study carried out for the Massachusetts Advisory Council on Education to survey the use and implementation of new programs in elementary science, we found that almost everyone in the schools, from teachers to principals, gave program priority to reading, mathematics, and science, with social studies ranking a poor fourth as an important area of instruction at the elementary level.[2] If the priority is elsewhere, this can't help but affect testing, as well as teaching.

To prepare ourselves for writing this article, we conducted an informal survey of our own, talking with several social studies supervisors in school systems across the country. The theme of the 1972 study was echoed in a variety of ways. Some supervisors acknowledged openly that testing in the social studies at the elementary school level was of no concern. We learned that in systems where comprehensive testing was ongoing, the test battery for assessing student growth was selected for the strength of its tests in the major areas of concern—reading and mathematics. The social studies subtest was the tagalong, used because it was part of a battery. We found no case where a social studies test influenced the choice of the battery. While our reporters were admittedly few in number, the major reviewers of achievement tests—such as *The Mental Measurements Yearbook*[3]—mention this same phenomenon.

In some respects, then, the tests we get may be the tests we deserve. For example, the STEP social studies test, published by Educational Testing Service, does contain items that require more thoughtful response and a higher level of analysis and problem solving, by comparison with other major achievement tests. Yet even the STEP test leaves much to be desired, both as an instrument to foster the growth of the child's mind and as a reflection of what we believe should be the goals of social studies education.

A social studies coordinator in a Massachusetts school system mentioned to us the narrow and restricted range of items in existing social studies achievement tests and his own interest in instruments that would tap larger concepts and cognitive skills. But when he tried to convince test makers at ETS to develop a test that went beyond the STEP, he was told that schools have not shown interest in such an instrument. In fact, they said, items of a broader nature were considered for the STEP test but were not included in it because of this lack of interest. The market for the broader items just isn't large enough, in the view of the test developers and publishers, to justify including them in the tests.

Is it possible that we are caught in a double bind of our own making? As educators, we speak of the need for tests that assess the full range of the child's cognitive and attitudinal development; as public servants, we seem most comfortable using measures of accountability in areas where we are more sure of what we are teaching—facts, definitions, sequences of events. We are encouraged in this by parents who find traditional content and nationally normed test scores acceptable, and by our own persistent belief that specific content is "teachable," ignoring all we have come to know about the lack of staying power of content learning and about the skills and understandings that better contribute to the child's growth of mind.

A classic instance of this dilemma was presented to us by the principal of an elementary school in the Midwest. As we note elsewhere in this article, we found the SRA social studies test particularly lacking in items that move beyond factual recall and definition levels. The principal we spoke to mentioned this inadequacy and added that the SRA test didn't match his school's curriculum and goals. But despite these limitations, the test is used in his school, and a great deal of analysis of the results is carried on, with comparisons made across grades and from year to year. The social studies subtest does not assess growth in areas this principal is concerned about, but he is generally pleased with the SRA because group scores can be compared from year to year and used for public relations purposes with the community. Again, this school chose the SRA battery in the first place because the mathematics subtest seemed more satisfactory than the mathematics component of the Iowa Test of Basic Skills, which they had used previously.

•

How do the major tests in the social studies look? A cursory comparison of four popular social studies achievement tests will give us a starting point.

STEP.[4] Of the major tests available in social studies achievement, the STEP (Sequential Tests of Educational Progress) appears to be the best. Items emphasize critical skills and understandings, rather than factual knowledge and simple application. Though some items of this type still remain, the items are varied, providing a large amount of data in a variety of modes to which students are asked to respond, including maps, pictures, cartoons, and reading passages. On some items, students are invited to develop a logical sequence of thought. The domains tested are classified as political science, sociology-anthropology, economics, history, and geography—a broad range of social sciences. The essential qualities of STEP seem more admirable than most such tests, but the central question is, how similar are they in what they measure to reading and general ability tests? Is there a uniqueness about social studies that

THIS IS HOW THEY SAY IT

Country→	Ivory Coast	Pakistan		Peru	
Language→	French	Urdu	Bengali	Spanish	Quechua
Hello	Bonjour bonh-*zhoor*	Assalamo Aleikum asa-*lah*-mo a-*lay*-koom	Assalamo Aleikum	Halo! Hola! a-*lo* oh-*la*	*ahl*-yin *yah*-ch
Please	S'il vous plait seel voo *play*	Meherbani meh-hair-*bah*-nee	Doyakoray doh-*yah*-koray	Por favor por fah-*vor*	ama-*hee*-na kaspa-*yi*-kee
Thank you	Merci mare-*see*	Shukria shoo-*kree*-a	Dhanyabad doh-*noh*-bad	Gracias *grah*-see-ahs	Dios pa-gra-soon-kee
Good-bye	Au revoir oh *vwáhr*	Khuda hafiz hoo-*dah* ha-*feez*	*ach*-cha *cho*-lee *ash*-cha *ash*-ee	Adiós ah-dee-*ohs*	*eh*-wa-*koh*-ma

9. How do people in Pakistan say "hello"?
   A Bonjour
   B Assalamo Aleikum
   C Hola
   D Halo

10. The French word for hello is written two ways in the table (Bonjour and bonh-*zhoor*). What does the second way show?
    A How to say the word
    B How to spell the word
    C What the word means
    D Where the word comes from

11. Where would you look to find out how to say "mother" and "father" in Bengali?
    A An encyclopedia
    B A social studies book
    C An English-Bengali dictionary
    D An almanac

STEP Social Studies Form 4A, grades 4, 5, and 6

they should indeed measure? For all their strengths, compared to other social studies tests, we doubt they tell you much that you didn't already know from your students' reading scores. Indeed, the correlations between social studies and reading scores for Form 4A of STEP are greater than .8. The series of items shown above illustrates this correlation. The items are classified as being in the domains of sociology and anthropology, but they seem to us far more closely related to reading and the language arts.

The step battery does not include a social studies test below the fourth grade.

Stanford Achievement Test.[5] Early editions of the Stanford social studies test have been widely criticized for the narrowness and information-specific form of the items. The 1972 version appears much improved, especially by the inclusion of items requiring inferences from maps and graphs. The items are intended to cover geography, history, economics, political science, anthropology, and sociology. The social science test is included in the battery for grades 2.5 and higher. Unfortunately, the item-content dilemma remains. For example, the following item, taken from Primary Level III (grades 3.5-4.4), seems to be the type of information item that does not deserve a place in a forty-four-item summary of an entire year's study:

The world's largest body of water is the—

- ☐ Indian Ocean
- ☐ Pacific Ocean
- ☐ Mediterranean Sea
- ☐ Mississippi River

The test for fourth and fifth graders is intended to emphasize "the structure of the social sciences, and a conceptual approach which relies heavily on inquiry skills" (Teacher's Manual). There are such items as:

The fastest way to make electric clothes dryers would be to:

- ☐ let two workers work together
- ☐ let each worker make a dryer
- ☐ give each worker whatever task he chooses
- ☐ give separate tasks to different workers

Intermediate Level I, Form A, grades 4.5-5.4, item 36

This question, however, only highlights the inability of such a simple item to serve as a medium for exploration of the significant underlying issue here: the truly interesting social issue of working patterns in our industrialized society.

A more interesting series of questions, also in Intermediate Level I, relies on chart reading and interpretation. A few of the items in that series follow:

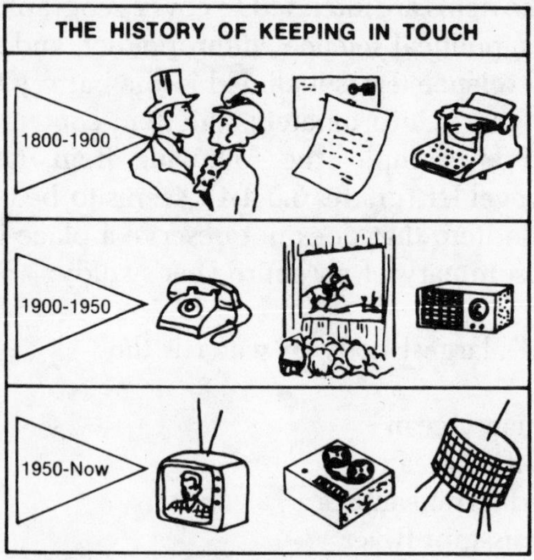

THE HISTORY OF KEEPING IN TOUCH

1800-1900

1900-1950

1950-Now

This chart shows that radio was invented before—

1 movies
2 typewriters
3 telephones
4 tape recorders

It should be noted, however, that the correlation between the social science and reading tests at the beginning of grade four is .87—almost impossible to improve on!

Norming and format for this series are adequate.

SRA Achievement Test.[6] Social studies is tested starting at the fourth grade. Judging by the reactions of school people with whom we talked, the SRA tests are well conceived and executed from a technical standpoint; that is, the tests have high reliability, and the age grading makes comparisons possible over a period of time and among schools. The range of domains covered is the same as in the previously mentioned batteries. However, the items draw heavily on recall and "reading" of graphs, maps, and cartoons, but demand little interpretation.

In this sample item, students are given a bar graph of percent of exports of different products from Latin American countries. They are then asked a series of questions, such as:

If everyone stopped driving automobiles, which country would be most affected by decrease in sales of gasoline?

☐ Chili ☐ Haiti ☐ Panama ☐ Venezuela

The economy of which country would be hurt if the sugarcane crop failed?

☐ Panama ☐ Venezuela ☐ Haiti ☐ Cuba

SRA Achievement Survey, Form E, Blue Level, grades 4-6.5

In this same Form E, a series of questions about an old political cartoon are somewhat more imaginative, albeit dated in today's world. Some recall and map-reading items of questionable social studies value round out this test. The next level test, for grades 6 to 8.5, includes twenty (out of forty) identical items—the poorer ones!

No one we talked to chose the SRA test because it seemed like a good test to them, but because it is part of a satisfactory battery (including reading and math) and because its technical strengths make it useful for public relations and accountability purposes.

Metropolitan Achievement Test.[7] Glancing through the MAT items, one quickly concludes that the authors have chosen a rather conservative route that does not reflect any of the curriculum changes occurring in social studies and that assumes, as one *Mental Measurements* reviewer stated it, that "such notions as process and the art of discovery have not yet contaminated teaching practice." In addition, specific items do not quicken an educator's pulse:

Which of the following is *not* a real factor in the growth of slum areas?

☐ disease ☐ unemployment
☐ crime ☐ climate ☐ don't know

What is the main crop grown today on the Great Plains?

☐ wheat ☐ apples ☐ citrus fruits
☐ timber trees ☐ don't know

Africa was long known as the "dark continent" because the—

- ☐ jungle foliage was dense
- ☐ area was largely unexplored
- ☐ native people had dark skin
- ☐ nights were long
- ☐ don't know

The chief reason that many qualified people don't vote is that they aren't—

- ☐ able to get to the polls
- ☐ interested in government
- ☐ knowledgeable about issues
- ☐ members of a political party
- ☐ don't know

Industry in the United States is concentrated in the—

☐ Southeast ☐ Northeast ☐ Midwest
☐ Far West ☐ don't know

Metropolitan Achievement Test, Form F, Advanced

All in all, the MAT is a test that helps us not one bit, except in a negative sense, to answer the question, what's worth knowing in the social studies?

•

In the world of standardized test making, there is a cluster of methodological concerns that are omnipresent in discussions of these instruments. It is unfortunate that such technical considerations as reliability and validity—often cited as indexes of effectiveness—tend to override educational considerations as the criteria for judging the merits of a test. While they are legitimate considerations, they are nevertheless part of a self-contained system of analysis. For example, the reliability of an item is generally determined by that item's correlation with the total test score. The assumption on which this internal system of validation rests is that the domain of knowledge to be tested is appropriately represented in the items. This is the assumption that ought to be challenged, given the nature of the social studies achievement tests we have inspected.

The most important dimension of a test is the fundamental quality of each item. What do we mean by quality? At the most general level, we mean knowledge that is "worth knowing." For example, in reviewing the major tests, we stumbled repeatedly on such items as:

The Eskimos never hunted
☐ buffalo ☐ seal ☐ walrus ☐ whale

Stanford Intermediate Level I, grade 5

In which part of the world does each family have more than one telephone?
☐ United States ☐ Asia ☐ Central America
☐ The graph does not say

SRA, grades 6-8 (based on a graph)

When a child takes a forty- or sixty-item test to summarize a year of thinking and studying in a subject; for even a small percentage of the items to be focused on such trivia raises questions about the value of the test to the child's development. The quality of an item, then, is our first criterion.

A second criterion is format. If we accept that human beings learn in several modes (through action, through image, as well as through symbol systems), at least the iconic as well as the symbolic should be represented in item formats. (We do see this trend in stimulus material in current tests, but the response choices are almost always in the language mode.) Otherwise, we are trying to measure learning that requires integration of a number of different mental operations through the single mode of language.

A third criterion for judging an item's worth would be its ambiguity level. If the item is set up for one correct answer, then there must indeed be only one correct answer possible. On anything "worth knowing," this is an all but impossible criterion to meet. These are dimensions on which the existing tests have long been criticized, and they are indeed appropriate areas for criticism.

Let's assume for the moment that the existing instruments are exemplars when judged by these criteria. In this best of worlds, what special value would the objective achievement test have to the educator? Three major advantages seem apparent:

- An administrative value: these tests are cost effective and easy to administer and score, and they provide explicit procedures for the teacher to follow before, during, and after the testing itself, plus an understood system for accounting to the community.

- A programmatic value: such tests allow tracking over a period of time of the performance of groups of children on a methodologically consistent measure. These tests also serve some diagnostic functions as tools to monitor individual and group performance in specified content and skill areas. They can also provide the data to help isolate problem areas by school or by classroom as a preliminary to providing support where it is needed.

- An educational function: if formulated to reflect something worth knowing, they can be one method, one evaluative tool for students and teachers to use in assessing learning and teaching.

These attributes are necessary but not sufficient in a system of evaluation in the social studies. By its very nature, the objective achievement test contains an inherent limitation: its format does not permit the development of sustained thinking or argument, but elicits a responsive, rather than an initiating or active, mode. School systems can become too dependent on objective formats—either the nationally normed tests or tests their own personnel have constructed—with the result that students develop great skill in selecting among options, but very little ability to develop and express their own ideas. In addition, no matter how exemplary an achievement test may be, it has other educational limitations:

- Such tests are derived from the basic notion of a right/wrong answer and invite an oversimplified structuring of the world, particularly of the social world, which is at the heart of social studies.

- Such tests seldom acknowledge differences in students' background, experience, and values that may legitimately influence interpretations of social studies content.

- The objective achievement test cannot assess some of the most critical dimensions of behavioral growth in the social studies, such as learning to communicate with others, to express and share ideas, to respect diverse points of view, to develop and defend one's position in the face of opposing argument.

This list could be expanded at some length, but the points seem so obvious that perhaps the better question is, what is the alternative to the existing nationally normed objective tests? Is it another achievement test in objective format? Probably not. Locally developed objective tests cannot help duplicating the problems of the published instruments, given the limitations of time and money in any local system. Criterion referenced testing, while a step in the right direction, is only a partial solution. In some ways it is, again, the easy way out. Item banks that are being built up by several companies around the country may eventually provide test items that are responsive to local goals and needs, but they do not solve the more basic problem of the "right answer" syndrome.

A fundamental problem—perhaps the most basic problem—is that teachers generally do not collaborate in developing instructional goals and a shared understanding of the purposes of the programs of their school. Without a shared view of goals and appropriate methods for assessing the degree to which these goals are achieved, teachers cannot present a coherent picture of learning outcomes to parents, and it becomes next to impossible for them to take a responsive and responsible role for evaluation in the classroom. It is our conviction that accountability must begin with teachers and students sharing responsibility for the many kinds of learning—from new ideas and methods of inquiry and analysis, to social competencies and personal insights—that should constitute the social studies.

In its most important sense, the process of evaluation is an extension of the human need to know, to reflect about where one has been in order to understand how far one has come and how far one can go. The term frequently applied to such activity is feedback—the use of information to judge the effect of previous experience and to consolidate or change behavior. So viewed, the process of evaluation becomes integral to the process of education, and forces different priorities. The most critical task becomes not measuring against a fixed standard, but giving the teacher and the class the tools for viewing in perspective, for summarizing and interpreting for themselves, what they are learning as they work together.

How do educators who wish to strike out in these directions in evaluating learning and teaching find examples of viable options? The next section takes on an admittedly personal tone and draws on our experience in attempting to devise just such options for new social studies curricula.

•

In evaluating learning from a humanistic perspective, we have found that it is important to take into account the special charactistics of the student age-group. Developmental psychologists have contributed much to our understanding of the stages of growth and development, from preschool children through adolescents. Knowledge about the expected parameters of the intellectual, personal, and social development of students in various age-groups is important not only in curriculum building but in developing evaluation techniques. For example, we know that students in upper elementary years are growing in social and intellectual maturity in the form of group orientation; cooperative behavior; orientations toward industriousness, reflective behavior, and language development; and the need to relate knowledge to personal concerns, to be imaginative, and to be expressive. Evaluation strategies that build on these natural resources of the students should include group as well as individual formats, permitting sharing of growth and learning as well as individual consolidation; they should emphasize problem posing and investigation; and they should include opportunities for imaginative and creative tasks.

In addition, knowledge and skills in the social studies cannot be fully defined by specified content outcomes; they involve sharing of learning, pleasure, and skill in expansion and exchange of ideas, along with personal immersion in knowledge and the process of knowing. Cognitive and psychosocial development go hand in hand. They must be seen as a unity, not divided into separate, sometimes competing arenas of learning.

Perhaps there is a dichotomy that is useful, however: that which distinguishes between the individual and the group. In terms of intellectual and personal development, students need to be self-conscious about their own growth of mind and their own competencies. They must also be able to find relationships between knowledge and daily living. In terms of social learning, students must have a means to judge their own behaviors and reactions in the classroom, because they affect the environment for other students, for the teacher, and for themselves.

We believe it is possible to support, as well as assess, the reciprocal nature of the learning process, involving groups as well as individuals in evaluation tasks and giving students a voice in educational assessment. It is ironic that youngsters have seldom been asked to participate in decisions affecting the process of their own education. Yet educators expect the social studies and humanities curricula in particular to provide young people with resources for making decisions affecting their public and private lives as citizens.

Figure 1, on page 277, shows an example of a simple classroom instrument to be used by a group of students.[8]

To allow the individual, the group, and the teacher to summarize the process of skill development—in in this case, developing and presenting a position and a logical argument to others, a core skill needed for participation in our society—instruments such as the one shown in Figures 2, 3, and 4[9] have proved extremely valuable and demonstrate how evaluation can serve an integrating educational function in the classroom.

This instrument is designed to be used by participants and observers whenever individuals role play, debate, or in some way try to convince others of something. The Position Sheet (Figure 2, page 278) is for an individual who is making some kind of presentation. The Observer Sheet (Figure 3, page 279) is filled out by members of the class, and the sheet entitled Analyzing Effectiveness (Figure 4, page 280) can be used by the teacher or players to learn how well their presentations were received and what improvements the class felt could be made.

In addition, at the EDC Social Studies Program, we use open-ended interviews to focus on the personal growth of ideas and the value of class activities; classroom environment checklists to give students an opportunity to evaluate materials and learning methods; and other self-evaluation exercises to permit review of concept mastery and reflection on attitudes.

The Social Science Education Consortium in Boulder,

FIGURE 1

Learning in a Small Group: What's Going On?

The following questions were developed for you to use with your group to help you understand better what has been going on while you were working on projects or other tasks. In addition to the concepts ahd information you used and learned, you also learned a lot about working together. The questions below may help you learn more about small group work itself and how it can operate effectively and efficiently.

Group Opinion

I. Where's the Group in Solving the Problem?

How far did you get in	Very far	Fairly far	Not so far
—defining the task?	____	____	____
—collecting the data?	____	____	____
—exchanging information?	____	____	____
—analyzing and evaluating data?	____	____	____
—making a decision?	____	____	____
Was the group			
—moving toward solving the problems? Why?	____	____	____
—bogged down? Why?	____	____	____

II. How Well Is the Group Working Together?

Are the members	Very well	Fairly well	Not so well
—sharing information?	____	____	____
—expressing different points of view helpful in seeing all sides of the issue?	____	____	____
—clarifying ideas of others?	____	____	____
—building on ideas of others?	____	____	____

III. How Well Are the Group Members Helping Each Other?

Are members	Very well	Fairly well	Not so well
—encouraging each other?	____	____	____
—keeping communication channels open?	____	____	____
—helping to settle disputes?	____	____	____
—getting the discussion off dead center?	____	____	____
—getting and giving feedback (i.e., checking out how you or others feel or think)?	____	____	____

IV. What Are the Problems You Think the Group Needs to Work on?

How can you work on these problems?

FIGURE 2

PRESENTING A POSITION TO THE CLASS

Position Sheet

Your Name______________________________

Your Position____________________________

1. What are your objectives in the case you are trying to present?
2. What arguments will you use to reach your goal?
3. What arguments do you think your opponent will make?
4. How will you counteract your opponent's arguments?
5. What arguments will you use to open your case? To close your case?

PRESENTING A POSITION TO THE CLASS

(AFTER YOUR PRESENTATION)

6. What arguments do you feel you presented most convincingly?
7. Did you think of new arguments as you went along? What were they?

FIGURE 3

PRESENTING A POSITION TO THE CLASS

Observer Sheet Your name________________________

Player you observe________________ Position he takes________

1. List all of the arguments you remember that this person presented to support his position. Beside each argument tell how you feel he supported the argument: e.g., by evidence, reason, emotion, no support, etc.

ARGUMENT	SUPPORT FOR THE ARGUMENT
________________________	________________________
________________________	________________________
________________________	________________________
________________________	________________________

2. Are there arguments you feel could have been made that were neglected? What are they?
3. Was the presentation convincing? _____Yes _____No
4. List below the things other than arguments in this presentation that you think were:

THE BEST FEATURES	COULD BE IMPROVED
________________________	________________________
________________________	________________________
________________________	________________________
________________________	________________________

5. Did you agree with this position before the presentation?
_____Yes _____No _____Don't know
6. Did the presentation change your opinion? _____Yes _____No
7. If "Yes," did it change your opinion in its favor?
_____Yes _____No

FIGURE 4

PRESENTING A POSITION TO THE CLASS

Analyzing Effectiveness
(based on Position and Observer Sheet)

1. List below all arguments you *intended* to make, and check how often each argument was remembered by an observer:

YOUR ARGUMENT	Check each time an observer noted the argument
______________	______________
______________	______________
______________	______________
______________	______________

2. Add the arguments the observers felt you *ignored:*

______________	______________
______________	______________
______________	______________
______________	______________

3. Were the arguments most often noted by observers the ones you felt were most convincing?
4. Did students find you convincing? Number Yes_____ Number No_____
5. What, besides your arguments, were the best features of your presentation?
6. What in your presentation did observers feel could be improved?
7. How many students changed their opinions in your favor? Number Yes_____ (Question 7, OBSERVER SHEET)

Colorado, has also taken a step in the right direction by building a repertoire of alternatives in evaluation and developing guidelines for their use. This effort will soon be available to the educational community.

We have provided only two examples from our work, but the response of teachers to these new approaches has encouraged us to believe that much can be done to reshape the field.[10] We will need cooperative enterprise within our own profession and involvement of the school community to determine what and how we want to test—what we want to be held accountable for. But a more comprehensive and humanistic system of evaluation is possible. In the final analysis, the responsibility for bringing about this quiet revolution rests with the schools.

NOTES

1. Neil Postman, "The Politics of Reading," *Harvard Educational Review* 40 (May 1970): 244.
2. Dean K. Whitla and Dan Pinck, *Essentially Elementary Science: A Report on the Status of Elementary Science in Massachusetts Schools* (Boston: Massachusetts Advisory Council on Education, 1973).
3. Oscar K. Buros, ed., *Mental Measurements Yearbook*, 5th, 6th, 7th eds. (Highland Park, N.J.: Gryphon Press, 1959, 1965, 1972).
4. *Sequential Tests of Educational Progress* (STEP) (Princeton: Cooperative Test Division, Educational Testing Service, 1972).
5. *Stanford Achievement Test* (New York: Harcourt Brace and World, 1964).
6. *SRA Achievement Series* (Chicago: Science Research Associates, 1972).
7. *Metropolitan Achievement Tests* (New York: Harcourt Brace and World, 1959).
8. Figure 1 is from Janet P. Hanley (Whitla), "Learning About Learning: Evaluation Strategies for Teaching About the American Revolution," *Social Education* 38 (February 1974): 175-84.
9. Figures 2 through 4 are from Karen C. Cohen, *Strategies for Measuring Learning* (Cambridge: Education Development Center, 1972).
10. Other examples can be found in Hanley (Whitla), "Learning About Learning," and Cohen, *Strategies for Measuring Learning.* See also Hanley (Whitla), *MAN: A COURSE OF STUDY Evaluation Strategies* (1969, 1970), and Cohen, *Goals and How to Assess Them* (1974), both published by Education Development Center, Cambridge, Massachusetts.

MATH TESTS

JUDAH L. SCHWARTZ

Judah L. Schwartz is professor of engineering science and education at the Massachusetts Institute of Technology, Cambridge, Massachusetts, and codirector of Project TORQUE, a group at Education Development Center, Newton, Massachusetts, that is developing new test instruments in mathematics for elementary school.

It is generally conceded that the primary reason for emphasizing mathematics in the elementary curriculum is our conviction that it is important for children to learn to handle the quantitive aspects of their environment with some ease and comfort. We teach our children to count, measure, and compute. We teach them to represent selected features of complex situations by numbers, symbols, maps, or graphs. How well does this enterprise work? How well do children learn and teachers teach? The standardized mathematics achievement test is the instrument parents and school boards tend to rely on heavily in answering these questions. They need to know how good the answers are that they are getting.

Typically, mathematics achievement tests for the elementary grades are divided into three parts:

- computation
- concepts
- applications or problem solving.

Some of these examinations claim to be diagnostically useful to the classroom teacher in one or more of these areas. Some do not. Some of the commercially available tests are norm referenced, and some are criterion referenced. Some are machine scored, and some are teacher scored. Sometimes the tests are used as devices to assess in part children's performance, and sometimes they are used to assess in part the performance of teachers, of principals, or even of school systems as a whole. It is my purpose in this article to examine more closely some of the prominent features of currently available mathematics tests, in order to see how well they serve the ends their makers claim they serve. In so doing, I will not address a number of broader testing issues, such as linguistic complexity, cultural bias, or the logistics of administration and scoring. These questions—which are discussed in other articles in this issue—are, of course, as vital in the assessment of mathematics competence as they are in the assessment of any other competence.

COMPUTATION

There's not a great deal of ambiguity about the problem 177 + 259 + 346, or the problem 14,621—7,514. The teacher who learns that a particular child has carried out these computations properly no doubt feels a certain sense of satisfaction and pleasure. But suppose the child does not compute the answers correctly. On a machine scored test, some inference about the nature of the child's difficulty can be made from the particular choice of wrong answer, but not much. Further, if that information becomes available to the teacher two months after the tests are administered, its utility for shaping classroom instructional practice and helping meet the needs of specific children is questionable, at best.

Tests need not be machine scored. Indeed, many teachers score papers themselves and thus generally learn whatever the tests can tell them. But does the classroom teacher really need the full machinery of a standardized test to find out whether any particular child knows that $8 \times 7 = 56$?

There is a further difficulty with computation tests. They do not reflect the dynamic and evolving character of human computation. One thousand years ago, the problem $6734.51 \div 2.8$ could be performed only by highly skilled mathematicians, if at all. When I was a child, I was taught to solve problems of the form $\sqrt{24.} = \_\_$. It is now almost reasonable to ask children routinely to solve computational problems of the form $(3.5)^5 - (5.3)^3 = \_\_$. The point is simply that the amount, complexity, and sophistication of the computation we can do depends strongly on what tools we have available to do it with. Sometimes these tools are procedures to be carried out by people; sometimes they are procedures to be carried out by machines at the direction of people. (This is not the proper forum for analyzing the problem of the calculator in the classroom. Suffice it to say that those who argue against its use are limiting children's computational agility to that of the fifteenth-century mathematician.)

CONCEPTS

In addition to computation, every primary mathematics curriculum includes measurement, and properly so. We constantly measure lengths, areas, volumes, weights, times, temperatures, angles, velocities, and many other quantities. If schooling is to succeed, it must help people become comfortable with being quantitative about their surroundings. This means they must learn to measure, and one cannot measure without estimating. Let us see how informative the achievement tests are when they try to tell us about children's ability to measure.

Consider this problem:[1]

Which pencil is one inch shorter than the blue pencil?

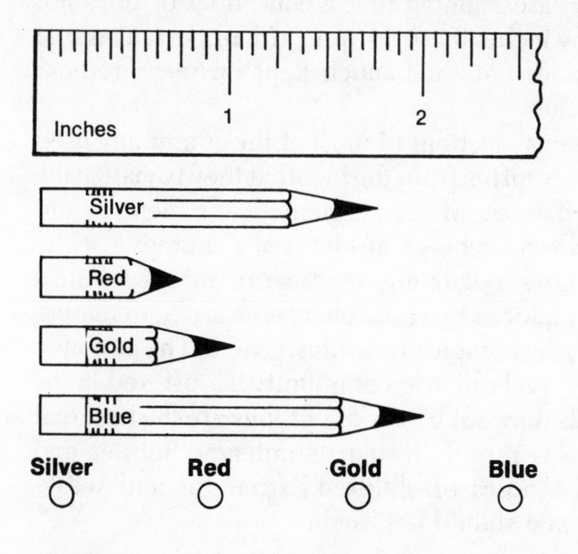

or this one:[2]

How many inches are there in a yard?

☐ 12 ☐ 16 ☐ 3 ☐ 36 ☐ DK

Do these questions, typical of the questions on measurement in present standardized achievement tests, really elicit the subtlety of a child's understanding of the measurement process? Do they tell the interested adult what the child understands about choosing units appropriate to the attributes being quantified, about adequate as opposed to spurious precision, or about the thoroughly intertwined processes of estimating and measuring?

If ever there was a competence to be ascertained by observing active, hands-on behavior, it is measurement—measurement of real things with real measuring instruments. A picture of four pencils, ranging from three-quarters of an inch to two inches in length, alongside a picture of a broken ruler, hardly constitutes a real situation in which one can make reasonable inferences about a child's ability to measure. Moreover, ascertaining that a child does or does not know how many inches there are in a yard, important as that fact may be, does not shed much light on measurement competence either.

The "concepts" sections of most of the commonly used achievement tests suffer from the fact that they trivialize the concepts. The richness of the mathematical structures and the complementary richness of children's cognitive structures is only now beginning to emerge in the clinical observation of children by researchers who are both mathematically and psychologically sophisticated. The rationalization that the psychometric community has offered in the past—"The tests may not be good, but they are the best that can be made"—is rapidly losing its potency. Subtler and more useful diagnoses of children's strengths and weaknesses can be, and should be, made.

PROBLEM SOLVING

Hapoalim hitchilu livnot binyan b 1932 vgamru b 1951. Kama shanim ovru?
(A) 83 (B) 19 (C) 21 (D) NG (E) DK

Despite the fact that this problem is a translation into transliterated Hebrew of a problem from the mathematics problem-solving section of a standardized test,[3] the reader will probably have little difficulty identifying the correct answer.

The reason is simple. One presumes, usually correctly, that four-digit numbers beginning with 19 and otherwise unpunctuated are dates. Given two dates, there is little to be done in the way of computation other than to take their difference. Neither adding, multiplying, nor dividing dates is sensible. If we are indeed interested in children's problem-solving competence, let us try to assess it with instruments that are capable of exhibiting children's ability to model reality—the process that lies at the heart of such competence. Problems such as the one quoted above are of little help in furthering that end.

BY WHOSE STANDARD?

It is hard to understand why any constituency that is interested in achievement test scores should be satisfied with knowing that their children, teachers, schools, and school systems compare well or poorly with the publisher's norming group. It is particularly difficult to understand when all too often what is being compared is performance on wrong, ambiguous, misleading, and trivial items. But regardless of the items themselves, if a child does not compute well enough, it seems to me of little comfort to know that he computes more skillfully than 50 percent of the norming population.

Performance measured against criteria is, in my view, a more reasonable strategy. The problem is that there don't seem to be any reasonable models of sensible criteria for any but the most mechanical sorts of chores. The most common form of criterion setting is the rephrasing of specific pieces of curriculum content into the appropriate syntactical form. It is not unusual to find lists of several hundred criteria for mathematics in grades K-6, each one narrowly and somewhat tautologically tied to the problems meant to elicit the child's competence with respect to that criterion. For example, the following problem[4]

What is the total number of triangles in this figure?

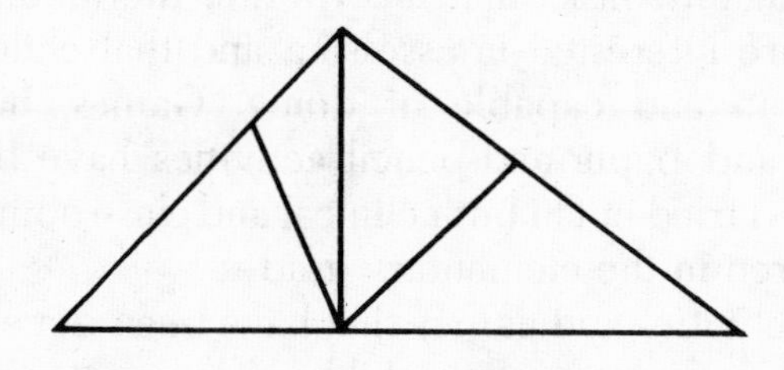

is designed to test the criterion, "The student will be able to solve a word problem to determine the number of triangles in a drawing."

In my view, this form of test does not benefit the child, the teacher, or the school.

•

The partition of mathematics into computation, concepts, and problem solving is a relatively unthoughtful breakdown of a very complex competence, one that serves neither the child nor the subject matter well. Within this division, mediocre items probe superficial formulations of mathematical skills, and little is learned about what is undoubtedly the object of the whole exercise: the child's ability to symbolically represent his or her environment, manipulate that symbolic representation, and make inferences about the real world from the symbolic representation.

We need not conclude, however, that the situation is hopeless. I believe we *can* learn to assess children's mathematical competence and diagnose their strengths and weaknesses. But it will take time, and the close and continuing collaboration of sensitive and perceptive school people and researchers who are responsive to the subtleties of both the mathematical and cognitive phychological issues. This is the approach being taken by Education Development Center's Project TORQUE. The Project's test development is centered around a new kind of validation strategy: tests are validated against tasks that incorporate the mathematical skills we are interested in assessing and that children are interested in and capable of doing. Games, hands-on-materials, and paper-and-pencil activities have been developed and tried out in both clinical and classroom settings with children in the elementary grades.

The activities and games that have been developed to date are designed to assess children's competence in the estimation and measurement of length, area, weight and volume, time, temperature, and angle.

The following thumbnail sketches of some of TORQUE'S measurement games and other activities[5] should suggest something of the subtlety of diagnosis that is possible without relying on standardized, machine scored tests:

- *Measure and Move*, a board game in which moves are determined by measuring various line segments associated with circles, ellipses, and polygons. This game allows the teacher to observe the child's ability to attend to the attribute that is being quantified; for example, perimeter-diameter confusion is quickly evident.

- *What's My Line*, a booklet containing a clearly graded sequence of linear measurement problems. Students are asked to estimate and then measure various rectilinear paths, beginning with a straight line and ending with complex spirals. This booklet allows the teacher to observe whether the student uses the zero point on the rule, what sorts of estimation strategies he or she employs, and what awareness of the symmetry of the figure the student has.

- *Area-Plane*, a board game in which students compete in covering up rectilinear figures using squares of various sizes. Children frequently confuse the notion of area with that of perimeter. The game focuses on the concept of an area as a covering and introduces the notion of a unit of area and its use in measuring area.

- *Tic-Toc-Rummy*, a card game that focuses on four types of time representation—digital, verbal, and two types of circular time "scales"—to reinforce the concept of equivalency of these different notations.

- *City Blocks*, a territory game in which the scoring depends on the computation of volumes.

- *Escribador*, a board game based on the measurement of angles. The notion of angle as a "turning" is emphasized. This is an important departure from the standard procedure of presenting angles statically. Under those circumstances, children frequently use the length of the rays bounding the angle as the measure of the angle.

Logistically manageable tests are then constructed and validated against games of this sort. The games used in the validation process are also available to the classroom teacher for fine-grained diagnosis of, and therapy for, a youngster's difficulty.

Efforts such as those of Project TORQUE in mathematics will probably result in the formulation of a new paradigm for educational research. That's fine, because the problem of language—reading, writing, speaking, and listening—lies ahead. It's a much harder problem, and we're further behind on it.

NOTES

1. *CTBS/QI* (Monterey, California: CTB/McGraw-Hill, 1968), p. 7, problem 12.
2. *Metropolitan Achievement Test, Intermediate Form F* (New York: Harcourt Brace Jovanovich, 1970), test 6, problem 8.
3. Ibid., test 7, problem 4.
4. *Prescriptive Mathematics Inventory* (Monterey, California: CTB/McGraw-Hill, 1972), orange book, problem 102.
5. For further information, write to Project TORQUE, Education Development Center, 55 Chapel Street, Cambridge, Massachusetts 02160.

SCIENCE TESTS

EDWIN F. TAYLOR

Edwin F. Taylor is a senior research scientist in the Department of Physics and the Division for Study and Research in Education at the Massachusetts Institute of Technology. He has written several textbooks in physics at the college level, participated in curriculum development projects, and studied some alternative modes of teaching and learning. He is editor of the American Journal of Physics, *which is "devoted to the instructional and cultural aspects of physical science" at the university level.*

The two theses of this article are simplicity itself: 1) standardized science achievement tests for the elementary school are almost uniformly poor in quality. They are incorrect, misleading, skewed in emphasis, and irrelevant; and 2) *any* quick-answer, paper-and-pencil science test that has consequences for the child or the school is likely to be irrelevant and perhaps harmful to those activities most likely to interest children in science.

The conclusion is also simple: do not administer these elementary school science achievement tests. Anyone who already agrees with this conclusion may want to skim the accompanying tables for amusement before skipping to the next article.

THE TESTS

Adult readers who examine elementary school science achievement tests for the first time are in for a shock. The shock is more severe for professional scientists who care for the subtleties of education and research in this fascinating field. In the course of preparing to write this paper, I have quoted some of the worst questions (Tables 1 and 2, see pages 296-305) to visitors in my office. Many people are incredulous and have to be shown the test itself before bursting into laughter or wincing with pain.

Happily, there are not a great many elementary school science achievement tests (see references 1 through 9 on page 308 for a sampling), and most of them are for use by the last three elementary grades. Therefore, one can corral and brand most members of the herd so that they may be recognized and avoided on the open range.

Some of the *general* difficulties with achievement tests have been pinpointed by Judah L. Schwartz and Jerrold R. Zacharias in Project TORQUE materials. They are describing mathematics achievement tests, but the same remarks apply to science tests:

> *The tests are permeated by items that test the names of concepts rather than the concepts. Over and over, one finds examples of children being asked to parrot prose statements that cannot possibly be meaningful to them.*
>
> *The test maker's intent can only rarely be discerned.*
>
> *There is no evidence that the tests are designed for use in any sort of diagnostic fashion, except at the grossest level of aggregation of concepts, computation, and problem solving.*
>
> *The two column format is confusing.*
>
> *Asking the child to mark the name of the answer (A, B, . . . H) rather than the answer is confusing.*

To this list one may add the following specific difficulties for the science tests examined here:

- The test items are often wrong scientifically

or confuse several different principles (see Table 1).

- Many items simply test for recognition of technical terms.

- Many items are "aptitude items" in the guise of "science items."

- The scientist is pictured as a technician who applies a limited and uniform method to investigate nature.

- In multiple-choice items, very often more than one alternative is correct (see Table 2, page 302).

These faults appear in even the best of these tests (see Table 3, page 305).

DISCRIMINATING AGAINST THE DISCRIMINATORS

There may be one defense against these critisisms. A test maker may say, "No matter how incorrect or silly these test items may appear to be, our trial testing shows that they discriminate between children who perform well in other measures of science achievement and those who perform poorly." Several responses to his argument might be: "What are the 'other measures' of science achievement?" "If incorrect or silly items discriminate between children, then you are testing something other than science achievement—goodness knows what." Or, "Not with *my* child, you don't!"

But the situation is worse than that. Anyone who knows how these tests are constructed is aware that a large number of questions are composed and tested. The items retained for the published version are those that discriminate in the ways that test makers decide the items *should* discriminate. Typically, items that discriminate between boys and girls are eliminated, while those that discriminate between white suburban children and black inner-city children are not.* Thus the discrimination defense is perverse and selfserving.

WHAT MAKES A SCIENTIST?

What quick-answer, paper-and-pencil tests do best (namely, to verify recognition of technical terms) is largely irrelevant to the enterprise of science as it is practiced in real life. Moreover, it is irrelevant to the *process* by which children are attracted to science.

Since starting this project, I have asked numerous scientists, "What experiences did you have between the ages of six and twelve that influenced you to become a scientist?" Common answers are "hobbies" and "projects" and "the profession or interests of my parents." One scientist mentioned "differential praise from my teachers between different subjects in school." A Nobel prize winner remarked that school science influenced him only by telling him things he doubted, and which his own investigations found to be wrong! My own summary would be "messing around and the accompanying growing sense of playful power over my surroundings."

Let the elementary school classroom be rich with things and people that stimulate messing around and arrange to support projects that students find to be fun and power evoking. Evaluate the program—not the child—by asking sensitive visitors to sample the energy, attention, and noise level of the classroom. Invite them to report on the plans, the playfulness and enthusiasm of the children, and the support systems of the materials. Have the children describe what they are doing and demonstrate the results, if any. Let the high schools and colleges condense experience into "laws" and familiarize students with terms and symbols that express these laws—even then, let laws be keys to greater

*Mary Jo Bane in *Tests and Testing* (McLean, Va.: National Council for the Advancement of Education Writing, 1974).

and more varied kinds of power and appreciation.

And now the ultimate danger of the elementary school science achievement tests can be simply stated: they direct the attention of students, teachers, and academic decision makers away from the activities and resources that lead children into powerful relationships with the natural world.

MOUSE HAIR AND INSECT PARTS

Nothing that has gone before should be read as criticism of the use of tests by teachers within the confines of their own classrooms. In some ways, the teacher is like a personal physician employed by the patient to diagnose individual medical difficulties and to prescribe a particular treatment. Society rightly permits the doctor wide latitude in the use of medical procedures for diagnosis and treatment, some of which would not be acceptable for use by the population as a whole. Similarly, we allow those who teach our children wide latitude in the tests they use to discover and overcome individual academic difficulties. I have doubts about the usefulness of quick-answer, paper-and-pencil science tests for the purpose of helping a child's involvement in science or understanding of it. Still, I would be inclined to consent to their use if everyone involved, including the child, could sit down and argue about the possible results of the tests and the meaning of the results for that child.

In stark contrast to our liberal attitude toward individually prescribed medical treatments, public health measures designed to apply to the general population are (or should be) subject to the most rigorous limitation. A treatment that leads to death in 1 percent of cases may be justified for an individual patient with a serious illness; when applied to one million patients, however, the same treatment could result in ten thousand deaths. The U.S. Food and Drug Administration permits only minor traces of mouse hair and insect parts in foods sold in supermarkets and medicines sold over the counter. Similarly, achievement tests taken by a significant fraction of elementary school students must be free from pollutants. They are not free from pollutants, and even if they were (like cigarettes made of cornsilk), they do no apparent good.

Almost every science test examined here is one small part of a larger test booklet that also contains achievement tests in reading comprehension, mathematics, social science, and so forth. If, after reading other articles in this issue of the journal, you wish to administer these other tests, you may feel that you "might as well" administer the science test also, in order not to "waste the money" spent on the entire booklet. My advice is: don't do it. Leave the polluted side dish untouched, even if you have to pay for the entire dinner anyway.

Table 1: THE WORST

Here are some of the more outrageous items gleaned from the science achievement tests examined. In each case the urge to comment proves irresistible.

Item

Scientists study three basic kinds of things—animals, vegetables, and[2]

people
stars
minerals
foods
religions

Comment

So *that's* what scientists do!

Item

What does this picture of a boy looking at himself in a mirror illustrate?[1]

focusing
transparency
dispersion
reflection
don't know

Comment

Focusing (of his eyes and yours).
Transparency (and dispersion?) of the glass.
Reflection (at the backing).
I don't know (because real situations illustrate many things).

Item

Which one of these drawings most nearly shows the way sound waves travel from their source?[1]

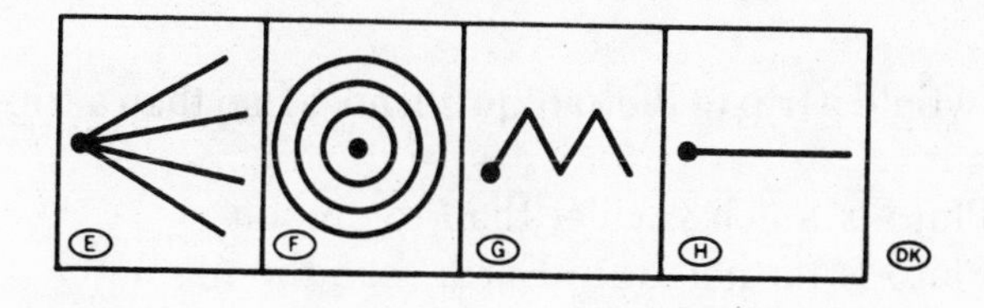

Comment

Every one is a valid representation of the propagation of sound waves, including the single line showing propagation to a single observer and the zigzag line showing echoes between parallel walls.

Item

If the earth's axis were "straight up and down" instead of being tilted,[2]

there would be no night or day
one side of the earth would be too hot to live on
there would be another Ice Age
the earth would no longer revolve around the sun
the seasons would not change

Comment

What's "straight up" in space?

Item

A man would die *most quickly* if he could not get any[2]

food
clothing
shelter
water
air

Comment

The author of this item will die *most quickly* for frightening my child if I get my hands on him.

Item

Why would a trip to Pluto require more fuel than a trip to the moon?[4]

Pluto is much smaller than the moon
Pluto is farther from Earth than the moon
Pluto moves faster than the moon
Pluto is closer to the sun than the moon

Comment

The key idea, difference in gravitational potential in the field of the sun, is not mentioned. The fact that "Pluto is farther from the Earth than the moon" is by itself irrelevant: in a frictionless environment, going far takes no more fuel than going near.

Item

The best explanation for breezes and winds is that[4]

the earth spins rapidly on its axis
temperature varies from place to place
the earth moves very rapidly through space
air pressure varies from place to place

Comment

Three of the named *conditions* contribute to winds, but none of them constitutes an *explanation.*

Item

Scientists learn the most about the plants and animals that once lived on the earth by[4]

studying fossils found in rocks
making trips into unexplored regions
studying the minerals in different rocks
reading the histories written by ancient men

Comment

Moral: the scientist limits himself to a narrow range of experiences in decoding nature.

Item

A damp towel is placed in a warm, dry room. After one hour, the towel probably weighs[9]

more than before
about the same
can't tell
less than before

Comment

Does "the towel" include the water it holds?

Item

What do scientists use to make small things appear larger?[4]

a barometer
litmus paper
a balance
a microscope

Comment

What are "small things":

small differences in pressure?
small changes in acidity?
small weights?

Item

Our bodies do not collapse because[5]

blood pressure is stronger than air pressure
the air pressure inside our bodies is about equal to the air pressure outside our bodies
our skin protects us
we have muscles

Comment

Could a doctor "choose one answer"? What does "stronger" mean? If blood pressure is "stronger" why don't we blow up? Is there "air" inside our bodies to provide pressure? Are elementary school pupils supposed to know about partial pressure of dissolved gases?

Item

In the following food chain, which is the primary producer?[8]

corn→mice→snakes→hawks

Comment

Code word recognition. But what is "primary"? The hawk fertilizes the corn.

Item

One illustration of this [the Law of Gravitation] is the fact that[1]

you are thrown forward when an automobile stops suddenly
rain can turn to snow
you weigh more on Earth than you would on the moon
trees lose their leaves in the fall

Comment

The first answer illustrates the fact that acceleration of a frame of reference yields effects indistinguishable from the effects of gravitation (the so-called "principle of equivalence").
The second has to do with falling objects.
The fourth discusses leaves that fall in the fall.

Item

What is the most important source of the energy we use?[4]
coal
the sun
natural gas
petroleum

Comment

Confusion between proximate and ultimate source.

Item

The universe is called {1. a primary 2. a secondary 3. an energy 4. a vital 5. a space} system.[6]

Comment

Huh?

Item

Radiant energy travels at {(1) 186,000 (2) 133,333 (3) 185,000 (4) 187,000 (5) 190,000} miles [sic].[6]

Comment

Honest!

Item

If the earth did *not* turn on its axis, there would be no[8]

phases of the moon
summer and winter
months and years
day and night

Comment

and no test makers.

Table 2: CHOOSE ONE ANSWER?

Elementary school science achievement tests use a multiple-choice format or the equivalent. Invariably, the student is instructed to select the best answer from those given in each case. But what does "best" mean? Most often it appears to be a way of invoking the "common understanding" that surrounds middle-class homes and schools. Yet the only real clarity of multiple-choice questions is the decisive distinction they can provide between "right" and "wrong." Here are some examples of questions for which more than one answer is clearly "correct." I would claim that for eight of the following fourteen items all *of the alternative answers given are correct.*

How is your hearbeat affected by skipping rope?[1]
it beats slower
it beats faster
it beats the same
first it beats faster and then slower

A material is *translucent* if light passes through it, but you cannot see through it. Which of these is *translucent*?[2]
foggy air
window glass
plastic sandwich bags
tinted automobile windshields
frosted glass on shower doors

Green plants are often called the most important living things on earth, mainly because they[2]

produce pretty flowers
are the basic source of food for all animals
help stop soil erosion
provide homes for many wild animals
provide fuel and lumber for man

Which one of the following has potential energy due to its position?[3]

a road
tree roots
an underground rock
a tank of water on a tower

Ocean waves are caused by the[3]

earth's gravity
moon's gravity
earth's motion
wind's patterns

Which of the following would be the best place to study a crab to learn if its color change is caused by changes in the light?[3]

its natural surroundings
a room with a sunny window
a box made to look like its natural home
a place where light can be controlled

An orange seed grows into[4]

an orange tree
an orange
another seed
an orange blossom

The moon is seen by us because it[5]

reflects sunlight
is white hot
is a close star
appears at night

Sleet is frozen[6]
dew
water
vapor
rain
snow

Moonlight is[6]
reflected sunlight
reflected earth lights
radiant energy
moon energy
imaginary

A small pan of water is made to boil by placing it over a lighted candle. A mirror placed above the rising steam is soon covered with moisture. This example can be compared with the water cycle. The lighted candle acts like the[7]
warm earth
sun
rising air current
gravity moving the rivers

When fish take water into their mouths they are[8]
eating
drinking
breathing
tasting

Many kinds of plants are not able to live on the desert because of the[9]
high temperature

low rainfall
bright sunlight
poor soil

In warm weather, water changes into water vapor and rises into the air. Later this water vapor changes into rain or snow and falls to the earth. This [which?] process is called[9]
evaporation
condensation
precipitation
the water cycle

Table 3: THE BEST

The least objectionable of the tests examined is the Stanford Achievement Test,[7] Primary Level III, Form A, copyright 1972 by Harcourt Brace Jovanovich, Inc. This test is apparently intended for grades 3.5 through 4.4 (middle of third year to middle of fourth year). In order to obtain a random sample of questions from this test for analysis here, I listed the numbers 1 through 42 on a piece of paper and asked the first person I met to circle five of them. Ten-year-old Andrew Taylor, a fifth grader, helped by acting as guinea pig for these five items. Here are the five and our analysis.

Item

6 Starting with the eggs (A) in the drawing above, which order of letters best shows how an animal develops?

A→B→C→D
A→B→F
A→B→C
A→B→D→E

Comment

6 Does "an animal" mean "*any* animal" (clearly wrong) or "a *particular animal*," in which case it is natural to assume, as Andrew did, that all six figures represent stages in the development of a single animal. It is the order of *pictures* that show development, not the order of *letters* (Andrew chose ABCD). What does a newly hatched fish look like: is ABC possibly correct? Clue: the correct sequence of pictures lies on a straight line. What does this item test besides past acquaintance with polywogs and ability to manipulate labels?

Item

Questions 17-20 are based on the pictures below. Observe the pictures in the box.

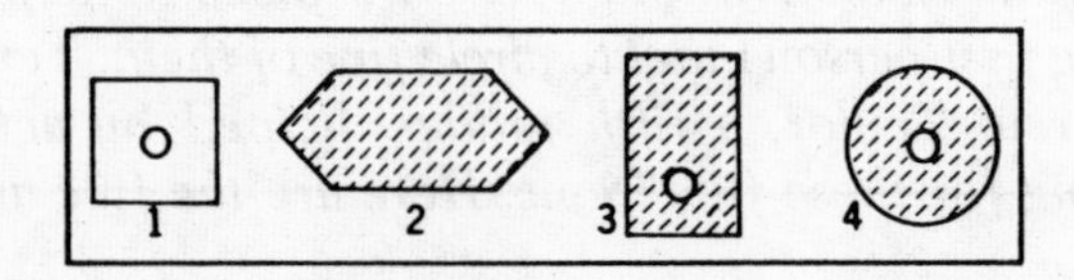

20 Place your hand over objects 2 and 4 and look at the other two objects. How are they alike?

They are the same size
They are both shaded
They have four sides
They are both unshaded

Comment

20 The last of four similar questions on this set of figures—10 percent of all "science" items! Looks like an "aptitude" test to me. I first noticed that objects 1 and 3 both have holes: try again.

Item

Use the graph below to answer questions 23-27. A class collected eye color data. They made the graph with their results.

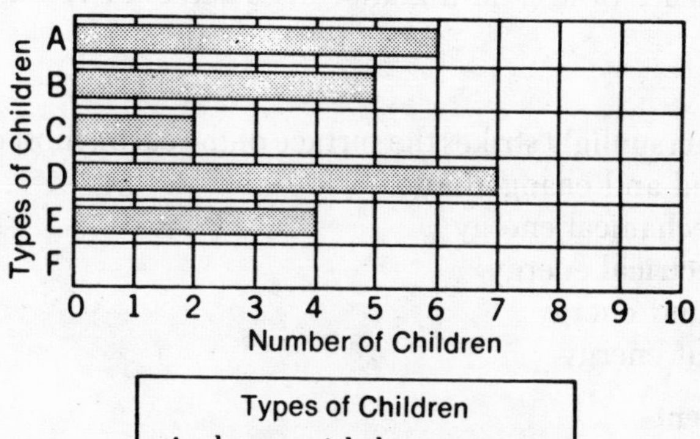

Types of Children

A. boys with brown eyes
B. boys with blue eyes
C. boys with green eyes
D. girls with brown eyes
E. girls with blue eyes
F. girls with green eyes

24 How many children have blue eyes?
⑤ 9 ⑥ 7 ⑦ 2 ⑧ 5

Comment

24 The second of five similar items on this graph. An exercise in sequential decoding of labels, graphs, and numbers. Andrew, who loves paper-and-pencil puzzles, did fine, but is it science? Possible confusion between the number *of* the answer and the number that *is* the answer.

Item

32 Amphibians are animals that
always live in burrows
can fly and climb

live both on land and in water
always live in oceans

Comment

32 Recognition of a technical term. Fifth-grader Andrew never heard of it. (Ninth-grader Criss had to be reminded.)

Item

40 When sunlight strikes the surface of the earth, most of it is reflected and changed into
mechanical energy
electrical energy
sound energy
heat energy

Comment

40 *Reflected* energy is presumably *not* changed but stays in the form of light, so the initial statement is wrong. *Absorbed* energy can be changed into any of the indicated forms; the key word "most" is required to funnel our thoughts to "heat energy."

TESTS CITED

1. *Metropolitan Achievement Test: Intermediate, Form F* (New York: Harcourt Brace Jovanovich, 1970).
2. *Scholastic Tests: Educational Development Series, Elementary Level, Form B* (Bensenville, Ill.: Scholastic Testing Service, 1972).
3. *Comprehensive Tests of Basic Skills, Level 2, Form S* (Monterey: CTB/McGraw-Hill, 1973).
4. *Achievement Series, Blue Green Series* (Chicago: Science Research Associates, 1968).
5. *Elementary Science and Health, Second Every Pupil Test, Ohio Scholarship Tests* (Columbus, Ohio: State Department of Education, 1965).
6. *Every Pupil Achievement Test, Elementary Science* (Emporia: Bureau of Educational Measurements, Kansas State Teachers College, 1966).
7. *Stanford Achievement Test: Primary Level III, Form A* (New York: Harcourt Brace Jovanovich, 1972).
8. Ibid., Intermediate Level I, Form A.
9. Ibid., Intermediate Level II, Form A.

READING TESTS

DAVID HARMAN

David Harman is lecturer in education and research associate at the Center for Studies in Education and Development, Harvard University Graduate School of Education, Cambridge, Massachusetts.

Mr. Harman was formerly director of the Center for Pre-Academic Studies at the Hebrew University of Jerusalem. He has also designed programs and curriculums for adults, and adult literacy programs in several developing countries as well as in the United States. He is the author of Community Fundamental Education, *published by D. C. Heath in 1974.*

*Si duo idem faciunt, non est idem.**

The ability to read is widely considered to be one of the most significant of the basic skills. Some people have gone as far as to suggest that the teaching of reading is the *raison d'etre* of schools. Whether one is in complete agreement with this statement or not, reading skills and their instruction have clearly been an overriding concern among educators and parents, predicated, at the very least, on their being a prerequisite for all subsequent learning tasks.

It is hardly surprising to learn, therefore, that there has been more activity related to the teaching of reading (development of methodologies and creation of teaching material) than to the teaching of any other school subject. It

*If two people do the same thing, it is not the same thing.

might come as a surprise, however, to learn that there is not a universally accepted definition of what reading precisely is, and consequently what the act of reading entails. Definitions of reading range from the relatively straightforward notion of decoding written symbols into their phonetic sounds, to the far more complex premise that reading requires the comprehension of written material. Largely influenced by the work of Edward Thorndike early in this century, many American reading authorities subscribe to the second definition, arguing that the basic purpose of reading is comprehension. This argument begs the question of whether reading in itself and understanding what is read are separate or complementary activities.

The issue can be illustrated with the following example: most readers will find little difficulty in reading—that is, decoding—the Latin phrase at the beginning of this article, but many will have to search for the translation in order to understand it. Certainly, this does not mean that they cannot read, although inability to comprehend the words will be interpreted by some measures as a reflection of reading ability.

The lack of clarity and resolution of the reading-comprehension issue extends to the multitude of standardized tests used to measure attainment in reading. Through the years, concern with reading and its instruction has resulted in the production of a great many testing tools. Indeed, more tests are available to measure reading attainment than to measure accomplishments in any other area of the school curriculum. Since 1914, when Edward Thorndike devised the first two standardized tests in reading comprehension—known as the "Visual Vocabulary Scale" and the "Scale for Measuring the Understanding of Sentences and Paragraphs"—literally hundreds of standardized tests have been developed in an attempt to measure a wide variety of what are considered to be reading skills and abilities. Of these, some twenty tests or batteries of tests are in wide use at all levels of schooling throughout the United

States. Ironically, despite this "embarrassment of riches" of testing tools for reading, as a result of the definitional confusion, there is little agreement on the basic question of what should be tested.

A brief look at the current common practice is instructive. One finds that reading skills are usually assessed at three distinct stages of development: the preparatory stage, or reading readiness phase; the development of reading skills phase; and the reading for comprehension stage.

Reading readiness tests are predicated on the notion that an identifiable group of motor skills and cognitive abilities exist that are required for the initiation of formal reading instruction. Subtest titles in some of the more prevalent testing batteries indicate the range of these skills: Listening Comprehension, Auditory Discrimination, Following Directions, Letter Recognition, Visual Motor Coordination, Visual Discrimination, and Word Recognition (*Gates-MacGinitie Readiness Skills Test*, 1968); Word Meaning, Listening, Matching, Alphabet, Numbers, Copying, and Draw a Man (*Metropolitan Readiness Test*, 1964); Using Symbols, Making Visual Discriminations, Using the Context, Making Auditory Discriminations, Using Context and Auditory Clues, and Giving the Names of Letters (*Harrison-Stroud Reading Readiness Profile*, 1956).

A child who achieves a given composite score on any of these batteries is considered ready for formally learning how to read. One whose composite score is below that given figure requires additional "readiness" preparation. Underlying the use of such tests is a distinct notion that readiness for reading and reading itself are two separate stages, the latter of which requires the existence of the former as a precondition. Consequently, the two phases are considered different activities in a hierarchical, time related framework. In recent years, this point of view has undergone modification, and there is growing agreement that different children attain "reading readiness" at different paces, and that the skills and competencies considered necessary for reading develop as part of actual reading tasks. To some extent, this change has been manifest in most reading readiness tests. For example, we find that in tests of visual discrimination, geometric forms have been substituted for letters of the alphabet. Clearly, identification of letters is a reading associated task while the identification of geometric forms is not overtly related to reading.

Readiness tests are essentially administered for two purposes: first, for use in predicting subsequent reading attainment; second, for diagnosis of skills or competencies that might appear weak and in need of further development before the onset of formal reading instruction. A great deal of research has been conducted over the past forty years to determine the validity of reading readiness tests for these purposes. Research findings tend to cast a shadow of doubt on claims of validity issued by test producers. While some studies indicate that one or another battery of tests might have predictive validity, other studies strongly suggest that such predictability is more likely valid for children who score high on tests than for children who score low. Assessment of student potential by teachers, as well as utilization of test batteries that do not purport to measure reading readiness (various IQ tests) appear, according to some studies, to have as much if not more validity in predicting future reading ability.

It is significant that the "future" reading ability to which existing research relates is usually exhibited at the end of the first grade and does not represent ultimate reading capabilities. Although some of the readiness tests propose precise formulas for the number of months before formal reading instruction should begin or should be delayed (on the basis of test results), most research indicates that among children whose reading instruction was put off in an attempt to increase readiness, the delay neither improved performance nor accounted for it in any important way. It remains highly dubious whether reading readiness tests perform what they claim. Many test publishers caution, in accompanying manuals, against the use of individual subtest scores, suggesting that only a composite score might be valid. Does this imply that subtests do not specifically test what they attempt to test? Do the subtests provide only a rough approximation? Such warnings only serve to cast additional and severe doubts on the value of reading readiness tests. Nevertheless, they are in use in more than 80 percent of the kindergartens and first grades in the United States.

Beyond the reading readiness phase, standardized achievement tests are in wide use throughout the formal school years. In addition to the basic encoding and decoding skills that are requisite for reading ability (reading skills have legitimacy only as they apply to a variety of written messages), reading tests attempt to assess comprehension and vocabulary. Most available tests for use in the early primary school grades contain subtests that evaluate decoding skills (letter or word recognition tests). In addition, they all contain some form of reading comprehension and reading vocabulary subtests.

Following this intermediate phase, during which the more technical decoding aspect of reading should have been mastered by students, most reading instruction is inexorably linked with the notion of comprehension. Consequently, all reading tests are concerned with determining the degrees of comprehension. Overall reading or comprehending ability consists of a wide variety of competencies. The following list of subtest titles, taken from different test batteries, identifies the type of competencies sought: Accuracy, Average Comprehension, General Comprehension, Speed of Comprehension, Specific Comprehension, Paragraph Meaning, Sentence and Word Meaning, Word Discrimination, Word Knowledge, Word Recognition, Vocabulary, Comprehension, and Rate of Reading.

These headings point predominantly to a concern with various perceptual and cognitive capabilities. The desired perceptual abilities relate to accuracy and rate of word perception as well as to techniques that are used in word perception. The cognitive skills all relate to the derivation of meaning from the printed message. They consist of literal meanings and abilities to draw inferences from literal messages, evaluation of messages, recall, and appreciation. Because of a lack of clarity in the basic definition of reading comprehension, however, there is a wide variation in the tests purporting to measure it, just as there is in the materials that attempt to develop comprehension.

All standardized tests undergo a norming procedure in which the test items are administered to a representative national sample of students, and norms for test scores at different grade levels are derived on the basis of the results. What are commonly thought to be reading grade levels do not, consequently, refer to reading tasks that are deemed appropriate for given age-groups, but rather to the mean score of the group participating in the norming procedure. By the same token, reading grade levels do not refer to actual, "real life" reading tasks, but rather only to those posed by the particular tests chosen. A child reading at a sixth-grade level, therefore, is not necessarily reading materials that have been designed for twelve-year-olds, but is exhibiting various comprehension capabilites that, on one or another of the existing scales, coincide with the norm calculated for a population of sixth graders. Since all standardized achievement tests assume a normal distribution of performance, 23 percent of those taking such an exam will score below average by definition, while another 23 percent will score above average.

Test scores have significant implications for people over and above their use as determiners of reading ability. They are widely used as criteria for placing students in different classes, for accepting or rejecting students for different schools, and for guiding and counseling students into different avenues of academic and vocational pursuit. It is, indeed, one of the distinct ironies of the American experience that a cultural heritage predicated on the notion of rugged individualism should spawn a system of education that places so much credence in standardized and normed achievement testing. Despite the lack of clarity surrounding the form, use, and validity of the tests—and the lack of agreement on the essence of reading itself—most schools throughout the United States make wide use of standardized reading tests in the determination of student performance, level, and potential.

•

It is interesting to contrast this situation with that pertaining in some other countries. Japan, Israel, and England might be of particular interest; the first because it boasts a remarkably high literacy level and low incidence of reading failure; the second because, until recently, it reported the world's highest per capita consumption of reading matter; and the third because it is another major country in which the language taught and read is English. Although standardized tests exist in these countries, largely as a result of American influence, in all three instances they are used primarily in the diagnosis of reading difficulties among those students who are obviously failing, rather than as general tools of evaluation and assessment. In all three countries, reading abilities are thought to develop as a result of actual reading rather than as a function of formal instruction in reading.

Israel and England, among other countries, have become disenchanted with standardized testing in general, and both have recently abolished national standarized examinations that served as indicators of potential and, hence, education beyond the primary school years. Research in all three countries has indicated the importance of parental involvement in the teaching of reading. Great importance is attached to the role of parents as reading motivators, stimulators, and, in many cases, instructors. Parents also play an important role in identifying reading difficulties and, through working in tandem with schools, they serve significant roles in alleviating them. Also of importance in all three countries is the attempt to determine areas of interest to schoolchildren so that reading material might be suitably planned and published.

These observations are not intended to imply that reading difficulties and failure do not occur in Japan, Israel, and England. They do, however, show that emphasis in areas such as parental involvement, student motivation and interests, and individualized—rather than standardized—approaches to student reading development might be more profitable avenues to the attainment of reading and comprehension abilities. The less frequent use of standardized exams in these countries has certainly not hindered instruction or caused greater general reading failure.

Understanding the dangers inherent in standardized achievement testing, both scholars and test writers in the United States have issued repeated warnings concerning the interpretation of test results. The gist of these warnings is that a test score tells nothing more than the achievement of a person in a given test on a given day. The implication of this seems clear: the same person given a different test on a different day might attain completely different test results. On the one hand, this warning bears ample testimony to the lack of efficacy of standardized reading tests. On the other hand, hidden in this warning, by implication, is a notion of great significance that warrants further exploration: the content of the tests.

Comprehension must be wedded to content, since without content there can be no comprehension. All comprehension tests must, therefore, present those being tested with some content. Here we find wide differentiation among existing tests. Content topics of different tests relate to areas as widely divergent as the social sciences, industrial processes, geography, philosophy, history, animals, sports, literature, and so forth. It seems appropriate to assume that the content of a message will influence its comprehension to a very large extent. If a person is given two reading comprehension tests with widely different content, it seems likely that the test results will indicate two quite different levels of comprehension.

Herein lies the major fallacy of achievement testing in all its phases and levels. What are considered to be a set of objective skills and competencies are tested against a wholly subjective criterion. Stated differently, motor and cognitive abilities are examined without sufficient attention given to the affective domain. Less is known about testing people's interests, attitudes, or character developments than is known about testing motor or cognitive abilities. Neither does the attempt to assess various affective factors lend itself to standardization. But all of these reasons for not attempting to assess these factors are completely inadequate. For example, many people read material they are interested in with total comprehension, although they may not do as well with material that does not interest them. Without a doubt, reading entails affective as well as cognitive and motor behaviors. Confining testing and instruction to the latter skirts what might, indeed, be the main component of reading capability.

The same holds true of reading readiness tests, which, again, purport to identify a variety of motor and cognitive abilities but do not, in the main, delve into basic questions of young children's motivation and desire to read. Beyond the accepted reading "readiness" elements of visual discrimination, letter recognition, and auditory discrimination, it seems most tenable that there is an affective aspect to readiness—the ambition that develops in a child to become an independent reader—that complements the others and emerges independently of their existence. Surely, then, it is as important to identify and encourage this affective aspect of readiness as it is the traditionally accepted cognitive and motor factors.

The suggestion looms large that the ability to decode written symbols and extrapolate their verbal meanings, coupled with sufficient interest and appropriate motivation, creates good readers. According to this premise, the onus of creating good readers is transferred from the student to the materials used in both instruction and testing.

Much can be learned from analyzing attempts to teach adult illiterates how to read. It happens that the acquisition of the more technical aspect of reading is relatively easy. This ability rapidly atrophies through disuse, however, unless newly literate adults are sufficiently motivated not only to read the materials on hand but to require that appropriate materials be provided for them. Experience in adult literacy programs has shown that, once they are convinced of the importance of being able to read and, as a result, are sufficiently motivated to acquire reading skills, adult illiterates learn to read very rapidly. Having mastered the technique of reading, the new literates read materials that are important and interesting to them with great facility and with complete comprehension.

Surely, this experience has implications for both reading instruction and the testing of reading attainment. Far more emphasis should be placed, in the initial phase, on the development of motivations toward reading and, in the subsequent phases of reading instruction and attendant testing, on the source of materials that are geared to the specific interests of the readers. There is a paucity of tools for identifying areas of interest. Such tools, rather than standardized achievement tests, should be on the developmental agenda of those concerned with the teaching of reading.

The experiences noted in Japan, Israel, and England suggest an additional avenue for future work: involving parents more actively in their children's acquisition of reading skills. At least some of the demand for standardized achievement testing comes from the expressed desires of parents to know how their children are reading in comparison with other children. These desires have been a major constraint in attempts to introduce change into achievement reporting. All too often parents of schoolchildren have successfully conspired against attempts to report the achievement of their children in any but standardized forms. Most parents tend to relegate the task of teaching their children how to read to the schools, and they are quick to place the blame for failure squarely on teachers and the often maligned education system. Parents' active participation, particularly in the affective aspects of reading, is surely as crucial to the furtherance of reading skills as what is done in school. The implications are broad, however, and a search for ways and means in which parents can be creatively involved in the reading development of their children is a potentially rewarding area of exploration and experimentation.

While there is a need to modify the notion and tools of testing, there is also a real need to educate parents about the notion of reading and the importance of their participation, and a real need to report reading achievement in individualized formats.

Standardized reading achievement tests are at best a reflection of the prevailing approaches and attitudes toward reading and the teaching of reading. Reading, however, is a very personal skill; people read best what they want to read. Perhaps more than with any other skill, the aphorism at the head of this article holds true: *si duo idem faciunt, non est idem.*

SOME EXAMPLES OF TEST ITEMS

The following examples are taken from the *Gates Basic Reading Test* series (New York: Bureau of Publications, Teachers College, Columbia University, 1958). While dated, the Gates series is still in use throughout the country. The Reading Vocabulary Subtest (Type RV, Form 1) includes words such as:

crystal 1. glass 2. building 3. cold 4. hard 5. watery

pasture 1. water 2. clouds 3. cows 4. barn 5. land

genteel 1. colorless 2. polite 3. rich 4. stupid 5. nervous

serpent 1. fish 2. bird 3. snake 4. plate 5. sermon.

torrid 1. heavy 2. hungry 3. tasteless 4. hot 5. light

proffer 1. offend 2. open 3. speak 4. destroy 5. offer

debility 1. scorn 2. certainty 3. weakness 4. alertness 5. frankness

recumbent 1. aloft 2. reclining 3. courageous 4. defiant 5. apologetic

taciturn 1. colorful 2. silent 3. sticky 4. strange 5. obstinate

These are only several of the sixty-five word definitions appearing in the test. They certainly are not very common words, nor are they words that might be used in regular daily conversation, particularly not by primary-school-children. Knowledge of these words, therefore, requires a certain amount of a particular kind of reading experience. It is difficult to assume that all third graders will have read the kinds of materials, or would have been motivated to read the kinds of materials that might contain these words. Word choice within this subtest, then, is clearly biased and would tend to work against those students whose reading interests might lie in totally different directions.

The following examples are taken from the Reading to Appreciate General Significance Subtest (Type GS, Form 1):

> *Nan and Bob wanted a pet rabbit. With a box and a stick they built a trap that would catch a rabbit without hurting it. They baited the trap with carrots and lettuce. The first night nothing happened. The*

next night the bait was taken, but the trap had not worked. On the third morning as they came near, they could see that the trap had worked.

Draw a line under the word that tells what Nan and Bob found in their trap.

rabbit wildcat lion ant dog

A child with some imagination might very easily think that an animal other than a rabbit had been caught by the trap. Answering *dog*, for instance, would be considered by the examiner an error, although it is a very plausible answer, easily defensible, and on the surface indicates that the child can read and has seen fit to put a different animal into the trap.

Sally and Betty went to the circus together every year. They looked forward to it with pleasure. Every time they went, they laughed at the clowns' tricks and gasped at the daring of the high-wire artists. They ate popcorn and hot dogs and drank pink lemonade as if it were their last chance to enjoy these delicious treats.

Draw a line under the word that tells how Betty and Sally felt at the circus.

bored excited indifferent ill pained

The correct answer to this question, according to the check sheet, is *excited*. Obviously, the words *ill* and *pained* are also plausible responses. After having eaten all the things mentioned and consumed gobbles of pink lemondade, it stands to reason that one might feel *ill* or *pained*. However, the child with more imagination who responded with *ill* or *pained*. would be considered wrong and, in the final test score, unable to read as well as the child with less imagination.

Sally and Betty had been good friends ever since they were in the first grade. They had had their disagreements, but they liked each other too well to let any quarrel last long. One day Betty was chosen to play the queen in the class play. Sally had wanted to act that part herself, so at first she felt a little cross with Betty.

Draw a line under the word that tells how Sally felt toward Betty two day's later.

cross jealous angry distant friendly

The answer sheet indicates that *friendly* is the correct answer. However, could one not answer any of the other four words and make a very plausible argument about why they, too, are appropriate answers? The ambiguity in this and similar questions discriminates against children who read the short paragraphs perfectly well but allow their imaginations or own interpretations to dictate what, to them, are the correct answers. Answering differently from what is expected does not necessarily indicate that the person being tested cannot either read or appreciate the significance of the passage.

The following question is taken from Subtest on Reading to Understand Precise Directions (Type UD, Form 1):

Fred is going to build a model airplane. The wooden parts of the plane, a knife to shape them, and the glue to hold them are all together on the table where they will be handy. As he begins to work, he finds something in his way. Put an X on it.

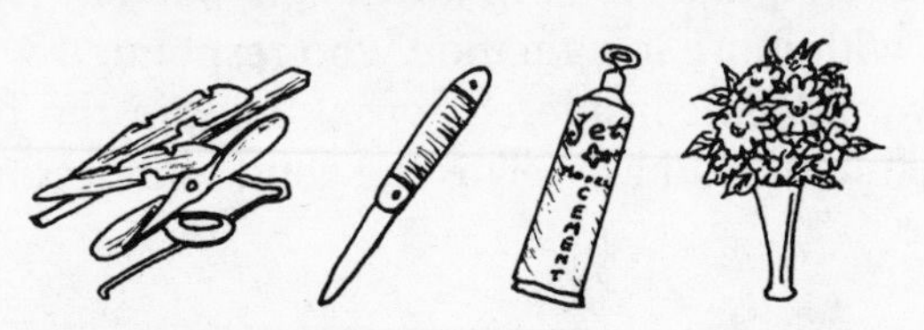

The correct answer is a vase with flowers. However, one could easily argue that the answer might be the cement, or the handle of the knife, or one of the objects in the drawing of the parts of the model plane. This kind of ambiguity might clearly work against the person who can both read the paragraph well and understand the directions he was given. Clearly, placing an X on any of the other objects could be as correct as placing it on the vase.

On the Misuse of Test Data:

A SECOND LOOK AT JENCKS'S "INEQUALITY"

MITCHELL LAZARUS

Mitchell Lazarus is director of nonbroadcast media for Project ONE, a group at Education Development Center, Newton, Massachusetts, that is producing a television series about mathematics, primarily for minority children, with related hands-on activities.

More than two years have passed since the appearance of Christopher Jencks's *Inequality,** and its conclusions are widely known by now. (Robert Hassenger provided a brief summary of the book's main points in the January 1973, and again in the November/December 1974 issues of *Principal.*) Among other things, Jencks and his colleagues concluded that differences in quality of schooling have very little effect on differences in adult success, and that improving schools can do very little toward improving society.

The strong and immediate public controversy that *Inequality* touched off has still not died down completely. Discussions of the book have so far overlooked an important point, however: the quality of the source data. In fact, *Inequality* is a good case study of what can happen when data from large-scale tests are taken too seriously. Among the various kinds of data that Jencks uses in his analysis, test

---

*Christopher Jencks et al., *Inequality: A Reassessment of the Effect of Family and Schooling in America* (New York: Basic Books, 1972).

scores play a large part—especially achievement scores and IQ scores. These turn up often in his calculations and contribute heavily to his conclusions. Indeed, without test data to draw on, the book could never have arrived at its conclusions. Thus, if there are serious basic flaws in the process of achievement testing and IQ testing, the book's conclusions must come into serious doubt. And, in fact, this is just the case.

Jencks's use of test score information is questionable in several ways. But before coming to these in detail, let us look at a more general and pervasive issue.

Throughout, the book consistently uses inadequate measures to stand for phenomena being measured. For example, it reflects a student's academic achievement in terms of his or her scores on achievement tests. These are not at all the same thing. If they were, the only effects we would seek from schooling would be changes in test scores, which is simply not true.

The link between measures and phenomena being measured is much clearer in the physical sciences than in education. An astronomer doing an orbit calculation might represent the earth as a point mass of so many quintillion tons, but he would never confuse the earth itself with this large number. The earth has animals, rocks, fish, trees; the number is just a number. The social sciences, on the other hand, sometimes do seem to mistake the number for the thing itself—the score on an IQ test for actual intelligence, or the score on an achievement test for actual achievement. True, many sociologists would deny this heartily. But remember the Jencks book: again and again, Jencks and his colleagues rest their conclusions on test scores just as if the scores were the real thing.

Let us look at this in more detail. Jencks used achievement scores and IQ scores heavily in his analyses, and in particular took achievement scores as a direct measure of what schools accomplish. For his conclusions to be sound, therefore, the following underlying assumptions would have to be true, or nearly so:

- The only important outcomes of schooling are those that achievement tests look for.

- Achievement tests are valid; they actually measure what they claim to measure with a good degree of accuracy.

- The analyses carried out on test scores are sensible, consistent, sound, and reasonably complete.

- IQ tests are good measures of intelligence, which implies that intelligence can be described adequately by a single number.

All of these assumptions are false, and so Jencks's use of test scores to support his conclusions is very much in question.

First of all, achievement tests try to measure only a small part of what schools try to do. Achievement tests look most of all for the acquisition of knowledge, the collection of facts that a child may have picked up while in school. More specifically, reading tests look for meanings of words, points of grammar, and the like; mathematics tests look for the ability to calculate and for some familiarity with terminology; and science and social science tests are tied even more directly to particular accumulations of facts.

But there is much more to education than learning particular facts and individual skills—especially in a time when "common knowledge" changes noticeably from each decade to the next, and even "common sense" does not stay quite the same. Good teachers and good principals try to develop sound judgment, creativity, insight, and understanding, as well as many other accomplishments that achievement tests make no effort to tap. The old picture of education—the child coming to school empty and the school filling him with facts—is thoroughly obsolete, surviving now mostly through the large-scale achievement tests. Conclusions based on test results, such as those in the Jencks book, reflect a distorted picture of what schools seek to accomplish.

Second, there is good reason to doubt that achievement tests measure properly even the characteristics they are designed for; that is, their "validity" is very much in question. For the most part, achievement tests are judged valid if they meet three conditions: 1) superficial appearance of validity; 2) internal scoring consistency over a sample of students; and 3) correlation with other tests of a similar nature. None of these tell us if the tests are doing their job properly. And hardly ever are tests validated against independent, outside criteria. Thus any defects common to most tests of the same type will likely be overlooked.

For example, virtually all large-scale achievement tests put a heavy demand on students' reading abilities—even if the test is supposedly one of social sciences or of mathematics. Thus every such test is a reading test first, and a test of anything else only afterward. Also, the tests demand performance under time pressure, which some students react to badly. Other traits, such as motivation to do well on the test, orderliness, ability to guess constructively, and resistance to panic, are also important to good scores, even though they may be completely irrelevant to the knowledge that is supposedly being tested.

A score in, say, mathematics achievement might in part reflect the student's mathematical abilities, but the score will be heavily contaminated by factors totally unrelated to mathematics performance. A social analysis based on such scores can be very unfair to some students and social groups, especially if the extraneous traits important in the tests are "middle class traits" that are not spread evenly through the population. If this is true, then the results of analysis based on test scores can be very misleading.

Note that Jencks seems undecided about the appropriateness of test scores in his analysis. Early in the book he asserts: "We take a very dim view of test scores, both as measures of schools' effectiveness and as measures of individual talent" (p. 12). But forty pages further on, he discusses test scores in markedly more positive terms: "Our intuitive conviction, however, is that standardized tests *do* measure certain basic cognitive skills . . ." (p.52; original emphasis)—although he then goes on to define these skills, circularly, in terms of "whatever it is that standardized tests measure." Nevertheless, these basic cognitive skills (as reflected in test scores) play a large part in his subsequent arguments.

Throughout the book, Jencks reminds us that standardized tests do not tap all of intelligent behavior, but still he uses test scores as complete reflections of cognitive skills.

The model that Jencks uses for his analysis adds some further troubling assumptions. His mathematical picture of a school is a box, with dollars-per-pupil going in at one end and standardized test scores coming out at the other. No other factors come into account: "We did not look in any detail at things like morale, teacher expectations, . . . and school 'climate'" (p. 95). From this very restricted model, Jencks draws his now famous conclusions that school resources have no important effect on educational accomplishment (p. 8). Jencks claims a dislike for the model, but this does not stop him from using it as the basis for a great deal of analysis.

Again, the model is a case of quantifying the quantifiable and ignoring the rest. The tactic makes a mathematical analysis possible and seemingly provides an atmosphere of scientific authority. But it overlooks the fact that schools are made of people, and that we are not very good at quantifying people yet. "Ignore what you cannot measure" is a dangerous doctrine, for it can give quasi-scientific respectability to conclusions that come from very weak data.

•

Finally, let us turn to the problems involved in using IQ scores for any kind of analysis. Apart from the issues of test design and contamination (which are at least as troublesome for IQ as they are for achievement testing), there is a serious conceptual matter here: the notion of assigning a single number to represent a person's intelligence. People are more complicated than that, and it makes no sense at all to collapse the different facets of intelligence into a single IQ score. Worse, doing so will badly misrepresent what people are really like. And it invites simpleminded comparisons among individuals and among groups.

If it means anything, intelligence is the ability to survive and flourish *in one's own environment*, and even in a single environment, that ability can take many forms. People are different. We cope in different ways, and we bring to bear different kinds of skills and traits. Each of us is good at some things and poor at others. A single-number measure of intelligence makes far less sense than a single-number measure of beauty, or of character—and who would be foolish enough to try pinning single numbers on these?

Jencks's book fails in several ways, many of which stem from his use of test score data. The book uses measures that look at only a small part of the picture and then see that part in very distorted ways. It relies on analyses that consciously overlook the most significant parts of the situation being analyzed. And it presents results that may be due far more to poor measures and inadequate analysis than to the schools and the society they try to represent. The final outcome is simplistic, and perhaps wrong.

About his mathematical techniques, Jencks wrote: "The [statistical] methods we have used may involve considerable error. In self-defense, we can only say that the magnitude of these errors is almost certainly less than if we had simply consulted our prejudices, which seems to be the usual alternative" (p. 15).

Not necessarily. Jencks's analysis may be no better in the end than his prejudices, if the numbers he uses bear little on reality. Worse, the mathematical trappings may intimidate readers into taking the conclusions far too seriously—much more seriously than they would regard bare prejudice without the quasi-scientific trimmings. Test scores have an official, no-nonsense look about them that leads to misguided respect for the testing system, even though they actually mean little. Worst of all, test scores invite us to lump people together in a kind of mathematical stereotyping.

Once we understand the flaws in the testing process, we cannot take the Jencks book too seriously. More important, we can begin to set aside test scores for the time being and focus instead on people: students, teachers, school systems, and cultures. The outcome of education is not test scores, but young people. We must never again let that point become confused.

TWO PRINCIPALS LOOK AT STANDARDIZED TESTS

ARTHUR S. LAUGHLAND
WILLIAM CORBETT

Arthur S. Laughland is principal of Hyde School in Newton, Massachusetts.
William Corbett is principal of Lowell School in Watertown, Massachusetts.

No people on the face of the earth have been bitten quite as hard by the testing bug as the American people. We take quizzes on every aspect of our lives and derive self-satisfaction or self-mortification from the results we achieve. We have even been known to cheat a little in order to get that warmth and security we feel when the little computations at the end of the quiz yield a result indicating that we are "above average" or even "superior" to others.

We have an unfortunate belief that every skill, every talent, every body of knowledge, and even our personalities, can be broken down into finite parts; that we can draw a sample of those parts, test ourselves with that sample, and thus prove our ability in any particular area.

We employ this technique in business and industry to determine the "right" people for the "right" job. In colleges, we use this same technique to determine which "labels" to assign to people and to sort out those who should be admitted from those who should be refused admission. In our private lives, the technique reassures us that our personalities are "OK" and that our sex lives are "normal"; and in schools it "assesses" the progress of children and reassures parents that educators are doing a proper job.

This blind faith in testing is matched by no other belief. Yet, if we let it, testing can mark innocent children with stigmata for the rest of their lives, tarnish schools' reputations, and ruin teaching careers.

In recent years, despite such risks, the administration of commercial, standarized tests to schoolchildren has become widespread. One large factor in its growth has been the desire of state and federal agencies to obtain objective data to prove the efficacy of programs funded by state and federal grants. The growth in size of federal and state financial support for local educational facilities has led to an understandable desire to ensure that such funds are wisely spent. School systems should be held accountable for the quality of education that they provide. Federal, state, and local monies are too hard won to allow school officials to spend them unwisely.

Surely there can be no objection to educators being held accountable. It is, rather, the method of accountability that should be questioned. For example, several states have passed legislation that makes objective, standardized testing one of the criteria by which the quality of education shall be judged. Colleges have done this for years through Scholastic Aptitude Tests. Entrance to a particular college may be determined by the scores achieved by any particular individual. The basic effect of this system has been that college entrance requirements have determined, in large part, what the curriculum—at least in the high schools—will be. It is obvious that one of the criteria by which a school system is judged is simply the number of youngsters from that school system who gain entrance to college—preferably to the college of their choice. Therefore, any school official, any high school principal, will see to it that the young people in his charge are exposed to, and even practiced in, the materials that comprise the SATs. In short, teaching to the test has become a way of life for many of our high school teachers.

During the last several years, the high costs of a college

education, the greater number of places available in the colleges, and changes in the aspirations of a large part of our student population have caused some shift in attitudes to college entrance. Many schools have responded more to the individual needs of their students by broadening the school experience and becoming more concerned with the thinking process and the development of values and personality.

One would assume that this is better education, but it does not necessarily yield high scores on college entrance examinations, for the old yardsticks are being used to measure new pathways. Already, the lament is appearing in the newspapers and other media that the decline in scores on college entrance examinations is evidence that the quality of education provided for young people has also declined.

And now, several states are proposing to repeat old mistakes. Objective, standardized testing will become the criterion for assessing the quality of education in any particular community. Teachers, being human and knowing that they will be judged on this criterion, will teach to the test. As a result, once again we will be locked into a test determined curriculum, and schoolhouses will become—for at least a portion of the day—the plodding, pedestrian, soul-destroying places they were in the past.

But it is not merely on the grounds of curriculum determination that I object to standardized testing in our schools. Objective, standardized testing breaks down a certain body of knowledge and certain skills into discrete, manageable parts. It samples these parts and constructs a test that is then administered to a sizeable population in order to determine "norms." The norm is determined in various ways, but essentially it means that half the sample population scored above the norm and half the population scored below the norm.

If the sample population, by some miracle, matches the local population, then one should expect that half the local population will score above the norm and half will score below the norm. By such reasoning, then, a school is doing fairly well if half the children fail. Yet how many parents and how many public officials would accept such results as evidence of quality education?

There are further objectionable factors built into the tests. Objective testing means that the examiner provides the "right" answer. The testees choose from alternatives. They may know the answer; they may make an informed guess; or they may make a little mark at random to get the job over and done with. How many of us have seen youngsters marking randomly to complete the page?

Moreover, for the examinee, the enemy is time. Time pressure stimulates some testees and frustrates others. The ability to respond quickly does not necessarily reflect the quality of thought or knowledge. In fact, children with imagination and creative abilities can easily become confused if they think too deeply about some of the problems posed.

Finally, a standardized test is impersonal. It makes no allowances for individual peculiarities. It cries out for a kind of gamesmanship, and perhaps that is what it tests best.

If we understand these things about testing, maybe it is not so dangerous; it may even be fun for some of us. But it is not fun for the child who freezes; it is not fun for the child who struggles for small successes to be labeled a "failure" time after time; and it is not fun for the child whose one bad day yields results that must be lived with until the next testing time.

Are we to continue with these standardized, sterilized judgments? Is there to be no account taken of backgrounds, opportunities, and personalities? We test ourselves every day as we meet or fail to meet the challenges the day presents. There are teachers who know their children, care for them, and guide them. It appears, however, that we have lost our trust in them and, yes, in ourselves. We need something more than the reassurance of another human being, and we seek it in objective, standardized testing—preferably untouched by human hand. We need confirmation or denial of what we know in our hearts already.

If this be so, then let us, at least, make our judgments with compassion and understanding. If we need outside sources to determine whether schools are doing their jobs, let's establish teams of knowledgeable people to spend time in the schools; to learn the difficulties and frustrations of school people and students; to identify the strengths and the weaknesses of the system; and to suggest ways for significant improvement.

I read recently that our children's lives are far too precious to entrust them to professional educators. How much more foolish to entrust our judgments about quality education to the cheap panacea of easily administered tests.

A.S.L.

* * * * *

Once again standardized educational testing is enjoying considerable attention. Reexamination of testing procedures, which took place during the 1960s, when many were concerned with the affective needs of children, has been brushed aside as the "accountability" movement that began in the early 1970s has taken hold. How can we have educational accountability, some legislators and school board members ask, without massive doses of achievement tests? After all, we have neat examples of measurement and cost analysis in industry. Why, then, should we not measure and cost-analyze education?

Unfortunately, the recent phenomenon of publishing achievement test scores of school districts—or indeed of individual schools—has given false credence to the preciseness of standardized tests. (In some cases elaborate statistical procedures are used, further compounding an illusion.) The scores purport to be measures of the educational health of a community or a school. But, in fact, it would make as much sense to take the blood pressure of each student, apply the usual statistical procedures, and publish the results district by district, to measure the health of the student body. If a test on morality existed, and if there were enough people with funds who wanted one, its results could be similarly published to describe the moral condition of a school district.

Do standardized achievement tests tell us anything at all? I believe they tell us approximately as much about a student as blood pressure tests tell a medical doctor about an individual patient. If a community chooses to buy these crude instruments at all—and the investment is questionable—the results should be used by teachers as *one* factor in the process of assessing an individual child's progress.

Since the tests have such limited value, the reader may well ask how we have reached the position of using standardized achievement testing in such an extensive way. First, there is little question that the use of SATs (Scholastic Aptitude Tests) and then PSATs (Preliminary Scholastic Aptitude Tests) as a varying factor in college entrance has had a telling domino effect on standardized testing all the way down the line to grade testing in primary school. In addition, in a number of cases there is a belief that some teachers and some principals may not be maintaining academic standards as well as they should and that standardized test scores are an adequate measure of this performance. By the same token, there is also a lack of definition in these communities about what schools should accomplish, and this leads to the feeling that schools should accomplish all things that well-intentioned groups feel they should.

What, then, is the answer to this complex problem? I believe it is this: that the educational strength of a school lies in the leadership ability and integrity of its principal; in the quality of preparation, dedication, and empathy of its teachers; and in the strong interest and support of parents in the school district. Given these factors in generous quantities, coupled with appropriate financial support and some integrity at the university level, the contemporary mania for standardized testing should eventually become one of educational history's least read footnotes.

W.C.

REPORTING READING TEST RESULTS IN NEW YORK CITY

JEROME GREEN

Jerome Green is principal of the Ochs Public School 111 in New York City and past president of the New York City Elementary School Principals Association.

Mr. Green is also chairman of the elementary section of the National Council of Teachers of English, and president-elect of the New York State English Council.

Many educators who have dedicated their professional lives to the right to read for all students are now watching with concern as reading scores become ammunition in public discussion over pupil achievement and professional accountability. In New York City, if we look at our largest city as an example, one would have imagined that information about educational accomplishment could have been more meaningfully presented to the public than by publishing the reading scores of the schools. Unfortunately, what has happened has not created the kind of understanding that leads to public support of public education.

Since group IQ tests are neither given nor used in New York City, published reading scores have assumed an importance in the public mind that has become synonymous with educational success or failure. Every spring, standardized reading achievement tests (usually the Metropolitan Achievement Tests) have been administered in all grades, two through nine. The results of these tests have tended to obscure other important evaluative criteria relating to cognitive and affective domains of the curriculum, and to blot out other successful achievements and programs in the schools.

When the board of education began to release the reading achievement scores of the elementary and junior high schools in the decentralized school districts, these results were printed in the *New York Times* and other newspapers. The public was given a list of schools and a comparison of the median or mean reading scores in selected grades for the last two school years. No other data were listed for each school, and so other factors of possible relevance—such as pupil attendance, health, mobility, or bilingualism, as well as poverty or a school's Title I status—were not available for consideration in connection with their possible correlation with the results.

In fact, the progress of individual children tended to be completely ignored in these published results; no attempt was made to do more than list the results of the selected grades, and no attempt was made to identify pupils who were actually in them from year to year. Furthermore, no data were listed about the school's professional personnel. As a result, although the teachers and supervisors in the various schools knew what was actually happening to individual children, the public was given only a "number" by which to judge a school. Public opinion and parental attitudes were formed from such questionable quantitative data.

Even more misleading was the second way in which the public was given a picture of how well the city's schoolchildren were achieving. According to the State Decentralization Law of 1969, which led to the dividing of the giant New York City School District into thirty-two presumably more manageable community districts, the chancellor had to rank all schools on the basis of their reading test results so that those schools listed in the lowest 45 percentile ranking could use an alternative method of hiring teachers. This provision of the law allowed a school in the lowest rankings to hire teachers through a state certification and national teacher examination route rather than through the usual procedure of a civil service, competitive, teacher examination administered by the board of examiners of the board of education.

Although no one seems to have made a study of how schools using alternative hiring have fared in their quest for reading (test score) improvement, newspapers usually ran another story listing school rankings according to reading scores; but again, it was done with no other school-by-school educational data that might help the public to understand educational problems, such as why one school was "up" and one school was "down." And once more, the public was implicitly encouraged to make invidious and superficial comparisons.

Assumptions and inferences made by the public about these rankings were obvious, although not necessarily accurate. Schools that ranked "high" were considered "good" schools, presumably doing well because of superior teachers and supervisors. While this assumption may or may not be a fact, no one ever tried an experiment in which the professional staff of a "good" school with high scores was transplanted into a "bad" school with low scores in order to verify whether theories about professional accountability were tenable or justified. Some skeptics have even concluded that legislators and boards of education may have been looking for ways to divert attention from their own roles and responsibilities to the schools and found that playing the reading score "numbers game" was a diverting simplification of a complex problem.

In a time of increasing stress on accountability, the misuse of reading test results could become even more pernicious in the educational environment. Those who work directly with children in the schools and care about their development, and who also consider themselves teachers of the language as well as teachers of the values of our society, cannot accept a simplistic approach or stereotyped thinking that reduces a child, an educational process, a class of students, or a school environment to a statistic. Unless educators draw attenton to the responsibilities that society and all adults have to the youngsters in our schools, standardized group reading test scores will continue to be used as weapons, rather than as tools for analysis that can strengthen the teaching and learning process. Teachers and parents of pupils really need to know more, analytically, about reading.

We should no longer support the indiscriminate and mechanical use of each child's group tests, the results of which are publicized without sufficient analysis that everyone can understand. Instead, we must work for the funds and assistance to develop and put into use an individualized, diagnostic testing program supplemented by all the supportive services—remedial, psychological, linguistic, and medical—that might be necessary for those readers who otherwise might be cut off from the full personal, intellectual, and social development that is their birthright. Some steps in this direction are now being taken in New York City, but within limitations of critical funding problems.

The right-to-read concept will never be fully realized until society and its government put priorities and money where the needs are greatest: to help the urban and rural poor, the disadvantaged, and the bilingual child, who need better individualized services rather than group labels and ratings. Until we have commitments that will provide superior programs, materials, services, and trained personnel for reading development and improvement, and until reading test results are concerned with qualitative needs of individual children rather than with quantitative statistical generalities, we will be unable to say in a sanguine way, "Of such stuff are better readers made, and of such stuff are informed, affirmative public opinion and parental attitudes made."

HOW TO AVOID THE DANGERS OF TESTING

JERRY L. PATTERSON
THEODORE J. CZAJKOWSKI
ELAINE HUBBARD
GLENN JOHNSON
CHARLIE SLATER
DARWIN KAUFMAN

Jerry L. Patterson, Theodore J. Czajkowski, Elaine Hubbard, Glenn Johnson, and Charlie Slater are curriculum coordinators in the Research and Development Department of the Madison, Wisconsin, Public Schools.

Darwin Kaufman is coordinator for research and evaluation for the Research and Development Department of the Madison, Wisconsin, Public Schools.

The authors were members of an ad hoc Testing and Evaluation Committee, which drew up these guidelines and developed a framework for program evaluation.

Here is a hypothetical news story that might have appeared in the local paper almost anywhere across the country. Does it sound all too familiar?

TEST SCORES DECLINE

Test scores for Typicaltown sixth graders fell below the national average this year, for the first time in memory. Thomas Jefferson Elementary School, located in the central city, scored lower than any other Typicaltown school, while suburban Frank Lloyd Wright Middle School scored highest. These were among the results reported to the Board of Education last night by Director of Testing Q. A. Abbott.

Several board members expressed worry and concern about the decline. Newly elected board member B. L. Tighten, who ran on the campaign promise of cutting the budget, suggested that the low scores were the result of people who did not do their jobs. "It's time to cut some of the deadwood," he said.

Community criticism was unusually loud. One representative of Citizens for Better Schools said, "These results are yet another indictment of the inattention to inner city schools. Why isn't something done about conditions at Jefferson?"

Even teachers were critical. Clara Contract, president of the teachers' union, suggested that the lower scores resulted from large class sizes, and an unidentified teacher said that the tests bore no relation to what she taught. "What do these tests have to do with my classroom?" she asked angrily.

Standardized testing can generate a great deal of political controversy. As the scores go down, the discussion gets more heated. Interest groups tend to interpret the results in such a way as to support their own positions. In fact, the same data are often used to support a variety of conflicting arguments and causes.

Despite the difficulties surrounding the issue of testing and evaluation, however, we believe that tests can be useful sources of information for planning instruction, estimating student performance, and assessing success in achieving goals. This statement is qualified by two major ifs: *if* certain guidelines for the use of tests are followed, and *if* these guidelines are applied to a larger framework for evaluation.

While many scholars have discussed testing in measurement and evaluation primers, such information is usually not readily applicable to school testing situations. The guidelines that follow have been synthesized from several sources and can, we hope, be directly applied in most school districts:

- *Tests should be given for a specific, clearly stated purpose that is agreed on in advance by those who are to use the results.* When an adequate purpose has been formulated before the test is administered, there is little question about how the data will be used. Too often educators give the tests routinely and then wonder aloud, "Now what?" Failure to establish the reason for testing obviously contributes to the kinds of misinterpretations cited in the news account.

- *Tests should be viewed as only one source of data for decision making.* School districts often rely on a set of test scores for drawing major conclusions about programs and pupils. Seldom, if ever, should test results be the sole criterion on which educational decisions are based; educational settings are too complicated to support such a practice. Other information should be combined with test results to enable educators to make sound decisions. The following questions suggest the kinds of information that can interact with and modify the relative importance of test results: What is the relationship between test results and other indicators of student performance, such as teacher observations and judgments? How are the test results influenced by variables unrelated to the school program, such as environmental background? What goals of the program—students' social development, for example—are not evidenced in test results?

- *Standardized tests should be administered with the expectation that information derived from them will be helpful in making better decisions than could be made without them.* Since standardized tests are relatively expensive to purchase, administer, score, and interpret, their use is warranted *only* when the information they may elicit is not readily available from other, less expensive sources. Because such tests have been used in the past and are relatively simple to administer, their use continues to grow. We hope that adherence to this guideline will begin to restrict the inappropriate use of these instruments.

- *Measurement and curriculum specialists should supervise both the selection of tests and the interpretation of test scores.* Both measurement and curriculum specialists can assume an important role in deciding which test best fits the needs of a particular population and program. From a measurement point of view, for instance, tests need to be examined for technical features, such as reliability and norming procedures. Curriculum personnel, on the other hand, may look at the relationship between test goals and curriculum goals when choosing appropriate instruments. Once tests are administered, measurement specialists play an equally valuable role in clarifying terms, such as standard scores and standard deviation. In addition, curriculum specialists can use technical information—such as content analysis of tests—to gain the most accurate interpretation of scores.

- *Test data should be released to the media and public only when accompanied by proper background information and interpretation.* Since people who work in the news media rarely know all the many factors affecting school performance, they should not be left the responsibility of interpreting test results. An important element of any testing program is the dissemination of the information. Consequently, the data must be presented in the context of the questions and decisions it was gathered to address. Furthermore, the factors that limit the use of the information must be made explicit. To accomplish these functions, the dissemination format should be easily understood by the public.

Following these practical guidelines should minimize the testing problems that school administrators face. In addition, as we mentioned earlier, school administrators should see testing as but one part of a larger framework of program evaluation and should apply similar guidelines to that framework.

A DUE PROCESS PROCEDURE FOR TESTING

EDWIN F. TAYLOR
JUDAH L. SCHWARTZ

Edwin F. Taylor is a senior research scientist in the Department of Physics and the Division for Study and Research in Education at the Massachusetts Institute of Technology, Cambridge, Massachusetts.

Judah L. Schwartz is professor of engineering science and education at the Massachusetts Institute of Technology, Cambridge, Massachusetts.

Young children are not permitted to participate in certain medical experiments (even with their parents' permission) because we feel they are incapable of giving informed consent to potentially dangerous medical procedures. But without so much as a "by your leave," we routinely subject millions of children to "standardized" tests that may have far-reaching consequences for their academic and personal futures.

Most children do not have sufficient self-confidence to challenge adult educators, so it is an empty exercise to compose a written bill of rights for them to invoke. Instead, we are outlining here a procedure designed to protect the legitimate interests of all those involved in testing. The procedure itself is intended to be educational, as well, in that it encourages parents and children to inform themselves in a situation in which they are being asked to make a specific decision.

This procedure should be used whenever any communitywide, state, regional, or national test of either "achievement" or "ability" (including IQ) is to be given. Tests used by individual teachers with their own classes are not included, and we honestly do not know how—or whether—these small-scale tests should be controlled.

Before any "standardized" test is given, a permission slip (similar to those used for field trips) should be sent home. The permission slip, signed by the school principal, would include the following information:

- Description of the test to be given
- Who will be taking the test
- Who is expected to benefit and in what ways
- Who will use the results and for what purposes
- Whether or not the student's name will be known to those studying the results and what control student and parent have over dissemination of results
- Whether or not the test results will become part of the student's permanent record
- The consequences of *not* taking the test for the student, the school, and those administering the test or using the results
- Description of the report that will be made to the parent and the child (the parent must be accompanied by the child) after the test results are available.

In addition, the principal would offer to show a sample test to the students and parents in advance. (A student may see the sample test in the absence of his or her parents, but the parents may see it only in the presence of the student.) Blanks would be provided for refusing permission for the child to take the test, or for specifying conditions on which acceptance depends. The permission slip would be signed by the child and by one parent, and a copy provided for the files at home.

QUESTIONS YOU SHOULD ASK ABOUT YOUR TESTING PROGRAM

J. PARKER DAMON

J. Parker Damon is principal of McCarthy-Towne School in Acton, Massachusetts, a public exploratory school with five hundred students, kindergarten through sixth grade.

Mr. Damon has fifteen years of teaching and administration experience, which includes positions at the elementary, secondary, and college levels. He is a specialist in reading and language development.

"Standardized tests are the only objective measure we have to determine how well schools, programs, and students are doing." "Standardized tests are not perfect, but until something better comes along, they are better than nothing." "Standardized tests are too often misused; therefore, they should not be used at all."

Statements such as these represent the different views professionals and the public have of achievement and aptitude tests. Although the use of some standardized tests has been challenged for well over a decade,* the debate has intensified over the past five years. The issues involved are complex, diverse, and emotional. Community pressure groups, professional vested interests, and concerned parents all want to be heard. Who is right? Whose opinion should be followed? Unless the people who use the tests ask the right

*In the 1930s and again in the 1960s, the advisability and necessity of using College Entrance Examinations was questioned, with the result that many schools and colleges adopted alternative measures.

questions, there will be no resolution to the issues and there will be a breakdown of whatever cooperation and communication now exist among the public, educators, and educational publishers.

The words "standardized tests" mean different things to different people. IQ tests, college boards, job preference inventories, aptitude tests, curriculum achievement tests, and attitude scales are all forms of standardized tests. Some are given to large groups all at once, while others are administered individually; some are designed to be gross indicators of trends, while others are meant to diagnose particular problems.

In a public school, any one of a variety of professionals may use different standardized tests with the same students, or the same tests with different students. The classroom teacher, guidance counselor, learning disabilites specialist, nurse, principal, psychologist, remedial reading teacher, and speech therapist all rely automatically on certain tests. Yet each of them may refer to "tests," "testing," and "test results" without specifying which tests or kinds of tests they mean. In fact, school committees, parents, and even teachers are often unaware of some of the more significant distinctions in testing; for example, the difference between a criterion referenced test and a norm referenced test, or a domain referenced test. How are these different meanings going to be sorted out, and who is going to do it?

A few years ago, several national magazines and professional journals presented arguments both for and against IQ testing. Heredity, environment, and professional qualifications became equally weighted topics in the debate. To some, any discussion of the possible influence of heredity on the development of intelligence meant raising all the issues of racism as well. To others, any analysis of the influence of environment on intelligence meant examining all aspects of life in ghetto squalor, suburban affluence, or rural deprivation. And to still others, who was speaking, where they expressed their views, and the particular view they expressed became more important than clarifying the nature-nurture issue, examining assumptions, or changing practices. The argument was charged with emotion, but there are still no clear definitions of intelligence, IQ, or aptitude. There is still no satisfactory means of relating performance to creativity, values, and future experiences. And the tests are being used now more than ever.

Of course, the public should hold school systems accountable for wise spending and for meeting educational goals. Parents have a right to know how well their children are progressing and what additional measures they or the schools need to take. School committees and administrators need to know which programs are succeeding in order to allocate resources and set priorities. Teachers need to know the effectiveness of their teaching methods and materials. The requirements and expectations of these groups are different and should be treated differently. To assume that any one particular test is capable of providing such a wide variey of information is absurd.

Most people would agree to that point in theory, but unfortunately, actual experience indicates otherwise. A disproportionate amount of the money spent on evaluating systemwide or schoolwide programs is spent on testing; very little goes for teacher inservice or for curriculum development, even though these improvements are far more costly and important. A system that allots $10,000 for both testing ($3,000) and inservice and curriclum development ($7,000), out of a $3 million dollar budget for five schools and 2,500 pupils, is fooling itself if it expects to know very much about what is going on and also make improvements. A system that size might have a professional staff of 150 to 200, and thus spend only about $35 to $45 per professional to improve each person's skills in diagnosing difficulties, developing appropriate materials and methods, and implementing improvement.

It is not surprising, then, that test results receive so much emphasis. They are relatively easy to use, and they carry the weight of many years of authority. As a result, the scores are squeezed for every bit of information they can deliver, and everyone's attention—parents, educators, and citizens—is focused on what has already happened, not on what will.

Assuming for a moment that standardized tests should continue to be used in public schools, how might their use be improved? One way would be for students, teachers, parents, administrators, school committeee members, and taxpayers to ask some very specific questions about the school's testing program. Asking these questions challenges a long-held belief that giving tests is the prerogative of the educator. One can almost hear the retort: "Take away my right to test, and you've taken away one of my most vital instructional tools." Perhaps, but how vital to the teacher is data that is not received until many weeks later? (Standardized tests should not be confused with tests made by the teacher, of course, or with tests that are components of specific curriculum materials and methods.)

The assumption that an educator—administrator, specialist, or teacher—has the right to give any test to any student needs to be challenged, particularly when the results of the test will be stored in a computer. Who controls this information? The individual's right to privacy and the individual's right to know what is being done before it is done both need to be protected. One does not grant permission to a lawyer or doctor after the fact, except in emergencies, and how many standardized testing situations are emergencies? People should start asking questions *before* standardized tests are given, and they should accept only clear, specific, and comprehensive answers. If the answers are not satisfactory, then whoever has raised the questions should refuse to administer the tests, or take the tests, or allow the test results to be used. The remainder of this article deals with some specific questions that educators ought to raise about standardized tests.

How does the proposed standardized testing supplement other forms of assessment and evaluation already in use? Many systems and schools do not have a comprehensive testing plan; even if such a plan exists, not everyone in the system knows about it or its components. Frequently, a particular test is given long after its original purpose has been achieved, without being reexamined for appropriateness.

Many educators do not stop to ask if the same information could be acquired in other, more effective ways. Random sampling of a particular group, for instance, can provide information about that group that is as statistically significant as if every member of the group had been tested, and at a much lower cost. Similarly, not every test must be taken in its entirety by each student, nor must each student fill out the same answer sheet for every part of a test. On successive days, different students can be given different answer sheets so that, on completion of the testing, any one answer sheet may have been filled out by as many different students as there are parts to the test.

How much time will administering the test involve? How much will it cost? These are deceptive questions, for involved in a standardized test situation are not only the students taking the test, but also those who are administering it and who will ultimately use the test data. Could everyone's time be more profitably used? Many standardized tests require several days to a week, or more, to complete. During this period other in- and out-of-school activities are curtailed or interrupted, and the school climate is disrupted. And in addition to the price of purchasing and scoring the tests are the not-so-hidden costs of sorting, distributing, administering, packaging and mailing, interpreting, recording, and explaining. Some of these tasks may be performed by volunteers, but others must be done by school personnel in order to protect the students' privacy rights.

A typical standardized test may have nine parts, each

requiring an average of twenty minutes; the entire test will therefore require, on the average, more than three hours to complete. Prior to test time, a school secretary will already have spent several hours counting and sorting the tests, answer sheets, instruction booklets, and pencils for distribution to the teachers who will be giving the test. The teachers, in turn, will then spend an hour or so making sure they have received the correct materials, studying the instructions for administering the tests, and, if necessary, arranging the room so that each student has the proper kind of seat and writing surface to use. In addition, the teacher may give sample test exercises to the students to prepare them properly for the actual test situation.

After the test is administered, another hour or more will be spent by the secretary collecting, packaging, and mailing the tests to the scorer. When the results are returned, the secretary has to distribute them to the appropriate people: this year's teacher and maybe last year's, the principal, the guidance counselor, the reading teacher, and the learning disabilities specialist. Each teacher will have to spend an hour or more reviewing the test results and several more hours interpreting them to parents. Finally, all of the results must be filed in each student's record folder, gummed labels with total scores attached, and printout sheets or answer sheets inserted, a job that requires several more hours of the school secretary's time.

For a school with twenty classrooms and 525 students, kindergarten through sixth grade, it may require a minimum of fifty-nine hours to give the tests to 225 students, three classes per grade, in grades two, four, and six. A summary of how all this is spent—and what it amounts to in terms of dollars—might look something like the chart on page 354.

These are extremely conservative estimates of time and costs; for example, teachers' post-test time is often considerably more than I have shown, and the time of other school or system personnel has not been included at all. The costs in

Pretest Time	*Hours*	*Cost*
1 school secretary, distributing tests	2 at $3/hr	6
9 teachers' preparation, 1 hour each	9 at $10/hr	90
	11	$96
Test Time		
9 classes, 3 hours per class	27 at $10/hr	270
		$270
Post-test Time		
1 school secretary, packaging tests	1 at $3/hr	3
1 school secretary, distributing results	1 at $3/hr	3
9 teachers' time to review results	9 at $10/hr	90
9 teachers' time to explain results	9 at $10/hr	90
1 secretary to file results	1 at $3/hr	3
	21	$189
Subtotals.	59 hrs	$555
Cost of Tests		
Booklets, answer sheets, and scoring		$600
Total testing costs		. . . . $1,155

terms of dollars per hour are also conservative. (The figure of $10 per hour is based on an average salary of $10,000 a year.) Obviously, the time a teacher spends on testing is time *not* spent on instruction, and that is another "cost"—albeit an indirect one—that should be weighed.

Are the test results worth this much time and money? *If* the tests actually measure what they say they measure, *if* the results are returned in less than six weeks, and *if* the information is interpreted and used properly, then perhaps the testing is worth the cost. But if the information is superficial, incorrect, or invalid, or if the results are dated, or if the information is poorly used or not used at all, then the tests have wasted a great deal of time and money.

How will students and parents be prepared for the testing? Unless students take standardized tests all the time, they need to be prepared for both the format and the content of the tests. Otherwise, the tests are measuring the students' ability to take tests as much as they are measuring what they claim to measure. In the manuals that accompany the tests, test publishers comment on how to prepare students to take tests and on the importance of administering tests properly. Some manuals are quite specific about what kind of preparation should occur, when it should take place, and how it should be conducted; for example, some point out the possible difference in test results if the test is administered orally by the teacher as opposed to orally by using a tape recorder.

Before a test is administered, students should have some experience with taking standardized tests. They should practice answering sample items from the test itself and discuss with other students and the teacher the appropriateness of one kind of answer versus another. Ideally, students should be allowed to see the test before it is given, and they should have experience filling out the kind of answer sheet that will be used in the actual testing. The purpose for giving the test, the limitations of the test, and how the test results will be used should all be carefully explained and discussed with students before the test is given. If students of any age say that they do not want to take the test, their request should be honored.

Parents should be given the opportunity to say whether or not their children will be tested. Not only should the purpose of the tests be described to them, but they should also have a chance to see the tests beforehand. A brief announcement in the local newspaper or a form letter sent home with the student are the usual ways a school system divulges information about its testing program. Neither way will thoroughly inform parents of the purpose and content of the tests or of the choices open to them. An unvoiced question haunts many parents: If I refuse to permit my children to take the test, will it be held against them? Educators should commit themselves to answering this question. Providing students with individualized curriculum materials and programs turns into hollow dogma when there is no accompanying provision for individualized standardized testing or, even better, alternatives to testing.

How will the test results be used and kept? Both students and parents should be able to see how the tests have been scored and compare the actual responses on the answer sheet with the questions in the test booklet. Interpretation, diagnosis, and planning are meaningless unless the answer sheet and test booklet are examined. What kinds of "wrong" answers the student chose and how the test items are worded and arranged are questions that should be answered along with the question of how well the student performed. Are the mistakes careless oversights, or do they indicate creative thinking? Are the items arranged in order of difficulty but given equal value in scoring? Did some subsections of the test have more questions than others but produce subtotals of equal weight? Do the results show that the student got tired or bored? Test publishers often suggest that, for best results, the tests should not be administered immediately before or after vacations and holidays, and that unusual occurrences should be noted and considered when interpreting the results. Similarly, they suggest that the answer sheets of students who get distracted or upset should not be scored. These points need to be considered as part of the test interpretation process, but since test scores are routinely considered by themselves, they are usually ignored.

The sheer volume of testing has created additional problems, such as storage of test results and access to them. The public's increasing emphasis on accountability, plus parents' concern about their children's possible learning difficulties and educators' mistrust of innovations that are not buttressed by test scores, have led to the administration of more and more tests. Less and less space is available for storing the test results and, because of recent legislation, more and more people have access to them. School files are bulging with students' response sheets; superintendents' offices are humming with computers and xeroxes, tabulating and copying test results, which pile up in boxes on the floor in corners and closets. Test companies maintain computer banks stocked with information about school systems, individual schools, classrooms, and students. Who has access to all this information? Do parents and school officials know where all of it—a piece here, a bit there—is kept? What safeguards exist to prevent unauthorized access to this information? How may the information be corrected or destroyed? How long will it be kept on file? Who actually refers to it more than once?

How else might the same information be acquired? Standardized tests actually provide little information about a system, school, or student that cannot be better provided by other means. The only data the tests do provide well are superficial comparisons that promote misleading generalities and unfortunate decisions. Instead of immediately turning to tests, the public, parents, and professionals should carefully specify, in concrete language, the exact information they want. For example, "information about student progress" may be another way of saying that someone wants to know more about the progress of a student, or a group of students, for any one of a number of purposes: grade-to-grade placement; changing the curriculum during the school year to rectify weaknesses; smoothing the transition between grade levels or between one school and another; preparing budget priorities or long-range curriculum plans;

or diagnostic assessments of students who are having learning difficulties. As one specifies exactly what information is required, one should be conscious of when it is required, who requested it, and who will provide the information and in what format. The chart below shows one way the answers to these questions might be organized and used to decide which alternative might best provide the information.

Useful alternatives to testing can be grouped into four broad categories; parent-school meetings, surveys and questionnaires, studies and evaluations, and students' work. Small, informal coffees, either at the school or in neighborhood homes, fall in the first category. These get-togethers

INFORMATION A SCHOOL OR A

TYPES OF INFORMATION	WHEN REQUESTED
Individual student progress for placement and promotion within one school	Mid-year and end of year
Individual student progress for diagnosing and planning	Fall, winter, and spring
Individual student progress for placement, promotion, or transfer between schools	Anytime
Effectiveness of materials and methods for setting budget priorities and curriculum development plans	Mid-year and end of year

can provide information about the school's philosophy, plans, programs, and procedures to parents; they can also elicit parents' concerns, ideas, and expectations and encourage the faculty to respond. Larger, more formal meetings once a year or oftener will give parents a chance to suggest priorities for school goals and programs, to hear how well previously suggested goals and priorities have been adhered to, and to find out first hand about specific programs and problems.

In addition, faculty members can run workshops for parents to help them learn to work with their children at home; to inform them about changes in curriculum materials and methods; and to encourage and enable them to

SCHOOL SYSTEM IS REQUESTED TO PROVIDE	
BY WHOM REQUESTED	**HOW PROVIDED**
State statute, parents, and teachers	Administrative survey of teachers' recommendations; diagnostic tests; report cards; and parent-teacher conferences
Parents, teachers, and specialists	Conferences, report cards, and 1-to-1 diagnosis
Parents, teachers, and administrators	Criterion tests, report cards, anecdotal summaries, conferences, student interviews, and samples of student work
Taxpayers, the school committee, superintendents, and administrators	Norm referenced tests given to large random samples of students; community, parent, and student surveys and questionnaires; faculty reports; and criterion and domain referenced tests given to random samples of students.

participate more actively in the operation of the school. Parent-teacher conferences two or more times a year provide parents with specific information about their children's academic, social, and physical development and enable parents to participate both in assessing their children's developmental strengths and weaknesses and in planning appropriate programs for them.

Another way of collecting information involves the use of surveys and questionnaires, which can be distributed to all students and parents or to a random sample. The surveys can be designed to: 1) determine if the values expressed in the school and the home are the same or at least complementary; 2) establish levels of expectations and chart degrees of satisfaction over a period of time; 3) serve as the basis for discussions at parent-faculty meetings; 4) identify possible cause-and-effect relationships between school programs and students' later performances; and 5) permit students and parents to give the school more information than might easily be elicited at meetings, conferences, and workshops.

Less formal kinds of opinion polls can also be effective. For example, students who are transferring or graduating from the school can be interviewed with an eye to identifying the school's strengths and weaknesses. These interviews can help keep school personnel abreast of trends in students' interests, outlooks, and concerns, as well as pinpoint what individual students consider to be their most important accomplishments, areas of growth, and satisfying experiences. Other members of the system—school committee members, faculties of other schools, or community leaders—can be polled about their understanding of the school's programs and policies and their impressions of the school and what it might do to better meet the system's and the community's requirements.

The school's program can be evaluated in a number of ways. One way is to designate particular groups of the school population for random testing on certain skills, behaviors, or awarenesses, using tests made by parents or teachers, as well as newly developed commercial tests. Another way is to invite interested members of the community to study present programs and to work with school system personnel in developing improvements. Similarly, graduate students at local colleges can be encouraged to do research on the effectiveness of particular curriculum materials and methods. At the same time, the observations of volunteers, student teachers, other professionals, and visitors should be carefully considered.

Perhaps the most important basis for evaluation, however, is the students' work. Samples of student work should be kept and compared during the year for the same students; during the year for different students; and from year to year for the same and different students. In addition, pupil interaction can be recorded on audio-videotape for immediate assessment and future reference. To let parents and taxpayers see what is going on in the school, student work can be displayed in the community, or it can be published in local papers and magazines, accompanied by faculty explanations about how the work fits into the school's curriculum.

The foregoing alternatives may not only be less costly and time consuming than testing, they may also provide information that has more immediacy and impact. Some people might call such information more subjective, and thus more suspect, than test scores. Those who make this charge should be reminded of the highly subjective nature of test construction, to say nothing of the interpretation and use of test data. The issue may not be whether to use these alternatives, but whether the person requesting the information trusts the one providing it. Right now, the level of trust and confidence between the public and the professionals throughout the country seems low. Some of the alternatives I have suggested could actually increase this level of trust, for each of them can provide information about program effectiveness, maintenance of standards, student achievement, and emphasis on community values and traditions.

Standardized testing may be helpful or harmful. Any testing procedure has potentially dangerous elements, as well as useful and constructive ones. Tests may suggest questions that need exploring or provide insights that require further examination; tests may also contain inaccuracies, foster harmful attitudes, or encourage inappropriate interpretation. It is important, therefore, for parents to know why a test is being given, what it will consist of, and how it will be used. Some of the questions that parents should have answers to before they grant permission for their children to participate in any particular standardized test situation are:

- What test is being given, and what are its limitations?
- Why is the test being given?
- When and where will the test be given and by whom?
- Who will receive the test results, how will they be reported, and where will they be stored?
- When will the test results be destroyed?
- How will the results be used, by whom, and with what degree of confidentiality?
- What are the consequences if a student does not take the test?
- Will parents or students be able to see the test beforehand?
- How will students and parents receive the test results?

If alternatives to standardized tests are not used, and if parents grant permission to school personnel to give their children standardized tests, the next decision is how to use the tests. Part of this decision should be based on the way in which the school or system gathers all of its information about students and programs. By having an overall view of how information is collected, a decision maker may eliminate duplication of effort and expense and plan an information-gathering program that uses tests only as necessary.

Testing may, of course, provide useful information for evaluating programs, assessing individual student progress, diagnosing program and pupil strengths and weaknesses, comparing schools and systems, and preparing and evaluating long-range planning. To help prevent the misuse of test results, parents and professionals must be aware of the overall testing and information-gathering plan of the school or system. One way to achieve this comprehensive awareness might be to ban the administering of all standardized tests to large groups of students for five years. As they devised alternatives, test users would be forced to examine what they were doing and why they were doing it. A moratorium on test use would also encourage publishers to improve the content of their tests and to provide more meaningful assistance to their customers.

The best way to combat the unnecessary, inappropriate, and harmful use of tests is for educators and parents together to challenge some of the long-held assumptions about testing. Together, they must ask specific questions and demand concrete answers. The reasons and the means for challenging these assumptions already exist; the question now is whether the desire is there as well.

ON STANDARDIZED TESTING AND EVALUATION

VITO PERRONE

Vito Perrone is dean of the Center for Teaching and Learning at the University of North Dakota, Grand Forks.

Mr. Perrone is also associated with the North Dakota Study Group on Evaluation, a group at the University of North Dakota that is developing alternative methods of evaluating students. He is the coordinator of Testing and Evaluation: New Views, *published by the Association for Childhood Education International in 1975.*

Standardized testing, essentially a post-World War I phenomenon, has become a way of life in America. Tests exist for almost every human social trait imaginable, from "intelligence to alienation, self-concept to maturity, moral development to creativity. They are used to select people into and out of a wide range of educational programs, private and public projects and a variety of jobs."[1] Standardized tests affect Americans of all ages, in all fields; however, they come down most heavily on the young, those between the ages of three and twenty-one. David McClelland suggests that standardized tests are so thoroughly ingrained into American schools that "it is a sign of backwardness not to have test scores in the school records of children."[2]

As organizations having to do with the education and well-being of children from infancy through early adolescence, the Association for Childhood Education International and the National Association of Elementary School Principals are concerned about the effects of testing on individuals of all ages. We are especially concerned about its effects on young children at the primary school level. These are years when children's growth is most uneven—in large measure idiosyncratic—and when large numbers of skills needed for success in school are in rather fluid acquisitional stages.

The standardized tests most widely used *attempt* to assess intelligence, language, readiness, achievement, and self-concept. Commonly the tests are *norm referenced*, which implies they have been constructed to enable users to rank-order individuals or groups in relation to a norm population. (And most test publishers argue that the populations used to establish norms are representative of the general population for whom the tests have been devised.) We have become so accustomed to their use that we have often failed to ask ourselves whether the tests do in fact assess what they purport to assess or whether the assumptions that undergird the statistical and psychometric constructs used are acceptable.

SOME HARD QUESTIONS ABOUT STANDARDIZED TESTS

Sheldon White (1975) suggests that we are contending with "an affair in which magic, science and myth are intermixed."[3] He may well be offering an understatement! How many of us, for example, actually believe that the intelligence and competence of any individual can be adequately represented by any group administered test? Or, that there is *one* "normal curve" that can provide a distribution capable of classifying all children? Such assumptions defy almost everything we have come to understand about children's growth.

Even if one fails to take note of the implicit assumptions of the tests, an examination of the test items ought to cause enormous concern.* Are they clear? Are they fair? Do they

*A large number of recent articles have provided thoughtful critiques of sample test items from a variety of popularly used standardized tests. See: NAESP Journal.

address the *particular* educational concerns of teachers of young children? Do the tests as a whole provide *useful* information about individual children, about a class as a whole? Do they help young children in their learning? Do they support children's intentions as learners? Do they provide essential information to children's parents? In our experience, we have encountered few teachers able to provide an affirmative response to *any* of the foregoing questions. They do respond in the affirmative, however, to the following questions: Do teachers feel any pressure to teach to the tests? If the tests were not given, would there be fewer skill-sheets and workbooks, a broader range of materials, more attention to integrated learning? Would teachers prefer to use the time devoted to standardized testing for other educational activities? Do teachers feel they can assess children's learning in more appropriate ways than through the use of standardized achievement tests?

LABELS THAT CRIPPLE

We have many other concerns about the standardized tests. They have been used increasingly to make judgments about children. Those judged to be "below average" are not likely to receive, in most schools, the kinds of educative opportunities available for children judged "above average." Placement in "remedial" and other special education programs and in lower-level tracks is usually related closely to test results. Children placed in such settings are often viewed as failures; expectations tend not to be high for them. And children in such settings quickly learn to view themselves as failures, producing little. Children who are labeled in a manner that suggests limited ability find that their education takes on a narrow focus—one-dimensional tasks such as skill-sheets, workbooks and drills of one kind or another being most prominent.

Who are the children who tend most often to be labeled in a manner similar to the foregoing? The high proportion of children from lower socioeconomic populations, which include large numbers of minorities, represented in special education and lower-level tracks ought to give us serious pause. Jane Mercer provides rather stark data: namely, that from 50 to 300 percent more black and Mexican-Americans are identified as mentally retarded than could be reasonably expected from their proportion of the population.[4] Our commitments to democratic practice, equality of educational opportunity, forces us to speak out strongly against a process that consistently produces such results.

MULTIPLE PATTERNS, DIVERSIFIED PROGRAMS

As educators of young children we have long believed that children come to learning in many different ways, demonstrating in the process that they have multiple patterns of growth and achievement. This belief has given direction to programs that are diversified as to aims and goals. In these programs, we respect children regardless of their racial background or socioeconomic class. Their interests have become basic starting points for learning. Such developmental programs have tended to support more formal instruction in reading, for example, only when children are ready and not simply because they are six years of age. Because teachers in such settings have been committed to increasing children's opportunities for successful experience and high levels of self-esteem, many learning options are made available. The clock then tends not to determine to such a large degree when children begin and end learning activities. Peer interaction—communication—is encouraged. Integral, rather than peripheral, to a child's life in these classrooms are the creative and expressive forms of communication that have the capacity for developing feeling—the most personal of human possessions. (Too often a teacher does little with the creative and expressive arts because they don't relate particularly well to the normative testing programs. They are not *basic* enough![5]) Static expectations for children, rooted in an array of basal materials and common curricula, do not reflect the diversity that actually exists and is supported in responsive primary schools. Yet, the standardized tests are rooted in standard curriculum materials (basal textbooks, syllabuses, state guidelines) that have predetermined expectations and that everyone is expected to work through. To actually develop a responsive, developmental classroom environment is to risk lower scores on many of the standardized tests. Teachers and children do not need these kinds of external pressures.

HOW ABOUT CRITERION REFERENCED TESTING?

What is the potential of *criterion referenced testing*, which many see as a useful replacement for existing norm referenced achievement testing? In many respects, criterion referenced testing programs *are* an improvement. Unlike the norm referenced testing that has dominated the schools, they have potential for providing some useful information about children's performance in relation to the direct instructional purposes of teachers or of the *particular* math, reading or social studies programs that teachers are actually using. They also have significant limitations.

Criterion referenced tests have been typically constructed around items that lend themselves easily to measurements "directly interpretable in terms of specified performance standards."[6] They tend to measure *simple* tasks at the expense of higher-level thought processes [7] and to reinforce teaching of skills in isolation. They provide no more guarantee than the norm referenced tests that the behaviors expected are really important or that the curriculum will not be developed principally to meet objectives that have little significant challenge to children or assist them in their general development. They tend to stress end products; processes of learning and thinking may take on limited importance.[8] While we do not, on the basis of what we have seen, have very much confidence in criterion referenced testing programs, we are aware that efforts in this direction are still in their formative stages.

WE TAKE A STAND

Many educational organizations have called for a moratorium on the use of standardized intelligence and achievement tests.[9] Others have called only for a moratorium on group administered intelligence and achievement tests, believing that tests yielding normative scores can be used with young children "if the tests are administered on an individual basis by a skilled examiner who makes sure that he has the attention and interest of the child and that the child understands what he is supposed to do and wants to do it."[10] ACEI and NAESP believe the latter position seeks too much. A moratorium is needed and we wish to lend support to such a position. A moratorium, we believe, will intensify a critical reexamination of the politics of testing, the problems of misuse and the negative effects on children, teachers, and programs. It is needed also to encourage the development of—and to increase the legitimization for—alternatives to the standardized testing.

EVALUATION CONSONANT WITH PURPOSE

Does the foregoing suggest that evaluation is not important? Most definitely, we do not oppose evaluation; we consider it basic to the growth of programs, teachers and children. But evaluation needs to be routed in the classrooms. It needs to be consonant with *purpose*. Assessing children's growth, for example, is an intense activity, occurring daily, continuously. It is integral to everything that goes on in the classroom.

ALTERNATIVES TO STANDARDIZED TESTS

How might teachers and school programs proceed with an evaluation program that does not include standardized tests? Some alternative directions follow. They are clearly not all-inclusive; and many are, in fact, merely reaffirmations of practice that many teachers used to engage in before the disruptive pressures of increasing numbers of standardized tests.

Supporters of standardized tests often argue that the tests are necessary because teachers and schools are not often organized sufficiently to describe children's learning or school programs. It is true that to engage in a systematic process of documentation—"a selection of documents put together to portray a program or the life of a child in a classroom as clearly and as truthfully as possible with the significant elements represented"[11]—is to expend considerable effort. Fortunately, increasing numbers of teachers at all levels wish to make such an effort.

• *Systematizing Documentation.* What might a group of teachers in a given school want to look at? What might they view as especially important to document? *Answers need to come at the level of the school.* (Individuals external to the school have typically determined what is important to document. And such a process has contributed significantly to the negative character that evaluation has tended to assume.) For a school as a whole (or particular clusters within a school) to make such decisions is not meant to imply standard record-keeping procedures in all areas in every classroom; it does imply some consensus about what areas will be looked at closely by a group of teachers. Where such a consensus exists, individual teachers not only receive the support of their colleagues but also have others with whom to share their documentation and reflection. Moreover, such a condition provides a climate in which teachers can feel comfortable while observing in each other's classrooms, interviewing each other's children and seeking and providing assistance.

• *Process, Content, Context.* In documenting the *process of learning*, teachers in a school might wish to include information about the children's originality, responsibility, initiative and independence of effort. In relation to the *content of learning*, they might wish to consider materials the children produce (such as writings and drawings); evidence that instruction deals with important concepts as well as necessary skills; and evidence that children find meaning in their learning, that it is not merely rote. And in relation to the *context of learning*, they might consider the basic human relationships that exist—child to child, child to teacher, and teacher to teacher—and respect for the efforts and feelings of others.[12]

The Prospect school in North Bennington, Vermont, uses some of the following records for its basic documentation: children's work (for example, drawings and photos); children's journals and notebooks of written work; teachers' periodic assessments of children's work in math, reading and other activities; curriculum trees; and sociograms.[13] (The documentation is so complete that few individuals ask about a standardized test score.)

• *Interviews.* At the University of North Dakota, a process for documentation has been developed that includes interviews conducted with teachers, children and parents.[14] These interviews have been used extensively as a base for program evaluation and staff development. The *teacher interview* provides a context for individual teachers to reflect on their intentions, use of materials, relationships with children, organization of time and space, difficulties, successes, and so on—in other words, the teacher's own perspective of the classroom. The *child interview* provides another important perspective, focusing on such issues as how the child uses materials, pursues learning, understands what is occurring in the classroom, uses the teacher, and relates to other children. The *parent interview*, bringing in a third perspective, is aimed at a description and understanding of parents' perceptions and attitudes about what is occurring in the classroom, the degree and kinds of their involvement in the classroom, what they believe is important, how they view their children's progress, and their overall level of support (or lack of support). The three interviews provide an enormous amount of qualitative evaluation-information about classrooms and schools. No standardized test can provide as much data or make as much difference in what teachers do and how children learn—especially when the information gathered in the interviews is seriously reflected on and discussed.

• *Broadening the Base of Observations.* Teachers can keep up on children's progress in such areas as reading, language development and math through systematic observation and frequent conferences and recording.[15] Can a standardized achievement test really reveal as much as carefully kept records maintained over a period of time?

Many teachers make use of informal reading inventories as a means of monitoring reading, especially when they wish some rough comparative information.[16] Brenda Engel recently devised a number of reading tasks (similar to those used in informal reading inventories) to sample the reading level in the Cambridge Alternative School.[17] Defining reading as "the ability to get meaning from the printed page," she categorized children as "those who can read," "those who are still in the process of acquiring reading," and "those who are nonreaders." This process, one that teachers could replicate easily in their own schools, says far more than that the reading level in grade 4 is 4.1 or 3.6 or whatever.

Math checklists which teachers find useful are often provided along with the various math programs used in schools.[18] And individual teachers or groups of teachers can prepare their own checklists; they can also devise informal inventories of math understandings.

• *Teachers' Role.* All of the foregoing kinds of records can be particularly helpful to a teacher in planning learning activities that relate to a specific child or group of children. Teachers with whom we work feel this interplay of diagnosis and prescription is a critical aspect of their work.

For teachers to make a conscious effort to document in some of these ways, they must step back and observe from time to time. To make such observations meaningful, it is necessary to have a wide range of learning activities available for children to engage in during the observation. Otherwise, the activities are so undifferentiated that the observations will provide limited insight into children and their learning patterns, interests, and needs. Being free of standardized tests might encourage such classroom environments.

• *Children's Role.* How can children themselves contribute to evaluation alternatives to the testing? When children participate in record-keeping—maintaining daily or weekly journals, filing samples of their writing, recording the books they have read or the math concepts they understand—they not only provide information to the teacher, but they have an increased sense of where they are and what they need to do to extend their learning. Learning takes on a personal character, encouraging students to assume greater responsibility for their own learning. (Can any of the standardized tests do as much?)

• *Parents' Role.* In addition to children, parents can be actively engaged in the documentation process. For example, parents can conduct observations on the use of space and materials in a classroom, the task persistence of individual children, and various social relationships. They can also take photographs at various times during the year to record classroom changes, three-dimensional projects, and so on; and they can summarize reading biographies, questionnaires, and other materials. In the process there is potential for parents to gain increased knowledge about schooling and be able to enlarge their overall contribution to their children's education. And, of course, the information has enormous potential for the classroom teacher.

The foregoing suggestions, as mentioned earlier, are hardly meant to be all-inclusive; they ought to indicate that the means for evaluation are accessible if teachers organize their resources for such a purpose. Teachers need only decide what kinds of records they want to maintain, recognizing, of course, that they can't do everything in any one given year.

The outcome of engaging in alternative processes such as those suggested is the establishment of a basis on which individual teachers and schools can improve the quality of their efforts. This assessing of values, after all, is what evaluation must do to have any meaning and is what we wish to foster.

NOTES

1. Michael Patton, "Understanding the Gobble-dy-gook: A People's Guide to Standardized Test Results & Statistics," in *Testing and Evaluaion: New Views* (Washington, DC: Association for Childhood Education International, 1975), p. 18.

2. David McClelland, "Testing for Competence Rather Than Intelligence," *American Psychiatrist* (Jan. 1973), p. 1.

3. Sheldon White, "Social Implications of I.Q.," *National Elementary Principal* (Mar./Apr. 1975), p. 10.

4. A large number of publications have provided thoughtful critiques of sample test items from a variety of popularly used standardized tests. See: Deborah Meier, *Reading Failure and the Tests* (New York: Workship Center for Open Education, 1973); Deborah Meier, Herb Mack & Ann Cook, *Reading Tests: Do They Hurt Your Child*? (New York: Community Resources Institute, 1973); Banesh Hoffman, *The Tyranny of Testing* (New York: Collier Books, 1964); *National Elementary Principal* (March/April 1975 and August 1975)—among others.

5. Jane Mercer, *Labelling the Mentally Retarded* (Berkeley: University of California Press, 1972). See also Paul Olson, "Power and the National Assessment of Education Progress," *National Elementary Principal* (July/August 1975) for some of the cultural problems with tests as well as a review of some of the important court cases which are related. M. E. Leary, "Children Who Are Tested in an Alien Language: Mentally Retarded?" *New Republic* (May 23, 1970), pp. 17-19 discusses the *Diana et*

al. vs California State Board of Education case regardng the placement of Mexican-American and Black children in special education classes on the basis of test scores. *Hobson vs Hanson,* Civil Action No. 82-66, U.S. District Court for Washington, D.C., 1968, provides an excellent review of standardized tests and teaching. For readers interested in reading an excellent review of the serious problems of standardized testing and minorities, see Robert Williams, Chairperson, "Position Paper of the American Personnel and Guidance Association Committee on Standardized Testing and Evaluation of Potential Among Minority Group Members," 1975.

6. Robert Glaser & Anthony Witko, "Measurement in Learning and Instruction," in *Educational Measurement,* ed. by Robert Thorndike (Washington, D.C.: American Council on Education, 1971), p. 626.

7. Robert Stake and Dennis Gooler, "Measuring Goal Priorities," *School Evaluation,* ed. by Ernest House (Berkeley: McCutchen Publishing Co., 1973).

8. See Vito Perrone and Warren Strandberg, "A Perspective on Accountability," *Teachers College Record* (Feb. 1972), pp. 347-55.

9. The National Education Association passed a resolution calling for a moratorium in 1972 and has become during the past year increasingly aggressive in support of this position. The National Association for the Advancement of Colored People (NAACP) issued a similar statement in the spring of 1975. The Association for Supervision and Curriculum Development (ASCD) and American Association of School Administrators (AASA), while not calling directly for a moratorium, have used strong language about need to reconsider the uses of standardized tests.

10. Millie Almy, *The Early Childhood Educator at Work* (New York: McGraw Hill, 1975), p. 233.

11. Brenda Engel, *Handbook on Documentation* (Grand Forks: North Dakota Study Group on Evaluation, 1975), p. 1.

12. See Anne Bussis, Edward Chittenden & Marianne Amarel, "Alternative Ways in Educational Evaluation," *Testing and Evaluation: New Views* (Washington, D.C.: Association for Childhood Education International, 1975), pp. 10-11, for evaluation research.

13. See Patricia Carini, "The Prospect School: Taking Account of Process," *Testing and Evaluaion: New Views,* pp. 43-48, for an overview of how such records are kept.

14. This effort has been supported, to a large degree, by a National Institute of Education research grant (No. 00-160/3-0979).

15. See Dorothy Cohen and Virginia Stein, *Observing and Recording the Behavior of Young Children* (New York: Teachers College Press, 1972) for an excellent guide.

16. One of the most popular is Nicholas Silvaroli, *Classroom Reading Inventory,* 2d ed. (Dubuque, Iowa: W. C. Brown, 1973).

17. Brenda Engel, *An Evaluation of the Cambridge Alternative School* (Cambridge: Cambridge Alternative School, 1975). A summary of three years of this effort will be published by the North Dakota Study Group on Evaluation during the 1976-77 year.

18. *Project Mathematics* (Minneapolis: Winston & Co., 1974) is a

program that provides particularly effective checklists for teachers and children. The Nuffield Mathematics Project provides "check up" guides to determine children's growth in a variety of concepts. See also Nancy Langstaff, *Teaching in an Open Classroom: Informal Checks, Diagnoses, and Learning Strategies for Beginning Reading and Math* (Boston: National Association of Independent Schools, 1975) for some excellent ways of using informal checks productively. Langstaff's case studies provide a realistic context and should be useful to teachers and principals. We need many more such descriptions, written by classroom teachers or careful classroom observers, in order to enlarge teachers' understandings of such record-keeping and evaluation processes.

SELECTED BIBLIOGRAPHY

SELECTED BIBLIOGRAPHY

The literature on the educational and social consequences of standardized ability and achievement tests has grown rapidly in the last few years, reflecting both the increasing controversy surrounding the tests themselves and the public's concern over declining test scores. Rather than citing the classic works in psychometrics and educational measurement, we have focused this brief bibliography on recent critiques of standardized testing published by and for the education community and on publications that explore the larger public policy questions inherent in the use of the tests.

American Federation of Teachers. "To Test or Not To Test: An Examination of the Educational Testing Controversy." *American Educator*, Winter 1977.
A special issue focusing on an analysis of current trends in the use and abuse of standardized tests and on teachers' attitudes toward testing.

American Psychological Association. *Standards for Educational and Psychological Tests*. Washington, D.C.: the Association, 1974.
Proposes "essential," "very desirable," and "desirable" considerations about the development and use of standardized tests.

Association for Childhood Education International. *Testing and Evaluation: New Views*. Washington, D.C.: the Association, 1975.
A selection of essays on the problems inherent in the present standardized tests and suggestions for alternative approaches to student evaluation.

Block, N.J., and Dworkin, Gerald, eds. *The IQ Controversy*. New York: Pantheon, 1976.
Reprints articles by Jensen, Herrnstein, Jencks, Kamin, and others that are central to the debate over whether intelligence has a substantial genetic component; also reprints the 1922-23 debate between Walter Lippmann and Lewis M. Terman on the nature of intelligence.

Buros, Oscar K., ed. *The Seventh Mental Measurements Yearbook*. 2 vols. Highland Park, N.J.: Gryphon Press, 1974.
Lists more than 1,100 published tests, over half of which are reviewed, plus bibliographies on the construction, use, and validity of the tests reviewed.

Buros, Oscar K., ed. *Tests in Print II: An Index to Tests, Test Reviews, and the Literature on Specific Tests*. Highland Park, N.J.: Gryphon Press, 1974.
Supplements the *Mental Measurements Yearbook*.

Ebel, Robert L. "Educational Tests: Valid? Biased? Useful?" and Green, Robert L. "Tips on Educational Testing: What Teachers and Parents Should Know." *Phi Delta Kappan* 57 (October 1975): 83-93.
Two viewpoints on educational testing; Ebel focuses on psychometric theory, and Green focuses on the political, economic, and educational implications of testing.

Environment, Heredity, and Intelligence. Reprint Series No. 2. Cambridge, Mass.: *Harvard Educational Review*, 1969.
A collection of essays on the nature-nurture debate, including Arthur R. Jensen's controversial "How Much Can We Boost IQ and Scholastic Achievement?"

Fine, Benjamin. *The Stranglehold of the I.Q.* New York: Doubleday, 1975.
Restates for the layman many of the current criticisms of IQ tests and their potentially damaging effects on children.

Fry, Donald. "Against the Testing of Reading." *Urban Review* 9 (Summer 1976): 105-113.
A British view of the educationally pernicious effects of standardized reading tests and tracking of students.

Gartner, Alan; Greer, Colin; and Riessman, Frank, eds. *The New Assault on Equality: I.Q. and Social Stratification*. New York: Harper and Row, 1974.
Further essays on the nature of intelligence and the social implications of IQ testing.

Ginsburg, Herbert. *The Myth of the Deprived Child: Poor Children's Intellect and Education*. Englewood Cliffs, N.J.: Prentice-Hall, 1972.
Describes and evaluates psychological research on the intellectual development and education of children from low socioeconomic backgrounds, with emphasis on myths about IQ.

Harnischfeger, Annegret, and Wiley, David E. *Achievement Test Score Decline: Do We Need to Worry?* St. Louis: CEMREL, Inc., 1975.

Research report on declines in national standardized test scores and on societal and educational factors that could help account for them.

Hawes, Gene R. *Educational Testing for the Millions: What Tests Really Mean for Your Child*. New York: McGraw-Hill, 1964.
A general description of standardized tests and testing practices; written for parents.

Hein, George E. *An Open Education Perspective on Evaluation*. Grand Forks, N.D.: North Dakota Study Group on Evaluation, 1975.
One of a series of publications by the University of North Dakota's Study Group on Evaluation describing approaches to student evaluation that do not rely on standardized tests.

Herrnstein, Richard. "I.Q." *Atlantic Monthly*, September 1971, pp. 43-64.
A classic and controversial statement of the argument that intelligence is substantially genetically determined.

Hoffmann, Banesh. *The Tyranny of Testing*. New York: Crowell-Collier, 1962.
A witty and reasoned attack on the exaggerated claims of mass testing, the content and construction of the tests, and the unresponsiveness of the testing industry.

Houts, Paul L. "Behind the Call for Test Reform and Abolition of the IQ." *Phi Delta Kappan* 57 (June 1976): 669-673.
Surveys the ugly history of IQ testing and argues that group IQ tests should be abolished.

Institute for Responsive Education and National Association of Elementary School Principals. *Your Child and Tests: A Parent's Guide to Testing in the Schools*. Boston, Mass.: The Institute, 1977.
Answers parents' questions on the use and misuse of tests and outlines ways that parents can improve the testing programs in their children's schools.

Kamin, Leon J. *The Science and Politics of I.Q.* Hillsdale, N.J.: Lawrence Erlbaum Associates, 1974.
Focuses on the social history of IQ testing in the United States and disputes the classical studies on which theories of the heritability of intelligence have been based.

Karier, Clarence J. "Testing for Order and Control in the Corporate Liberal State." *Educational Theory* 22 (Spring 1972): 154-180.
An indictment of the U.S. corporate establishment's use of standardized tests to perpetuate the meritocracy.

McClelland, David C. "Testing for Competence Rather Than for

'Intelligence.'" *American Psychologist* 28 (January 1973): 1-14.
A critique of the rationale underlying IQ tests and of their use to predict success in school and career; recommends criterion referenced tests as an alternative.

Meier, Deborah; Cook, Ann; and Mack, Herb. *Reading Tests: Do They Help or Hurt Your Child?* New York: Community Resources Institute and Workshop Center for Open Education, 1974.
Contains actual items from standardized reading tests, plus comments and critiques by the authors.

NAACP Special Contribution Fund. *NAACP Report on Minority Testing*. New York: NAACP, 1976.
Discusses the effect of cultural and racial bias in standardized tests and recommends a moratorium on all current standardized testing.

National Association of Secondary School Principals. *Competency Tests and Graduation Requirements*. Reston, Va.: the Association, 1976.
An overview of one of the newest kinds of standardized tests; includes samples of competency tests and a list of the state legislation that mandates their use.

National Council of Teachers of English. *Common Sense and Testing in English*. Report of the Task Force on Measurement and Evaluation in the Study of English. Urbana, Ill.: the Council, 1975.
Includes criteria for selecting standardized tests in English and for interpreting and using test scores.

National Education Association. "Report of the NEA Task Force on Testing." In *Reports of Committees, Councils, and Task Forces 1974-75*. Presented to the Fifty-Fourth Representative Assembly of the National Education Association. Washington, D.C.: the Association, 1975.
Outlines the NEA's position on the proper uses of standardized ability and achievement tests and argues strongly against their use as selection or tracking instruments.

National School Public Relations Association. *Releasing Test Scores: Educational Assessment Programs, How to Tell the Public*. Arlington, Va.: the Association, 1976.
Handbook on interpreting test and assessment results to teachers, parents, and the public; directed to state and local education officials.

Richardson, Ken, and Spears, David, eds. *Race and Intelligence: The Fallacies Behind the Race-IQ Controversy*. Baltimore:

Penguin Books, 1972.
Reprints essays that approach the heredity-environment debate within the contexts of psychology, biology, and sociology.

Rudman, Herbert C. "How to Use Standardized Tests for Decision Making." *National Elementary Principal* 55 (March/April 1976): 59-64.
One of the authors of the Stanford Achievement Test in Science argues for the responsible use of test scores as the basis for making educational decisions at the individual school level.

Silberman, Arlene. "Tests—Are They Fair to Your Child?" *Woman's Day,* November 1976, pp. 54-62.
Focuses on how standardized tests can victimize children by mislabeling them and damaging their self-concepts.

Silberman, Arlene. "The Tests that Cheat Our Children." *McCalls,* April 1977, pp. 191 ff.
Reviews the growing controversy over IQ tests and urges parents to take a stand against using the tests to label and track students.

Weber, George. *Uses and Abuses of Standardized Testing in the Schools.* Occasional Paper No. 22. Washington, D.C.: Council for Basic Education, 1974.
An introduction to some of the current controversies surrounding the use of standardized tests, including group IQ tests.

Whimbey, Arthur, with Whimbey, Linda Shaw. *Intelligence Can Be Taught.* New York: Bantam Books, 1976.
Reviews the psychological research on intelligence and disputes the arguments of genetic determinists, outlining a program of "cognitive therapy" for improving intelligence through instruction.

INDEX

INDEX